GROUPTHINK OR DEADLOCK

SUNY series on the Presidency: Contemporary Issues
John Kenneth White, editor

GROUPTHINK OR DEADLOCK

*When Do Leaders Learn
from Their Advisors?*

By
Paul A. Kowert

STATE UNIVERSITY OF NEW YORK PRESS

Published by
State University of New York Press, Albany

© 2002 State University of New York

For information, address State University of New York Press,
90 State Street, Suite 700, Albany, NY 12207

Production by Christine Hamel
Marketing by Jennifer Giovani

Library of Congress Cataloging in Publication Data

Kowert, Paul, 1964–
    Groupthink or deadlock : when do leaders learn from their advisors?
/ by Paul A. Kowert.
        p. cm. — (SUNY series on the presidency)
    Includes bibliographical references and index.
    ISBN 0-7914-5249-2 — ISBN 0-7914-5250-6 (pbk.)
        1. Presidents—United States—Staff. 2. Presidents—United States—
Decision making. 3. Political Consultants—United States. 4. Political
leadership—United States. 5. United States—Politics and government—
1953–1961. 6. United States—Politics and government—1981–1989.
I. Title. II. SUNY series on the presidency.

JK552.K68 2002
352.23'233'0973—dc21   2001041148

10 9 8 7 6 5 4 3 2 1

Contents

v

Abbreviations

CEA	Council of Economic Advisors
CFEP	Council on Foreign Economic Policy
CIA	Central Intelligence Agency
DCI	Director of Central Intelligence
DLF	Development Loan Fund
EDC	European Defense Community
FBI	Federal Bureau of Investigation
GNP	Gross National Product
HUAC	House Committee on Un-American Activities
IBRD	International Bank for Reconstruction and Development
ICA	International Cooperation Administration
IDAB	International Development Advisory Board
IMF	International Monetary Fund
JCS	Joint Chiefs of Staff
LSG	Legislative Strategy Group
MBTI	Myers-Briggs Type Indicator
MSA	Mutual Security Agency
NAC	National Advisory Council
NATO	North Atlantic Treaty Organization
NSC	National Security Council
NSDD	National Security Decision Directive
NSPG	National Security Planning Group
OCB	Operations Coordinating Board
OECD	Organization for Economic Co-operation and Development
OMB	Office of Management and Budget

OPD	Office of Policy Development
PEPAB	President's Economic Policy Advisory Board
PFIAB	President's Foreign Intelligence Advisory Board
PLO	Palestine Liberation Organization
PRC	People's Republic of China
SHAEF	Supreme Headquarters, Allied Expeditionary Force
TOW	Tube-launched, Optically tracked, Wire-guided (missile)

Tables and Figures

Acknowledgments

This is a book about getting and using advice. It examines the decisions of two American presidents and explains why they were able to learn more from Cabinet officials, staff experts, friends, and even opponents in some cases than in others. Taking on such a project, I naturally sought advice myself. I now owe a great debt to many people. From the beginning, the guidance and encouragement of Peter Katzenstein, Daryl Bem, Susan Buck-Morss, and Ned Lebow at Cornell University was indispensable. Many others read drafts of one chapter or another, even the entire manuscript in some cases, and gave me the benefit of their reactions and insights. For this, I am grateful to Deborah Avant, Mike Desch, John Garofano, Thomas Gilovich, Charles F. Hermann, Margaret Hermann, Richard Herrmann, Walter Isard, Deborah Larson, Gil Merom, John Odell, Judith Reppy, Thomas Risse, Elizabeth Sanders, Jim Siekmeier, Richard Smoke, Christine Sylvester, and Nina Tannenwald. I also benefited from conversations or correspondence with Francis Adams, Jan Balakian, Eric Bein, Fred Greenstein, Hugh Gusterson, Janice Stein, Eric Stern, and the members of the Mershon Center Research Training Group (RTG) on Cognition in Collective Political Decision Making at the Ohio State University. The generous assistance of these friends and colleagues has helped me to avoid many errors and blind alleys.

For their expert archival assistance, I wish to thank Tom Branigar, David Haight, and Herbert Pankratz of the Eisenhower Presidential Library in Abilene, Kansas, and Kathie Nicastro at the National Archives in Washington, D. C. John Garofano also kindly made available to me materials he gathered at the Eisenhower Library. Portions of this book first appeared as an article,

"Leadership and Learning in Political Groups: The Management of Advice in the Iran-Contra Affair," *Governance: An International Journal of Policy and Administration* 14, 1 (2001). I thank Blackwell Publishers for permission to reprint that material. For careful editorial assistance, I am indebted to Christine Hamel at SUNY Press.

Finally, for their generous financial support at various stages of research and writing, I am grateful to the Graduate School, Government Department, and Peace Studies Program at Cornell University; to the Center for International Studies at the University of Southern California; and to the Mershon Center at the Ohio State University. Revisions of the manuscript were supported by a grant (DIR-9113599) from the National Science Foundation to the Mershon Center RTG for research on the role of cognition in collective political decision making at the Ohio State University, and also by a grant (P-97272) from the Social Science Research Council and from the Japan Society for the Promotion of Science for research leave at Ritsumeikan University in Kyoto, Japan. For her tolerance when work prevailed over other plans, I owe a special debt to Meagan Elmendorff. This book is dedicated to my parents, whose support of all kinds made it possible.

CHAPTER 1

Introduction

It may be lonely at the top, but hardly ever so lonely that important decisions in government and business are made by only one person. Even presidents and prime ministers must rely on others. In fact, the most powerful leaders generally confront such a range of problems that they require assistance and advice more frequently than less prominent figures. Small wonder, then, that the most important and time-consuming issue confronting newly elected presidents before they take office is not to determine their own position on various policy issues, but simply to decide how they will organize their staff.

In business as well as in government, this is a crucial problem. Schools of management debate ad nauseam the most effective and efficient way to fashion work groups of various sizes and functions. Does the Japanese *ringi* system of collective decision making, for example, produce better decisions than Western management styles even though it may seem less efficient?[1] Are cohesive groups more productive, or is some disagreement healthy?[2] How important is strong leadership for group efficiency?[3] Such questions are the staples of research on group decision making. And while their answers are debated, almost everyone agrees that groups deserve attention in their own right.

Yet no matter how indispensable a well-organized staff may be, even carefully assembled groups of advisors can sometimes create more problems than they solve. Many studies of presidential decision making argue that social pressures within high-level policy groups can lead presidents to make worse decisions than had they acted alone. The best-known work of this genre, Irving Janis's study of groupthink, holds that this danger is especially prevalent in highly cohesive groups.[4] Janis suggests that taking steps to prevent "excessive" conformity and to promote "devil's advocacy" will make the group a more benign setting.

Janis was not the first to recognize the danger of groupthink. It was probably common wisdom even when Aristotle wrote that "evils draw men together."[5] The danger is not simply that the presence of like-minded others can reinforce one's own sense of rectitude and virtuousness far beyond prudence. The mere presence of others is energizing in a way that can prompt rash action or even mob behavior.[6] Groups also provide a measure of anonymity; they make it easier to entertain the belief that, when plans go awry, someone else can be blamed.[7] This aspect of groups not only encourages risky behavior, but it creates problems of accountability that undermine democratic procedures. It is bad enough that leaders might be led by advisors to contemplate unwise adventures, but even worse when leaders purposefully distance themselves from the details of an operation to preserve "deniability," thus subverting their accountability before the public.[8]

One is tempted to assert that leaders (and their constituents) would be better off by themselves than in a room full of advisors.[9] Whatever its merits, no policymaker could really afford to adopt this maxim. Even the most knowledgeable leaders cannot be experts on everything. Neither side of the debate over the usefulness of advisors really takes issue with an underlying premise: that more information is always better, so long as there is sufficient time to consider it. Information, one might say, is the lifeblood of decision making. The assumption that it is intrinsically valuable is a truism among almost all of those who study group decision making.

MATCHING ADVISORS TO LEADERS

This book rejects the assumption that more information is always helpful—even when the information itself is important and even when there is sufficient time to consider it. For people as for computers, information is not helpful if it arrives in too great a quantity to process. For computers, the problem is simply one of processing speed. All that is necessary, for computers, is enough time. But for people, the problem is processing speed *and* tolerance for ambiguity, diversity of opinion, complexity, and many other features of the information itself. Computers are indifferent to the information they process, but people obviously are not.

To store knowledge efficiently, the brain simplifies and distorts learned information. One of the most basic assumptions of cognitive psychology is that people attempt to preserve consistency among their beliefs, fitting beliefs to simpler (and thus more efficient) mental frameworks.[10] When we are unable to preserve consistency, however, we do not merely experience this as another interesting fact. Inconsistency is uncomfortable; it produces anxiety. A quantity of discrepant information is merely input for a computer, but for a person it can be very disturbing. And this is more than a matter of "taking it all in." The complexity, inconsistency, and even "acceptability" of information are all distressing in their own right.[11] Emotion and learning influence each other in other ways too. Emotional arousal is beneficial in some circumstances. It draws attention to important problems and motivates hard work to solve them. Yet great anxiety can be distracting.[12] Mood also alters the way people gather and use information: those in a good mood pay greater attention to "positive" information and those in a bad mood, to "negative" information.[13] And emotion leads to certain characteristic errors in decision making. Happy people, for example, tend to make decisions faster, based on less information, and with greater tolerance for risk than do neutral individuals.[14]

When the stakes are high, as is often the case in the policy-making groups on which this book focuses, the relationship between emotion and information is even harder to ignore. For the reasons just given, some of which will be considered in greater detail in chapter 2, leaders are rarely indifferent to information. Sometimes they are well aware that the problems they face need closer scrutiny. At other times, they are equally sure that further discussion and debate is intolerable. For some leaders (and in some settings), learning more about a particular problem is a burden rather than a benefit. Certain types of leaders do not benefit from a smorgasbord of advice, should not endeavor to receive it, and will suffer if it is thrust upon them. Others, precisely as

Janis argues, do benefit (and can avoid costly mistakes if they get the right information).

It is entirely appropriate, then, for leaders to concern themselves with the organization of their staff.[15] Some adopt very complex staff systems designed to filter information at many different levels and through many different channels. Other place themselves at the center of the flow of information. And still others attempt to remove themselves altogether, as much as possible, from the flow of deliberations, preferring to delegate problems to their subordinates. Some prefer harmony among their associates. Others encourage friction in the belief that a little competition among subordinates promotes a more honest exchange of views. Yet despite the obviously great differences in the way leaders prefer to arrange their advisors, scholarship on group decision making tends to offer the same prescriptive advice: it is better to have more information rather than less and more opinions rather than fewer.

This book develops and tests a different claim. It argues that while some leaders thrive on diversity of opinion, others are immobilized by it. Some leaders should seek out many different perspectives on a problem, from a wide range of associates, just as Janis insists. But others must "ration" their attention. The latter sort of decision maker thrives in a carefully managed, hierarchical setting in which cohesion rather than discord is the norm. While this second type of leader may seem especially in need of devil's advocates, exposure to dissent can rapidly become too much of a good thing. Clearly, not all leaders actually employ the same decision style or use advisors in the same way. This book cautions them against trying to do so.

Chapter 2 explains in greater detail why policymakers differ in their capacity to use advice. It considers the appropriate management of advisory staffs for different kinds of leaders and concludes with a theory of group dynamics that predicts whether or not leaders are likely to learn from their advisors when making important decisions. Chapter 3 presents a more detailed picture of differences in leadership style through a comparison of two U.S. presidents: Dwight Eisenhower and Ronald Reagan. Although these two presidents (and their presidencies) resembled each other in many respects, they differed markedly in their tolerance for complexity, conflict, and contradictory advice.

Chapter 4 explores four cases—two from each administration—in which these presidents clearly learned from their advisors. In each case, the president reversed a policy to which he was personally committed after being presented with evidence that the policy was unlikely to succeed. In each case, moreover, learning followed changes in the organization of the president's staff in a direction consistent with the predictions of the theory. Chapters 5 and 6 discuss cases in which these leaders *failed* to learn, despite mounting evidence of their policies' improvidence. On the occasions when Eisenhower failed to learn, discussed in chapter 5, his decision process closely resembled the pattern of *groupthink* described by Janis. When Reagan was most unable to learn seemingly apparent lessons (chapter 6), the problem was not too much cohesion among advisors but rather too little—a situation that might be described as *deadlock*.

DOES LEADERSHIP REALLY MATTER?

Studying leaders and advisors is moot if one believes that individual leaders are not so important. It scarcely seems possible to understand modern India without a proper appreciation of Gandhi's influence, France without reference to Napoleon and de Gaulle, or Germany without understanding the roles of Bismarck and Hitler. But Louis XIV's famous dictum—*l'état, c'est moi*—overstates even a king's power. And three centuries later, despite his proclamation that "the buck stops here," Harry Truman was well aware that the buck also stopped at the other end of Pennsylvania Avenue.

Many prominent political scientists thus believe that it is a waste of time to study political leadership, preferring to focus instead on the political institutions within which leaders and followers alike must operate. As one former president of the American Political Science Association (APSA) put it, "an institutionalist approach does not deny the relevance of individual psychology but treats it as marginal in the context of the tremendous historical forces lodged in the laws, traditions, and commitments of institution."[16] From such a perspective, even when leaders do make a difference, they affect political outcomes only in unique and idiosyncratic ways that cannot form a solid basis for theorizing.[17]

Stephen Skowronek argues, to take but one example, that U.S. presidents are constrained by cycles in what he calls "political time."[18] Some presidents ride the crest of a new political wave, sweeping away much of the established institutional order that preceded them. Others consolidate and preside over the new order as caretakers. And still others must witness the decline and dissolution of the institutional patterns to which they have grown accustomed, preparing the way for yet another cycle in political time. In short, ruling coalitions form and prosper, consolidate their power and persevere for a certain period of time, and eventually weaken and die as they become outmoded. Whereas Bert Lance alone sufficed to bring President Carter's popularity rating to new lows, President Reagan survived a series of ethics scandals with his popularity intact. Skowronek's work offers a simple, institutional explanation for their differing political fortunes. Carter and Reagan simply held office, he would argue, at different points in the cycle of political time: Carter at the end of a dying coalition and Reagan at the head of a new one. Institutional arguments are good at explaining such patterns.

By the same token, however, they do not account well for abrupt changes in political patterns, such as Ronald Reagan's sudden inability to manage the Iran-Contra scandal after weathering so many others. Ad hoc explanations are certainly possible, but nothing in Skowronek's institutional theory suggests that such a popular president would suddenly have such difficulties. While institutional arguments may be able to account for gradual change, the "tremendous historical forces" to which APSA President Theodore Lowi alluded do not generally work rapidly or abruptly. Institutionalism is thus rarely useful for explaining important policy shifts or sharp breaks with the past.[19] To explain change, we must look to individuals rather than to their institutional roles. The perceptions and decision-making procedures of political leaders (and followers) connect institutional pressures to specific political outcomes. Even institutionalists thus need to know which institutional constraints a politician finds salient. And institutionalists must recognize that leaders may, over time, change their assessments of the constraints they face. In short, they may learn. Learning is particularly important when a single individual possesses sufficient power or influence to alter political outcomes decisively. This condition is not unusual even in international politics, as the historical contributions of Ronald Reagan,

Mikhail Gorbachev, Boris Yeltsin, and Saddam Hussein show. The lessons that each of these men learned (or failed to learn) from history mattered to a great many people.[20]

WHAT IS LEARNING?

It is a simple matter to insist that it is important for political leaders to learn the lessons of history, but much more difficult to specify exactly what *learning* is. Like the old saying about pornography, most students of political decision making believe they know learning when they see it. Generally, they have found it unnecessary to be more precise than the "ordinary language" meaning of the term.[21] When Janis writes that groupthink leads to "a deterioration of mental efficiency, reality testing, and moral judgment," one might readily conclude that groupthink results, in other words, in a general failure to learn.[22] Yet nowhere in his book on groupthink does Janis deem it essential to devote more attention to explaining exactly what learning, mental efficiency, reality testing, or moral judgment are. And in a compelling discussion of the Fashoda crisis and the Cuban missile crisis as "learning experiences," to take another example, Richard Ned Lebow associates learning with reassessing existing beliefs and dispelling "dangerous illusions," but he does not dwell further on how to define it.[23]

In this book, I will also adopt an ordinary language definition of learning. Even in conventional usage, however, *learning* can mean two very different things. One common meaning is *to gain knowledge about, or familiarity with, something through experience*. This is the way most cognitive psychologists use the term (though, to be sure, psychologists disagree among themselves about exact definitions).[24] In this definition, learning is acquiring information that one did not previously possess. The information may turn out to be incomplete or faulty, but one can be said to learn whenever the *process* of acquiring information occurs. Yet *learning* is often used in a second, more substantive way. In this second usage, *to learn* is a synonym for *to know*. When parents say, for example, that their child has "learned a lesson," they mean much more than that the child was exposed to new information. They are vouching for the correctness of what the child has learned.[25] In this case, it would be nonsensical to say, "she learned a valuable lesson, but she was wrong." Definitions of learning can thus be either procedural (the first kind of learning) or evaluative (the second).[26]

I will resist the temptation to *evaluate* the decisions of the presidents on which this book focuses. To a certain extent, history has already performed this task, apparently vindicating certain of their decisions and condemning others. But this book's purpose is not to enter into essentially unresolvable political or moral debates over their choices. What *can* be determined is whether or not these two leaders gathered and used the information and advice that was at their disposal. It is merely an assumption that doing so would have improved (and in some cases, did improve) their decision making.

To assess learning, this book seeks answers to two questions. First, to what degree do leaders gather diverse information and advice? To the extent that leaders get more advice from more perspectives, they can tentatively be said to learn. Unfortunately, commissioning studies of a problem may be more an effort at public relations than a sincere attempt to learn. And leaders might consult their potential adversaries only to marshall their support (or defuse their opposition) rather than to discover the reasons for their opposition. Merely acquiring knowledge, therefore, does not in itself constitute proof of learning. One must also ask whether leaders use this information to reassess their policy options, even when doing so might challenge cherished assumptions about the world. Clearly, questioning one's basic assumptions is harder than merely adapting to changing conditions. The former is what some students of policymaking refer to as "fundamental" learning. Both adaptation and "fundamental" learning are important skills for policymakers.[27]

Answers to these questions promise no precise, quantifiable indicators of learning. Although such measures may seem desirable, they would only be misleading in practice. It is impossible to say, for example, whether a leader who reads ten policy papers has learned twice as much as one who reads only five. It is more important to know whether the documentary record indicates that a leader found information and advice to be valuable or thought-provoking, regardless of whether the advice was contained in the first or tenth study. As a practical matter, another indicator of learning is a change in policy. In an effort to establish a "baseline" for learning in the Eisenhower and Reagan administrations, chapter 4 will thus pay special attention to the reasons for changes in policy and to whether leaders (or their subordinates) attribute these changes to information they acquired in the course of their policy deliberations.

CONCLUSION

There are larger issues in the study of high-level decision making that this book will not address. It will not ask, as many others have, whether the policy-making process is better characterized by essentially rational (i.e., economic) models or by the theories of cognitive or motivational psychology. It walks a middle road in this debate out of the conviction that economists and psychologists alike can agree that learning is valuable and that both leaders and their advisors have something to do with it. Nor, as already noted, do the following chapters make any effort to decide whether or not Eisenhower and Reagan learned the "right" lessons from history. The reader may draw his or her own conclusions.

This book will argue, however, that not every method of deliberating over important policy problems is equally fruitful. Some arrangements are more conducive to learning than others. Moreover, not every leader benefits from the same sort of staff arrangement. Students of policymaking would thus be wise to heed the advice that a famous turn-of-the-century medical researcher, William Osler, gave to his colleagues. He admonished them to study "not only what sort of disease the patient has, but also what sort of patient has the disease."[28] Considerable research on political and economic decision making has focused on the various alleged diseases (mental errors, emotional biases, etc.) that afflict policymakers. Paying a little attention to these individuals, and not only to their cognitive "diseases," promises to yield a more realistic and useful explanation of when leaders are likely to learn from their advisors.

CHAPTER 2

Who Learns, and When?

It is easy to think of moments in history when the fate of many hinged on the actions of a few. This does not mean that scholars would always be well-advised to concentrate their attention on the qualities of those few individuals. Apart from historical curiosity, investigating the character traits or decision-making abilities of world leaders has value only if one expects to learn something that can be generalized to other leaders, in other circumstances. The dubious quality of many generalizations about political leaders has undermined enthusiasm for the approach. Because this chapter argues that it is not only possible but necessary to generalize about leadership style if we are to explain whether or not leaders will learn from their advisors, it may help to begin by considering a few common objections.

Many accounts of Saddam Hussein that appeared after the Persian Gulf War noted that the Iraqi leader's father died before he was born and that he fled an alcoholic, abusive stepfather to live with his maternal uncle, who was a fervent Iraqi nationalist.[1] Later, the adolescent Hussein returned home to drive his stepfather out of his mother's home. Perhaps these and other facets of his childhood explain Hussein's preoccupation with power, his ruthlessness, and his well-known brutality. In one of the quirks of fate that make politics so interesting, another recent world leader grew up in surprisingly similar circumstances. Like Hussein, Bill Clinton's father died before his son was born. And like Hussein,

Clinton grew up with an alcoholic stepfather, left home at a relatively early age, and eventually returned to confront his stepfather. Fred Greenstein attributes a personal style practically opposite to that of Hussein to the same events: "Clinton's almost unsettling good cheer reflects the exaggerated need to be agreeable found in children (and stepchildren) of alcoholics."[2]

Or consider the case of another American president. Woodrow Wilson is probably second only to Richard Nixon as an inspiration for psychoanalytic studies of failures in the office of the presidency. Common wisdom remains, as Alexander and Juliette George argued, that Wilson's father—a Presbyterian minister of high standards who did not hesitate to enumerate the ways in which his son failed to measure up—is responsible for producing a lasting sensitivity to criticism and a stubbornness that later prevented President Wilson from compromising even slightly in negotiations abroad and at home on the League of Nations covenant.[3] The Georges' work is a model of careful documentation and research, and their hypotheses are more nuanced than this brief summation indicates. But even care and nuance leave important matters unexplained, such as the notable flexibility Wilson displayed earlier in his political career in his conversion from conservatism to pragmatism. The Georges conclude that Wilson was simply more adept at pursuing power than at wielding it.[4]

How can very similar childhood circumstances explain the apparently divergent leadership styles of Hussein and Clinton? And how can Wilson's domineering father explain both his flexibility in some cases and his extreme rigidity in others? Perhaps, such paradoxes can be resolved by scholarly fine-tuning. No doubt there were other important differences in Hussein's and Clinton's childhood experiences. Or, conversely, their leadership styles may actually be more similar than most people appreciate. And perhaps, in Wilson's case, additional hypotheses can be introduced to explain why he reacted strongly to criticism in some cases and adapted to it in others. None of these explanations, however, give the impression that a satisfactory general theory of political behavior can begin with a study of personality.

Such pessimism is one of the main reasons why social scientists have almost completely abandoned the study of personality and politics.[5] The inherent difficulty of studying character and leadership style is another reason. Personality traits (unlike behavior) cannot be measured directly. Efforts to be more scientific thus led scholars in many fields to de-emphasize personality in favor of social or economic explanations of behavior. Even psychologists redirected their attention away from personality and emotion and toward cognition and social psychology.[6] Many psychologists also complained that the few remaining, extended efforts to study personality actually suggested that most people's behavior is determined more by their environment than by any coherent "personality."[7]

These problems are all serious. To summarize, critics maintain that general theories of the effects of leadership style are impossible, that measuring leadership style is inherently difficult and usually fraught with bias, and that even psychologists often attribute behavior to situational constraints rather than to personality. None of these complaints, however, is quite as fatal to the future of research on leadership style as is sometimes supposed.

The last is the easiest to rebut. The perennial debate among psychologists over whether the "person" or the "situation" is the more important determinant of behavior can never be resolved definitively, although the truth is undoubtedly somewhere in the middle.[8] But the debate is really beside the point. Common sense and considerable research each confirm that "personality" is not simply a fiction of the psychoanalyst's couch or an artifact of research in college psychology laboratories.[9] Extensive longitudinal studies stretching over the past several decades offer strong support for the claim that people have stable personalities in adulthood.[10] The remainder of this chapter treats as axiomatic the claim that it is meaningful to speak of personality traits and that these traits exhibit some cross-situational consistency.

Defending claims about a particular individual's personality, however, is no easy matter. Personality and leadership style are obviously hard to measure. And it makes little difference whether one chooses to study living or historical figures: contemporary leaders are naturally reluctant to subject themselves to psychological evaluation, and the historical record is subject to various biases. But these measurement problems are hardly unique to research on political leadership; they are common in the social sciences. The best way to respond to this challenge is to insist on clear standards for evidence and, where possible, to "zero in" on the object of one's investigation by employing several different research methods. Chapter 3, which compares the personal and leadership style of two American presidents, will take this approach, using multiple methods and multiple sources of evidence to justify its claims.

Finally, skeptics about a general relationship between leadership style and political outcomes may well be correct. As the examples of Hussein, Clinton, and Wilson suggest, the causal chain connecting a leader's personality traits to successes and failures in office is a long one. Many things can intervene to cause different leaders to behave in similar ways, or similar leaders in very different ways. Yet this does not mean it is pointless to study leadership style. The error of many (probably most) studies of leader personality is to address questions that are too "large"—to attempt analytic leaps so daring that they are doomed to failure from the beginning. Even the best social science theories are probabilistic rather than deterministic. Scholars must therefore keep the chain between cause and effect short if there is to be any hope of finding a relationship. A study of leadership style should investigate things that personality can affect in a direct and systematic fashion. This book will make no grand claims about whether childhood traumas will lead leaders to pursue aggressive or conciliatory policies. It will not search for the origins of personality traits that make some leaders unwilling to compromise while others happily cut political deals. These are interesting questions, but asking them is not likely to lead to a satisfactory general theory of aggression, compromise, or conciliation.

The extent of this book's daring is to claim that different kinds of leaders learn in different ways. Simply put, some can handle more information and advice than others, and thus some benefit much more than others from large and diverse groups of advisors. Cause and effect are both situated at the same "level"—that of the individual decision maker. Although this claim is more modest than those just mentioned, the following chapters seek to show that it is nevertheless important. Whether or not leaders learn may not *determine* the policies they choose, but it almost always *affects* their choice of policies. Whether or not leaders are able to learn, to respond to the larger pressures and problems they face, is thus a crucial point for many "bigger" theories that focus on these problems.

The argument about leaders' decision styles offered in this book is easy to state: not everyone learns in the same way. The first implication of this claim, discussed in the next section, is that some leaders are more likely to learn than others. But all leaders are capable of learning. The following section thus addresses the central problem of this book. How should different kinds of leaders arrange their advisors and policy staff to take advantage of the advice they receive? As will become clear, not every leader can (or should) take the same advice about "advice." Scholars such as Irving Janis who dwell on the problem of too little advice from overly cohesive groups tackle only half of the problem.[11] Leaders can also fail to learn when they are overwhelmed by too many conflicting opinions. A theory of how best to learn from advisors must begin, therefore, by considering differences in the personal characteristics of leaders themselves.

LEARNING STYLE

Some leaders revel in political confrontation. Franklin D. Roosevelt was one who seemed to enjoy the heat generated by contentious debates so much that he often deliberately pitted one advisor against another.[12] This is the sort of leader that James David Barber called "positive"—a leader who thrives on the exercise of power and the "game" of politics.[13] Others, who Barber called "negative," find politics distasteful. Indeed, in a more general way than Barber describes, many people shrink from dispute and confrontation. They are thus negative not only about politics but about interpersonal conflict in general, and they typically withdraw, preferring private to public settings. When forced to participate in large social gatherings, they much prefer calm harmony to vocal (even if good-natured) debate.

We can begin, therefore, with a distinction between *open* and *closed* decision-making or learning styles. This distinction is an old one. It was, in fact, one of Carl G. Jung's basic insights into human personality. Jung proposed that people are oriented toward the world in one of two ways, which he characterized as introversion or extraversion.[14] Extraverts are intensely aware of, and interested in, the environment external to themselves. For introverts, on the other hand, the most important part of their experience is their "inner" world. The implication of this distinction for a study of decision making is that some people (introverts) need a greater incentive to attend to advice and evidence from their surroundings than do others (extraverts). The importance of this distinction is, by now, well established among psychologists. Indeed, almost all specialists on personality traits now regard introversion/extraversion as one of the fundamental dimensions of human personality.[15] Some even argue that it is a product of basic human biology (and not merely, as Jung would argue, of childhood psychosocial development). Hans J. Eysenck, for one, maintains that the reticular brain stem works as a "volume control" for the brain and that, when it is turned up too high, people will naturally recoil from their surroundings (producing introverted behavior).[16] Although such research on biological psychology may seem far-removed from any practical relevance to the study of decision making, the distinction between introversion and extraversion also forms the basis for what is probably the most widely used personality questionnaire in occupational settings: the Myers-Briggs Type Indicator (MBTI). Corporations often use the MBTI to inform their strategies for personnel management and even to guide decisions on promotion and hiring.[17]

So far, I have deliberately avoided muddying the waters with an overly technical discussion of personality research. But the distinction between open and closed learning style is more than—and slightly different than—the distinction between introverts and extraverts. Openness encompasses not only the sociability to which extraversion refers but other aspects of open-mindedness as well. Indeed, it is entirely possible for a gregarious and socially adept person to be, nevertheless, quite close minded and unwilling to learn. Some leaders—such as Lyndon Johnson and Ronald Reagan—who were forceful and outgoing in social settings nevertheless preferred a very small and carefully managed group of close advisors when making important decisions. Such men are "publicly extraverted," but privately rather closed.[18]

Another important trait that explains some of this difference in learning style is *locus of control*. First studied extensively by Julian B. Rotter, locus of control refers to convictions about whether one's own behavior matters. People with an internal locus of control believe that their actions will elicit positive (or negative) reinforcement from their environment. Typically, "internals" believe that hard work and/or talent will be rewarded, whereas laziness or ineptitude will be punished. Those with an "external" locus of control, on the other hand, see fate or the actions of powerful others as more influential than their own behavior. Rotter finds that such beliefs are stable in most people across a variety of settings.[19]

Locus of control is important because experiments conducted by Rotter and others have consistently shown that internals are more likely than externals to gather information about their environment.[20] Herbert M. Lefcourt argues that internals also tend to have longer attention spans, particularly when they view tasks as tests of personal competence.[21] The intense ambition and competitive streak noted by Jimmy Carter's biographers suggest an internal locus of control and thus help to explain Carter's well-known ability to work long hours and to master arcane details of policy.[22] Internals need a stimulating environment to maintain interest. Externals, on the other hand, may prefer routine tasks and "standard operating procedures." To put this in the terms of the preceding discussion of extraversion, "internals" have a large incentive (their own interest in exerting control) to pay attention to their surroundings; they should behave like extraverts. Externals, on the other hand, have little reason to seek such stimuli; they should resemble introverts. This terminology is confusing (it is one reason why I adopt the simpler label of *open* or *closed* learning style). Yet the argument is straightforward. It is simply that decision makers can be divided into two groups according to their learning style: *open* individuals who desire a great deal of diverse information and advice, and *closed* individuals who rely primarily on their own instincts and on a much smaller quantity and variety of information to make decisions.[23]

The distinction between open and closed decision makers suggests that a common assumption about the relationship between decision makers and their environment should be refined. As long ago as 1908, Robert M. Yerkes and J. D. Dodson found that people are able to learn more with "moderate" stimulus from their environment than with either very high or very low stimulus.[24] The resulting inverted-U relationship between stimulus or stress and decision-making performance, sometimes called the "Yerkes-Dodson curve," has since been noted by many other scholars.[25] High-level decision makers are subject to stress for many reasons: time pressure, uncertainty, the potential consequences of their actions, and even the simple abundance of information to which they must attend. Some stress may help to concentrate a leader's attention on a particular problem. But as stress increases, decision makers are likely to become distracted. At this point, more information is not only useless but actually harmful.

The distinction between open and closed learning styles suggests that stress will not have the same effect on everyone. In general, open decision makers are able to tolerate higher levels of

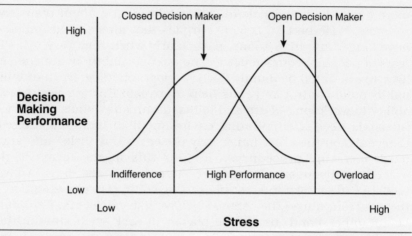

Fig. 2-1. The Relationship between Stress and Decision-Making Performance for Open and Closed Decision Makers.

stress than are closed decision makers. Because open individuals are accustomed to higher levels of stimulus from their environment, they subjectively feel less stress than would closed individuals in the same circumstances. The inverted-U curve describing the relationship between stress and performance thus shifts according to learning style, as shown in figure 2-1.

Barber's positive leaders, Eysenck's extraverts, and Rotter's internals are not the same sort of people in all respects. There are subtle differences among these descriptions of character. But research in each of these areas has roughly the same implications for learning style. The implication is not that only open leaders can learn. As figure 2-1 suggests, open and closed leaders are both capable of learning. But they tend to learn in different ways. Closed leaders prefer a constrained, highly managed flow of information. Open leaders, on the other hand, are more comfortable with a greater quantity of information and with contradictory information and advice. On balance, it is also true that open leaders are likely to learn more than closed leaders, a difference reflected in the height of their decision-making performance curves.

That some people are more comfortable in information-rich environments, and more likely to learn within them, does not sound like much of a revelation. Such differences between people are obvious. In any case, there is not much leaders can do to change their level of comfort in challenging, information-rich environments. Learning style is no easier to change than any other aspect of one's personality. The distinction between open and closed learning styles is important, however, because of its implications for the way in which leaders should organize their advisors. In short, open and closed leaders cannot afford to arrange their staff in the same way.

MANAGING ADVISORS

Leaders do not, in fact, use advisors in the same way. At the highest levels of government, policymakers may put considerable energy into deciding how best to organize their staff. Some prefer to delegate authority, others to hold the reins of power tightly. Some enjoy confrontation while others go to great lengths to avoid it. Some place themselves at the center of the flow of information, others at one end of a chain of advisors, and still others prefer to remove themselves from policy debates altogether, concentrating instead on the big picture and leaving details to their subordinates. Such variations in staff arrangements are the standard fare of research in public policy and organizational sociology. Yet the implications of learning style for leader-advisor relations have received little sustained attention.

Perhaps the most prominent discussion of high-level staff arrangements is Richard Tanner Johnson's typology of *formal, competitive,* and *collegial* groups.[26] Although it is popular, the typology is incomplete. It identifies two *dimensions* of advisory group structure: formal/informal and competitive/collegial.[27] In Johnson's view, competitive and collegial groups each combine elements of informality with political rewards that are allocated within the group either through constant-sum (competitive) or positive-sum (collegial) "games." The differences between formal competitive and formal-collegial staffs go unexplored, perhaps because Johnson expects formality to prevent such differences from expressing themselves.

Johnson and Alexander George (who adopts Johnson's classification scheme) treat staff organization largely as a matter of choice rather than of necessity. Any leader might choose to arrange his or her advisors in any of these ways. George suggests that leaders may also choose to mix elements of the different models. And

they may employ different staff arrangements for different purposes.[28] No doubt, leaders will have some general preferences
about the best way to organize their staff. Yet no single approach
can avoid trade-offs. More formal groups may be more efficient, for
example, but they may also be less flexible and less likely to consider out-of-the-ordinary solutions to problems. More competitive
groups may encourage debate, but potentially at the cost of building consensus in favor of any solution to a given problem.

Because of these trade-offs, George argues that any effort to
offer advice to policymakers must eventually move beyond such
simple, general models—a sentiment strongly shared by other specialists in the structure of policy-making staffs, such as John
Burke and Fred Greenstein.[29] George proposes a narrower focus
on precisely what this book will explore: the way groups handle
information and create (or interfere with) opportunities for leaders
to learn. The best way to promote learning, George argues, is to
institutionalize "devil's advocacy" in a system of "multiple advocacy decision making." To his credit, George recognizes that multiple advocacy is no panacea. Not every decision requires multiple
advocacy. And ironically, the higher the stakes involved in a given
problem, the more difficult it may be to encourage multiple advocacy. Senior advisors are usually reluctant to advocate solutions
they believe to be unpopular since doing so might tarnish their
own reputation or diminish their future influence. More subtle
social pressures to be a "team player" may also discourage multiple advocacy. In any case, a wider circle of advisors increases the
chances of potentially embarrassing "leaks."[30]

These are just the sort of problems that led Janis to suspect
"groupthink" as a major cause of decision-making "fiascoes."[31]
Janis prescribes the same medicine that George does—more
devil's advocacy. To encourage this, Janis suggests that leaders
make special efforts to establish a norm of "impartiality" that will
encourage critical thinking without fear of retribution. Janis also
recommends that important problems be given to multiple groups
and that leaders work to prevent these groups from becoming too
insular or cohesive.[32]

Janis and George (and many other scholars) agree, then, that
more multiple advocacy is better, ceteris paribus. As the previous
section of this chapter has shown, however, other things are not
equal—beginning with leaders themselves. Open leaders will be
much more comfortable with (and more able to benefit from) mul-

tiple advocacy than closed leaders. George is somewhat more sensitive to this problem than Janis, pointing out that an "executive's receptivity to multiple advocacy is . . . critical" and that it "is likely to suit the style and temperament of some presidents (and other officials who make lower-level policy at departmental and agency levels) more than others."[33] No single formula for organizing advisors is always appropriate, and leaders with different learning styles will function best and learn most when their staff is organized according to their particular needs and abilities.

Unfortunately, neither George nor other specialists in research on policymaking have offered much specific, prescriptive advice beyond a general injunction to take leadership style into account. Experimental research conducted by psychologists gives some indication of how to proceed. Eysenck (whose research on extraversion was briefly discussed in the preceding section) finds that "social conditions will act as additional drive to extraverts (sociable), but as distraction to introverts (unsociable), thus favoring the performance of the former."[34] Other psychologists have proposed an even simpler relationship between leader-advisor relations and performance. Evoking the inverted-U relationship between stimulus and performance, they argue that the presence of others in a group simply provides a higher "level of arousal" that stimulates extraverts to be more attentive but causes introverts to withdraw.[35] And taking a different approach, Jerry Burger finds that people with an internal locus of control are more resistant to pressures for conformity and thus more likely to resist groupthink.[36] The implication of such research is that open and closed leaders differ not only in their tolerance for information and stress in general, but in their ability to work with large, diverse advisory staffs in particular. There is, in other words, a range of inverted-U performance curves depending on the needs and personal learning style of decision makers (see figure 2-2).

Because open leaders are more comfortable with diverse and conflicting advice, and because they function well in group settings, they should benefit from precisely the sort of heterogeneous and freewheeling groups of advisors that Janis and George recommend. Leaders with closed learning styles, on the other hand, should prefer established routines, undifferentiated advisors, and a more carefully managed advisory group in general. Just as there are open and closed leaders, then, it is important to distinguish between open and closed advisory groups.

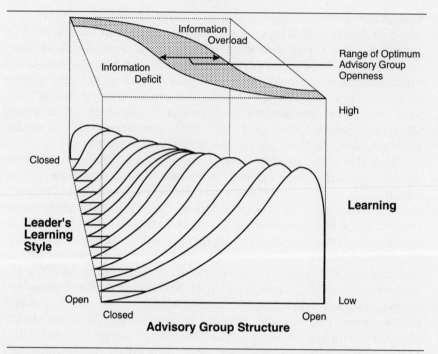

Fig. 2-2. Effects of Learning Style and Advisory Group Structure on Learning.

As with efforts to study the character of leaders, it is no simple matter to "measure" the openness of a group of advisors. In principle, if a leader consults many advisors with diverse backgrounds before making a decision, the group is open. If, on the other hand, advisors are few and share similar worldviews, the group is closed. At best, however, these are relative measures of openness. No group is absolutely open (representing all conceivable viewpoints), and there are only two ways a group of advisors could be described as completely closed: (a) if each member of the group shares identical views, or (b) if a leader consults no one at all before making a decision. For important, high-level policy decisions, neither scenario is likely. If the endpoints of the spectrum of staff openness have little practical relevance, then it will be difficult to say exactly how open a particular group is. Nor would it be helpful to designate an arbitrary number of advisors as the threshold for openness. It is precisely the argument of this book that such a threshold changes from one leader to another. The following chapters therefore adopt the expedient measure of searching for *changes* in the structure of presidential advisory staffs and then observing the consequences of these changes. It may be difficult to say, in the abstract, exactly how large or heterogeneous a group of advisors must be in order to be considered "open," but the implications of changes in staff organization are often much easier to discern.

A THEORY OF LEADER-GROUP RELATIONS

The principal argument of this book can now be stated more clearly. Unlike most other studies of the relationship between policymakers and their advisors, this book does not always recommend a more open staff or greater devil's advocacy. Leaders must guard not only against too little advice, but also against too much. Those with an open learning style are more likely to learn and improve their decision making if they receive advice from an open advisory group. Leaders with closed learning styles will benefit, on the other hand, from relatively closed advisory groups. An open group would overwhelm and frustrate the efforts of closed individuals to manage information and reach decisions. For such leaders, contentious discussions in a freewheeling atmosphere would be distracting or even threatening. *In sum, mismatches between the learning style of leaders and the structure of their advisory groups will inhibit learning and cause the quality of decision making to deteriorate.*

Open leaders in closed groups will not receive the information they need (and are capable of handling), will consider fewer options than they should, and will base their decisions on a distorted and incomplete understanding of the problems they face. The result will resemble what Janis called "groupthink." Closed leaders in open groups receive too much (and too challenging) information. They are more likely to suffer from a very different problem—one Janis, George, and others have ignored—which might be called "deadlock." In the face of conflicting advice and an overwhelming quantity and variety of information, they are likely to withdraw. In these circumstances, they will actually learn even less than had they been presented with fewer options and a more managed flow of advice. One might expect the problem of deadlock to be rare since important policymakers should be in a position to say how much advice they want. As chapter 6 will show, however, even presidents cannot always stop the flow of well-meaning (or not so well-meaning) advice. Indeed, senior policymakers (including American presidents) are often obliged to meet regularly with a wide array of individuals and representatives of various departments and bureaucracies. In some cases, it is practically impossible for leaders to find refuge from the advice and opinions of others. Cecil Crabb and Kevin Mulcahy argue, based on case studies stretching from the Roosevelt to the Reagan White House, that "the postwar American foreign policy process has become increasingly characterized by an absence of unity and cohesion."[37] As the news media has grown more intrusive, and as the internationalist consensus among postwar elites has evaporated, the danger of deadlock may actually be increasing.

Unsurprisingly, a corollary to this argument is that open leaders are generally more capable of learning and improving the quality of their decision making over time. It is for this reason that the "learning curves" shown in figure 2-2 are higher on balance for open leaders than for closed leaders, even when differences in staff structure are taken into account. This is so partially because an overload of information representing diverse viewpoints is more difficult for closed leaders to cope with than is a shortage of information for their open counterparts. As just noted, an open leader can always choose to seek more information, but a closed leader may have a hard time avoiding it. Of course, it is better for leaders to have access to more information if they can handle it. Consequently, open leaders are not only more likely to learn, but also likely to learn more than closed leaders. Figure 2–3 summarizes, in a simpler form than figure 2-2, the relationship between learning style and advisory group structure.

The implication of this argument for leaders is that they must take steps to avoid whichever "pathology"—groupthink or deadlock—they are most likely to confront, depending on their own learning style. In a series of thoughtful studies, Margaret Hermann and Thomas Preston argue that U.S. presidents ordinarily do just this, adapting the structure of their advisory groups to their own leadership style.[38] FDR is often taken as an example of an assertive president who consciously chose to pit advisors against each other in an effort to encourage debate and sharpen their arguments. Over time, Truman modified Roosevelt's contentious

Learning Style	Advisory Group Structure	
	Open	Closed
Open	Effective Information Gathering	Information Deficit - Groupthink Likely
Closed	Information Overload - Deadlock Likely	Moderately Effective Information Gathering

Fig. 2-3. Four Combinations of Learning Style and Advisory Group Structure.

staff arrangements, delegating more authority to his subordinates and, at the same time, allowing them freer access to the Oval Office. Reacting to what he perceived as disorganization, Eisenhower relied more heavily on a chief of staff and on a formal staff structure. Kennedy, in turn, reacted to Eisenhower's apparent formalism and sought to place himself at the center of a more relaxed and flexible circle of advisors.[39] One might interpret this evolution of advisory staff arrangements as providing support for Hermann and Preston's argument, revealing each president's conscious efforts to craft advisory groups appropriate to his leadership style. It is also possible that staff arrangements represent a cycle of reactions to the perceived shortcomings of a predecessor's methods.

In any case, the following chapters will show that leaders are often unable to regulate completely the structure of their advisory groups, whatever their preferences. Close, trusted advisors may suddenly resign. New appointments may arrive with unexpected agendas. And, in ways that can be particularly disruptive for closed leaders, advice often comes looking for presidents whether they want it or not. Achieving control over advisors is a political problem as well as a procedural one. Subordinates naturally fight for influence, and experienced leaders are well aware of the political stakes implicit in their decisions about who has direct access and who does not. Chapter 7 will take up the political problem of advisory openness in more detail. First, however, the intervening chapters must establish that advisory arrangements matter and that the consequences of mismatches are predictable.

The first issue in testing this claim is, as always, to identify an appropriate (and accessible) body of evidence on which to draw. Studies of presidential decision making pose special challenges in this regard. Most decision makers, and especially those in positions of national prominence, describe their decisions as the products of rational analysis and considerable hard thought. Their published memoirs tend to be self-serving. And for important decisions, other forms of documentation—if they exist at all—may be classified or otherwise unavailable. Fortunately, it is unnecessary to determine what a president felt, said, or perceived at a given moment in order to know whether his learning style was open or closed. The openness of presidential advisory groups may well be more fluid, but any changes that do occur (solicitation of new viewpoints) are frequently apparent.[40] Measuring the consequences of a mismatch between leader and advisors, however, poses a bigger challenge. To show how a particular combination of presidential learning style and advisory group structure leads to improvements in (or deterioration of) the quality of decision making requires careful historical process tracing and "behind-the-scenes" information about presidential learning.

Because the historical record is more complete for postwar U.S. presidents than for their predecessors, chapters 3–6 focus on the foreign policy decision making of two such presidents: Dwight Eisenhower and Ronald Reagan. Their presidencies make good choices for a comparative study of decision making for several reasons.[41] Both men were popular presidents, and yet both were strongly criticized in academic circles for their apparent failure to oversee subordinates and to provide leadership. Moreover, both were known for their "hands-off" administrative styles. As much as possible, therefore, these administrative similarities help to control for organizational differences not specifically related to learning style and advisory group openness.

Eisenhower's personality and learning style, however, was very different from Reagan's. As chapter 3 will show in detail, Eisenhower was comfortable with wide-ranging advice and conflicting opinions. He was inclined, particularly when making decisions on security policy, to consult widely before committing his administration to action. Reagan strongly preferred smaller groups of advisors in whom he had confidence. Neither leader was always able, however, to employ the staff structure he preferred.

Chapter 4 discusses policy deliberations during which they *were* able to use their preferred staff arrangements. These cases serve as a baseline for the analysis of learning failures that follows. Confronting the collapse of the French garrison at Dien Bien Phu (and the likely collapse of the conservative French government itself), and again in deliberations over the prospect of Alaskan statehood, Eisenhower reversed policies in which he personally believed after being convinced by his advisors that these policies were untenable. By almost any definition, Eisenhower *learned* in these cases. Similarly, when his administration faced economic disaster during the international debt crisis of the early 1980s and military disaster in Lebanon, Reagan too was able to reverse course at the behest of his advisors. These four cases correspond to the top-left and bottom-right quadrants (respectively) of figure 2-3.

Chapters 5 and 6 examine cases in which these presidents failed to learn apparently obvious lessons. Eisenhower never successfully responded either to McCarthy's red-baiting scare tactics (which the president personally despised) or to growing balance of payments deficits. Facing each of these problems, Eisenhower uncharacteristically refused to hear from a growing number of his own advisors who advocated a change in policy. Instead, he suppressed this internal dissent and encouraged his advisors to "toe the administration line" on these issues, resulting in deliberations that (when they occurred at all) resembled groupthink. Reagan, on the other hand, failed to learn for different reasons. During the Iran-Contra affair and, earlier, in the debate over the mounting budget deficits, Reagan got plenty of advice that challenged his administration's policies. At first, in each case, he made some effort to adapt his policies. Yet as criticism mounted, both internal and external, Reagan actually became less responsive. In striking examples of deadlock, he simply "withdrew" from these contentious issues and allowed administration policy to drift. It is no coincidence that the budget deficits and the Iran-Contra scandal became the Achilles' heel(s) of the Reagan administration. Table 2-1 classifies all of these cases by learning style and advisory structure.

Table 2-1. Classification of Cases by Leader and Advisory Group
Structure

Individual	Open Group	Closed Group
Open (Eisenhower)	Effective Learning, Good Adaptation, *Ex.: Dien Bien Phu, Alaskan Statehood*	Groupthink, Poor Adaptation, Inflexibility, *Ex.: McCarthyism, Balance of Payments*
Closed (Reagan)	Deadlock, Overload, Policy Drift, *Ex.: Iran-Contra Affair, Budget Deficit*	Moderate Learning, Incremental Adaptation, *Ex.: International Debt, Lebanon Withdrawal*

CONCLUSION

Because research on groupthink, and foreign policy decision
making more generally, has most often addressed the "high politics" of security policy, this book pays special attention to cases of
domestic and foreign economic policymaking as well as to security
issues. A leader's ability to learn may seem to be particularly crucial during a security crisis since poor decision making can lead to
armed conflict or even to global war. But decisions on other matters can also have striking consequences. As John Odell has
shown in some detail, for example, the decisions of President
Nixon and a handful of his key advisors on U.S. monetary policy
reshaped both domestic and international markets with far-reaching and lasting consequences.[42] The same president's behavior
during the Watergate scandal was a turning point in the relationship between the American people and their government.

Although none were quite so dramatic as the Watergate break-
in or the decision to abandon the gold standard, the cases examined in the following chapters also had lasting effects. Indeed,
Eisenhower's failure to reckon with the balance of payments problem helped to set the stage for Nixon's suspension of gold convertability. The outcome in several cases (e.g., the witch-hunts of
the McCarthy era or the chronic budget deficits of the 1980s)
caused lasting damage to the United States' reputation abroad.
Eisenhower's refusal to help the French at Dien Bien Phu was still
a vivid memory during the Suez Crisis and undoubtedly hastened

de Gaulle down the path of French independence from the U.S. and NATO. And the Iran-Contra affair became to covert operations what the war in Vietnam was to anticommunist intervention—a reminder that foreign adventures (even secret ones) lacking broad-based public support are unlikely to succeed.

Moreover, in each case discussed in the following chapters, the president had some freedom to act. It mattered, therefore, whether or not (and what) the president learned. A sense of manifest destiny or simple historical determinism may lead many Americans to assume, for example, that Alaskan statehood was inevitable. But it was not, at least not in the form that it ultimately took. A far greater part of Alaskan territory might have remained under direct federal control as a national defense exclusion zone, hostage to the strategic sensibilities of the cold war, were it not for the efforts of Eisenhower's secretary of the interior to alter the president's position. Or, to take another example, Reagan might certainly have chosen to retain American troops in Lebanon after his advisors recommended withdrawal. That he took their advice, even though it contradicted his own desires, undoubtedly saved the lives of many marines.

It is unfortunate that political scientists who study policy-making ordinarily limit their attention to security policy and decision making during international crises, ignoring domestic and foreign economic policy. It is also ironic, since economists and management specialists have long been enthusiastic students of effective decision making.[43] In fact, even those political scientists who specialize in crisis decision making are net consumers of economic and psychological theories, generating few of their own. Perhaps the tendency of political scientists to devote more attention to macro-level concerns such as class or state interests arises from unrealistic expectations about what micro-level theories can accomplish. Micro-level theories, such as the one offered in this book, cannot hope to reveal the larger patterns of international diplomacy or domestic governance. They make no attempt to do so—they are theories of policymaking (not of history). The debate over the importance of individual leaders and their ability to learn, briefly discussed at the beginning of this chapter, is something of a red herring. A good theory of presidential learning does not compete with institutional theories of American politics, class analysis of international markets, or claims about the stability of the international system. Micro-theories seek to explain behavior; macrotheories, to explain limits on behavior. Neither is really a substitute for the other. To change metaphors, it makes no more sense for a specialist in electoral institutions or global markets to deny that leadership and learning matter than it does for a specialist in riverbed topology to deny that heavy rain matters. Undoubtedly, there is room both for topologists and weather forecasters.

Perhaps the effects of heavy rain are more predictable than those of bad leadership, but bad leadership has consequences too. And unlike rain, about which flood control managers can do nothing, leaders *can* affect their prospects for learning. True, they cannot easily change their own personality, but they can certainly change the way they organize their staff and the way they go about making important decisions. Unfortunately, out of a misguided sense that class, state, or other "larger" interests are more important than political agency and the behavior of individuals, political scientists have contributed regrettably few innovations to the study of policymaking. Almost forgotten is Harold Lasswell's observation that "behind the façades of the class and skill struggle run the dialectics of personality."[44]

CHAPTER 3

Eisenhower and Reagan: Comparing Learning Styles

"He was enormously popular during his eight years in the White House. In contrast to Truman, Johnson, Nixon, Ford, and Carter, he not only entered but also *left* office riding high in the polls. Yet when he stepped down the experts who make it their business to observe presidents closely did not join in the public adulation."[1] The coy ambiguity of this description, written by one of the "experts," hints at the similarities between the Eisenhower and Reagan administrations. Fred Greenstein, who has studied each of these two presidents carefully, is describing both.

There are other similarities. Both leaders saw their election as a call to reduce the role of government in the private sector, as a "mandate for change." Eisenhower adopted this phrase for the title of one of his autobiographies, wherein he explained, "I wanted to make it clear that we would not be simply a continuation of the New Deal and Fair Deal. . . . In initiating a reversal of trends based on such beliefs—trends which by 1953 were twenty years old—we were setting in motion revolutionary activity."[2] Almost forty years later, Reagan explained his campaign for the presidency in nearly identical terms: "Now, people were rebelling, trying to get government off their back and out of their pocketbooks. . . . After a half century that had given them the New Deal and the 'Great Society'

and produced a government that took an average of forty-five percent of the national wealth, people were just fed up."[3]

Whether or not their elections were "mandates," both
Eisenhower and Reagan clearly were popular. They were the only
two postwar presidents (prior to Bill Clinton) to leave office after
serving complete terms with public approval ratings surpassing
50 percent.[4] Perhaps a good part of their success came from the
personal rapport each of these presidents seemed to have with the
American public. Eisenhower was a returning war hero who made
a bold promise to extricate the United States from Korea—and
then delivered. Reagan was a symbol of American resurgence who
vowed to eradicate the "malaise" of the 1970s and to replace it with
"a spiritual revival in America."[5] Both men radiated a supreme
confidence and optimism that responded perfectly to the American
public's yearning, in the early 1950s and late 1970s, for a renew-
al of American pre-eminence.[6]

Perhaps some of this popularity also stems, ironically, from
both presidents' unusual ability to dissociate themselves from
their own policies. In the 1950s, many observers considered John
Foster Dulles to be the real architect of the Eisenhower administration's foreign policies—and particularly of its foreign policy *failures*. Dulles's somber personality and strident anticommunist
moralism made him a lightning rod for popular dissatisfaction. His
rhetoric of liberation in Europe and his relentless opposition to
communism around the world caused the public, as Richard
Immerman put it, "to suspect Dulles of being a paper tiger, and an
irresponsibly hypocritical one."[7] Many also suspected Sherman
Adams, Eisenhower's chief of staff, of having undue influence over
the president, and he took a good deal of the blame for unpopular
domestic policies.[8] Eisenhower, meanwhile was portrayed by
Washington Post cartoonist Herblock as a smiling, vaguely naive
weekend golfer. Perhaps he was not entirely "in charge," but Ike
was easy to like.

In the Reagan administration, the "troika" of James Baker,
Edwin Meese, and Michael Deaver (and, in the second term, Chief
of Staff Donald Regan) appeared to be the real policymakers in the
White House—to such an extent that the popular media for a time
labeled Meese the "acting president." Scandals eventually forced
Meese and Regan out of the White House, but the "lightning-rod
effect" that had helped Eisenhower in the 1950s served Reagan
equally well in the 1980s.[9] A popular image as a grandfatherly

cowboy-actor who cared little for the details of his own policies may not have been particularly inspiring, but nor did it lend itself to pointed criticism. And so, in the cases of both Eisenhower and Reagan, their aides took the blame for their failures, while the presidents themselves took the credit for their successes. Both are aptly described by the term coined to describe the latter: the "Teflon president."

Each man, however, was ultimately responsible for his own administration's policies. And despite the many similarities between their presidencies, these two leaders tended to arrive at important decisions in different ways. These differences—in learning style and in the way each president preferred to arrange and use advisors—are the subject of this chapter. Chapters 4–6 explore the consequences of these differences.

THE EISENHOWER ADMINISTRATION

According to one view, Eisenhower was a hidden-hand savant whose "apparent artlessness" masked "extraordinary capacities for detached, orderly examination of problems and personalities."[10] The president's brother Milton downplays the notion of hidden-hand calculation, attributing Ike's reluctance to occupy the spotlight simply to a propensity to "[build] up the other fellow," and John Eisenhower also laments that "his father's tendency to subordinate his voice to others may have restricted his ability to galvanize public opinion."[11]

James David Barber offers still another explanation for Eisenhower's political detachment. Barber labels Eisenhower a "passive-negative" personality type meaning, as noted in chapter 2, that he neither enjoyed politics (negativity) nor did he actively participate much in it (passivity).[12] Yet Peter Lyon finds that, far from being passive, Eisenhower was driven by an unremitting "ambition and . . . determination to excel, to succeed."[13] For Arthur Larson and Andrew Goodpaster, moreover, Dwight Eisenhower was neither inherently active nor passive but, in their view, was above all a man of principle. As Larson put it during a retrospective evaluation of the Eisenhower administration at the University of Virginia's Miller Center, "I noticed very early . . . how often he said, 'I always' or 'I never' and then he would dredge down into some general principle of life or rule of life and come up with his decision."[14]

Even these brief sketches of the Eisenhower administration suggest that it may not be easy to distill a clear picture of Eisenhower's decision-making or learning style. As it turns out, two schools of thought about his skills as a leader have emerged over time. The first, especially popular among liberal intellectuals in the 1950s, portrays Eisenhower as an indecisive and uninformed weekend president, "typically with a golf club in his hand and a broad but vapid grin on his face."[15] This group believed that Eisenhower was "unduly impressed by wealthy businessmen and overly concerned for a balanced budget, and that he had reduced military expenditures to the point of endangering the nation's security."[16] Eisenhower's lack of interest in domestic problems, in the view of these critics, produced a string of missed opportunities. Even conservatives worried, moreover, about Eisenhower's weak leadership of the Republican Party and his failure to strengthen the position of moderates.[17] Perhaps the best that could be said of Eisenhower, according to the first school of thought, was that he "carried on a line-and-staff operation and delegated most work to others but . . . knew his mind and in the end kept from making the war blunder his successors made; . . . he vetoed the apocalypse whenever it was proposed."[18] Pessimists felt that Eisenhower had even less control, that he made little effort to inform himself about many of the pressing issues of the day, and that he was virtually a pawn of his own advisors (particularly Dulles).[19]

Most recent students of the Eisenhower presidency, however, paint a more flattering portrait. The "revisionist" version of the story portrays Eisenhower as a dignified, intelligent, and shrewd politician—one who was very much in control of decision making within his administration. This is the Eisenhower who presided over eight years of prosperity, who avoided U.S. involvement in Vietnam, and who extricated the country from Korea. In the revisionist view, President Eisenhower's public caution and restraint masked intense behind-the-scenes efforts to gather information about his policy options. Clearly, Eisenhower was not one to make rash or hurried judgments. As he put it himself, "unless circumstances and responsibility demanded an instant judgment, I learned to reserve mine until the last proper moment."[20]

During the recurrent crises over the islands of Quemoy and Matsu off the Chinese mainland, for example, Eisenhower received widely differing advice ranging from outright abandonment of Formosa to nuclear bombardment of the mainland, but he put off a firm commitment to action as long as possible. Ultimately, he resorted to a nuclear threat in the form of a press conference analogy between atomic weapons and bullets.[21] Yet although its implications were frightening, even this statement was far from a concrete plan for nuclear attack. What his critics might have considered both indecisive and irresponsible, others have come to praise. According to the noted cold war scholar Robert Divine, "Ike introduced a note of deliberate ambiguity into American policy. . . . The beauty of Eisenhower's policy is that to this day no one can be sure whether or not he would have responded militarily to an invasion of the offshore islands, and whether he would have used nuclear weapons."[22] Stephen Ambrose adds, "the full truth is that Eisenhower himself did not know. In retrospect, what stands out about Eisenhower's crisis management is that at every stage he kept his options open. Flexibility was one of his chief characteristics as Supreme Commander in World War II; as president, he insisted on retaining that flexibility. He never knew himself just how he would respond to an invasion of Quemoy and Matsu, because he insisted on waiting to see the precise nature of the attack before deciding how to react."[23]

This "flexibility" may have served Eisenhower well, but it bedevils efforts to arrive at a clear understanding of his personal character and decision style. As Barber complained, Eisenhower "comes as close as any President to being one who strays beyond our crude categories."[24] Fortunately, the following discussion need not concern itself with the full range of commentary on this president's character, or with whether the crude categories of the early school or those of the revisionist school are more applicable. If nebulous categories have contributed to unresolved (and probably unresolvable) debates, then let us turn to a more specific category of analysis: personal openness and the ability to learn.

Learning Style

One of the most vividly recounted stories in Eisenhower's memoirs concerns a boyhood encounter on his aunt and uncle's farm with a goose that was probably larger, and certainly more aggressive, than he. The animal repeatedly chased young Ike from the barnyard into the farmhouse. After he had unsuccessfully confronted his nemesis several times, his uncle Luther gave him a broom handle for a weapon and sent him back outside. As Eisenhower tells it,

> I was not at all sure that my uncle was very smart. More frightened at the moment of his possible scolding than I was of aggression, I took what was meant to be a firm, but was really a trembling, stand the next time the fowl came close. Then I let out a yell and rushed toward him, swinging the club as fast as I could. He turned and I gave him a satisfying smack right in the fanny. He let out a most satisfactory squawk and ran off. This was my signal to chase him, which I did.[25]

Eisenhower's memoirs tell many stories, such as this one, that emphasize the virtues of perseverance and self-reliance. He recalls that his mother "deeply believed in self-discipline and she preached it constantly."[26] Even when self-discipline failed and the Eisenhower boys got into fights, their parents rarely intervened:

> One day when relatives were visiting, Dwight and Edgar began scuffling in the yard. The relatives called (their mother) Ida's attention to the fight. She smiled and did nothing. . . . Another time Ida was baking in the kitchen. Dwight and Edgar began a fight on the kitchen floor. Soon the older and heavier Edgar was sitting astride the prostrate Dwight, giving him a pounding. "Give up?" Edgar shouted. "No!" Dwight gasped. Edgar grabbed Dwight's hair and began to thump his head against the floor. Earl (Dwight's younger brother) rushed in to help Dwight. Ida, without turning away from the stove, said sharply to Earl, "Let them alone."[27]

Along with self-reliance, however, came responsibility. Each boy had a share of household chores, and failing to complete them meant punishment. Eisenhower later recalled that his father was "never one for spoiling any child by sparing the rod."[28]

Through such reminisces in his memoirs, Eisenhower places great emphasis on his early education in personal responsibility. Perhaps the only event that really shook his faith in his control over his own destiny was an injury that ended his football career.[29] After Eisenhower had led Army to victories over Stevens Institute and Rutgers in 1912, his photograph appeared in *The New York Times* as "one of the most promising backs in Eastern football."[30] But he twisted his knee in a game against Tufts, and later that week "while participating in the 'monkey drill' in the riding hall— leaping off and back onto a galloping horse—his knee crumbled when he hit the ground."[31] The knee eventually healed, but Eisenhower's days as a running back were over.

> So great was his depression that several times his room-mate had to talk him out of resigning from the Academy. "Life seemed to have little meaning," he later recalled. "A need to excel was almost gone." His studies suffered. As a plebe, he had stood fifty-seventh in a class of 212; in his Yearling year, when he hurt his knee, he slipped to eighty-first in a class of 177. P. A. Hodgson wrote of him, "Poor Dwight merely consents to exist until graduation shall set him free. . . ."[32]

Only after returning during summer vacation to Abilene, Kansas, where he played the local hero, did his spirits revive. On his return to West Point, he became a cheerleader and, eventually, the coach of the junior varsity team.

The connection between events such as these and Eisenhower's learning style in the White House is not immediately obvious. What they do suggest—a point on which his biographers seem to agree—is that Eisenhower's childhood gave him every reason to become a self-assured, confident adult.[33] Even his knee injury serves to illustrate, by the intensity of his reaction, the depth of his commitment to self-reliance and to overcoming difficult odds through perseverance. People with such qualities might also be described by psychologists as having an "internal locus of control" (a belief in their own ability to shape events and to determine outcomes). Eisenhower's childhood was a model of the sort of upbringing that should encourage an internal locus of control. His parents consistently encouraged him to look to himself in both success and failure.[34]

As discussed in chapter 2, moreover, locus of control has important implications for learning style. An internal locus of control is strongly associated with an active and self-reliant orientation to the world.[35] "Internals" tend to gather information proactively, to be comfortable with relatively large quantities of it, and to make use of it in their decisions. Thus, the mature Eisenhower's propensity—noted by admirers and critics alike—to avoid taking firm stances until equipped with a maximum of information about a given subject may be one of the most significant consequences of the self-reliance he learned as a boy. Eisenhower entrusted the most important decisions only to himself.[36]

Like his self-reliance and "internality," Eisenhower's extraversion quickly became evident during his childhood. Perhaps growing up in a busy household with four other brothers helped to instill a certain tolerance for social contact. The family's modest house in Abilene, Kansas, was crowded (the older boys, in fact, slept two-to-a-bed in one small bedroom), but in this environment Dwight Eisenhower grew into a popular, easygoing young man. Childhood acquaintances later recalled that he "was just a jolly good friend," that he "was a real boy, associated with real boys, did the usual boyish pranks," and that he was a "regular guy."[37] By all accounts, he was optimistic and outgoing from an early age.

Later, after he became a high school football hero, he "was the most popular young man in town" according to one biographer.[38] At West Point, he continued to pay more attention to sports (and to pranks) than to conduct demerits or academic standing. When one of his lifelong friends, Swede Hazlett, came to visit him at the military academy in 1915, he found Ike to be "generally liked and admired. . . . Everyone was his friend."[39] After college, Eisenhower's outgoing good humor made him a popular young officer. "He played poker with the other junior officers, winning consistently, went drinking with them, and generally got along easily with the gang."[40] In 1916, he married Mary Geneva (Mamie) Doud, and the young couple loved to entertain so much that their apartment became known as "Club Eisenhower."

The easygoing social graces Eisenhower developed in childhood and in school held him in good stead as an adult. As supreme allied commander, perhaps his most important (and most difficult) task was to maintain the peace between strong-willed military commanders from several different Allied countries. Despite serious disputes with Churchill and de Gaulle, Eisenhower was, according to Divine, "able to retain the admiration and respect of these Allied leaders."[41] By the time he became president, "Eisenhower had spent his life working out compromises between strong willed people."[42] His social poise and outgoing nature, like his self-reliance, also improved his ability to learn about problems before making decisions. He was able to put his aides and advisors at ease, and he was very comfortable soliciting advice, even from opposing and contradictory perspectives. He was able to manage conflict among his associates and to learn from it.

In sum, then, Eisenhower's learning style closely resembles the "open" type described in chapter 2. Both his childhood and his adult life give every indication of a sociable, extraverted, and self-reliant personal character. Although this description may run partly counter to Barber's description of Eisenhower as passive, many other studies of presidential character—particularly those based on material released by historical archives during the past two decades—concur with the portrayal of Eisenhower as an active, involved, and generally open decision maker.[43]

This claim is also consistent with the findings of the relatively few quantitative studies of presidential character. In one, Dean Keith Simonton used a standardized list of adjectives (the Gough Adjective Check List, a common personality research instrument) to evaluate the personality of thirty-nine presidents based on various historical records. Eisenhower's scores were relatively high on both "friendliness" (with which adjectives such as *friendly, outgoing, sociable,* and *cheerful* were associated) and "flexibility" (the opposite of adjectives such as *stubborn* and *hardheaded*).[44] In another quantitative analysis of biographical materials, Lloyd Etheredge found that Eisenhower was relatively "extraverted" compared to thirty-five other "policy elites" (including secretaries of state, presidential advisors, and eleven other presidents from McKinley to Lyndon Johnson).[45] And using a different technique (asking historians, social scientists, journalists, and acquaintances of a president to describe him by ranking the items of the California Q-set, another standard personality research instrument), my own earlier studies also lend support to the description of Eisenhower as open.[46] Finally, Eisenhower's close associates and most prominent biographers have generally portrayed him as open. As his chief of staff during World War II, Walter Bedell Smith, observed,

> He has great patience, and he disdains no advice regardless of source. One of his most successful methods in dealing with individuals is to assume that he himself is lacking in detailed knowledge and liable to make an error and is seeking advice. This is by no means a pose, because

he actually values the recommendations and suggestions he receives.[47]

Similarly, according to Ambrose, Eisenhower "wanted to know all that he could about the world around him, and he would pursue his curiosity with a single minded concentration until he found the answer."[48] Just because a leader is open or curious, of course, should not cause us to predict that he or she will learn. Learning naturally depends on many other things, including the need for haste or secrecy, the importance of the decision, and—the factor most directly under a leader's control—the way advisors are used (or ignored).

Advisors

Twenty-five years after President Eisenhower took office, his White House staff gathered in Washington for a reunion. As one of the assembled group remembered it, a "camaraderie . . . filled the room," and when a reporter asked the purpose of the gathering, they responded, "Perhaps . . . it's the first time the members of a White House staff ever *wanted* to see each other again!"[49] Such abiding collegiality would be remarkable for many presidential staffs, but it characterized the Eisenhower administration. According to William B. Ewald, "Dwight Eisenhower, more than any other President in recent memory, was an organization man."[50]

Since his days as a football coach (which lasted, on an occasional basis, well into his army career), Eisenhower placed great faith in teamwork and careful organization. In a statement that could have been extracted directly from one of Herbert Simon's thick studies of organizations, Eisenhower himself observed,

Organization cannot make a genius out of an incompetent; even less can it, of itself, make the decisions which are required to trigger necessary action. On the other hand, disorganization can scarcely fail to result in inefficiency and can easily lead to disaster. Organization makes more efficient the gathering and analysis of facts, and the arranging of the findings of experts in logical fashion. Therefore organization helps the responsible individual make the necessary decision, and helps assure that it is satisfactorily carried out.[51]

Efficient planning and organization at SHAEF (the Supreme Headquarters of the Allied Expeditionary Force) seemed to be an essential component of the war effort, and Eisenhower believed that a similar organization was necessary for a president.[52] His penchant for formal, "military" organization was sufficiently pronounced that Harry Truman predicted before leaving the White House, "He'll say, 'Do this! Do that!' *And nothing will happen.* Poor Ike—it won't be a bit like the Army. He'll find it very frustrating."[53]

But Eisenhower did realize that the presidency differed from his previous experience. In a letter to Swede Hazlett not long after taking office, he noted, "I have always striven to prepare myself as much as possible for the known or calculable requirements of any job assigned me. In this particular post such intentions and practices have to be almost completely discarded. This is because of the infinite variety of problems presented, and the rapidity with which they are placed in front of the responsible individual for action."[54] To satisfy these demands, Eisenhower relied heavily on his advisors and White House staff. As he put it, "All of these individuals are the ones that help the Head in reaching a common sense, average solution. . . . They help to meet the deficiencies of a faulty memory, a deteriorating disposition, and any tendency toward the pessimistic or the morbid. The point of this recitation is that even the matter of reaching a common sense solution—or making an average decision—is not one that can be performed by an individual operating alone."[55]

Eisenhower expected his advisers to provide him information from a variety of perspectives and, consequently, was not inclined to surround himself with sycophants. Ambrose gives the following illustrative account of a Cabinet meeting:

During a Cabinet discussion over ways to cut spending, . . . [Henry Cabot] Lodge suggested reducing grants to the states for highway programs. Eisenhower replied that "my personal opinion is that we should spend more for highways." Lodge mumbled, "I withdraw." Eisenhower wanted none of that. "It's open to discussion," he told Lodge, and reminded him that "I've given way on a number of personal opinions to this gang."[56]

Even when their opinions ran counter to his own, Eisenhower generally listened carefully to his advisors. As he once told Andrew Goodpaster: "I have the best people I can find giving me advice, . . . and I take their advice. But, . . . I don't have to like it!"[57]

Within his group of advisors, several individuals were particularly important sources of guidance for the president. Primus inter pares on matters of foreign policy was John Foster Dulles. According to Richard H. Immerman, "one would have to go back at least to John Quincy Adams to find a secretary of state who as a student and practitioner of American statecraft was Dulles's peer."[58] Eisenhower would undoubtedly have agreed; he wrote in his personal diary that

> there is probably no one in the world who has the technical competence of Foster Dulles in the diplomatic field. He has spent his life in this work in one form or another and is a man of great intellectual capacity and moral courage.[59]

Although Dulles' public image as a dour and uncompromising moralist placed him among the least popular figures in the Eisenhower administration, the president clearly relied heavily on Dulles for foreign policy advice. And this advice was freely and copiously given. Eisenhower noted in his memoirs that the cables he received from Dulles during the secretary's foreign travels would make "a stack more than four feet high."[60]

On economic matters, the president looked initially to George Humphrey, during his first term, and then to Robert Anderson in his second term. Humphrey, in particular, was a close confidant—the only Cabinet member to become an intimate friend of the president.[61] On matters of policy, Eisenhower found him to be "persuasive in his presentations" with "his facts well in hand."[62] The president also greatly admired Anderson and placed him, according to Karl G. Harr (one of the president's special assistants), among his "favorite people."[63] Although Eisenhower had many other domestic and economic advisors, Humphrey and Anderson were "more-than-equal" voices in domestic affairs.[64]

Another close advisor, on matters of both foreign and domestic policy, was Milton Eisenhower. The president called his brother the "most knowledgeable and widely informed of all the people with whom I deal" and "the most highly qualified man in the United States to be President."[65] The two frequently discussed the pressing issues of the day over breakfast. Eisenhower's other advisors were too numerous to list exhaustively, but they included Sherman Adams (assistant to the president); Arthur Burns and Raymond Saulnier (consecutive chairs of the Council of Economic Advisors); Robert Cutler (special assistant to the president for national security); Allen Dulles (director of the CIA); Andrew Goodpaster (the president's staff secretary); James Hagerty (the president's press secretary); Gabriel Hauge (special economic advisor); Wilton Persons (White House congressional liaison); Walter Bedell Smith (undersecretary of state and Eisenhower's former chief of staff during the war); Charles Wilson (secretary of defense); Vice President Richard Nixon; and, on military-strategic matters, Admirals Arleigh Burke and Arthur Radford, and Generals Matthew Ridgway, Nathan Twining, and Maxwell Taylor.[66]

Like any president, Eisenhower relied on some more than others, and above all on a smaller group of close advisors and personal friends. Indeed, Sherman Adams was sometimes criticized for restricting access to the president.[67] But Adams appears to have served more to organize information than to restrict it.[68] And several other channels of "outside" information remained open to the president. Eisenhower held frequent "stag dinners," as he called them, to which a variety of prominent individuals were invited. Also, routine Cabinet meetings often included, in addition to Cabinet members themselves, more than twenty other members of the White House staff.[69] And, as Bradley Patterson observes, the Cabinet setting can help to guard against insular decision making:

> Cabinet members don't like Cabinet meetings. Particularly, they do not like having their favorite subjects brought up on the table for everybody to shoot at. They much prefer the "Amen Corner" philosophy, coming individually to the President and saying, "Mr. President, look what I've got here, please sign here and don't let anybody get in my way." Eisenhower, of course, was not going to conduct his government in this way.[70]

Instead, "he was going to have all the major questions of domestic policy laid out on the table in front of him and he didn't want anybody coming around the back fence and making an *ex parte* private presentation to him, and he was going to run the National Security Council (NSC) the same way."[71]

The National Security Council, in fact, was another important conduit of information to the president. Eisenhower attended 329 of the 366 NSC meetings held during his presidency.[72] He clearly regarded it as a vital source of information, so much so that he told President-elect Kennedy it was "the most important weekly meeting of the government."[73] To be sure, the NSC served more as a sounding board for foreign policy debates than as a high-level policy-making body. The most important decisions, and particularly those dealing with sensitive diplomatic or strategic matters, were discussed in detail among smaller groups of advisors.[74] But even when the president made a final policy decision in a meeting with a few of his close advisors, he ordinarily heard first from larger deliberative groups such as the Cabinet or the NSC.

Andrew Goodpaster summarized the president's access to advice as follows: "On the question of advisers, Eisenhower has a very large number. They extended over a quite wide range, and he used them in a variety of ways. . . . [Moreover,] he had a tremendous range of unofficial advisers or interlocutors."[75] Stephen Hess also notes that (with the partial exception, as just noted, of George Humphrey) Eisenhower "picked a cabinet of strangers. Not one member could have been considered an old friend."[76] As a result, Eisenhower was surrounded by relatively independent and diverse formal advisors and by an even larger group of informal ones.

Of course, Eisenhower did not want to run every department personally. Indeed, he often delegated considerable authority to his subordinates, perhaps contributing to his public image of passivity. Ewald offers an illustrative example of the president's willingness to delegate:

> In 1960 . . . (Attorney General) Bill Rogers reported the Department's readiness to seek antitrust indictments of leading executives in the electrical equipment industry, including some known personally to Eisenhower.
>
> "Did these men do what you say they did?" Eisenhower asked.
>
> "Yes, Mr. President."
>
> "Can you prove it?"
>
> "Yes."
>
> "It's a sad thing." And then, with no request for a review or a delay or a second thought, "Go ahead and indict them."[77]

Herbert Brownell, Bill Rogers's predecessor, put it more succinctly: "It was almost scary how much power he delegated to you."[78] On domestic matters, in particular, Eisenhower preferred to let others shoulder the burden of routine decisions. Such issues were not in the realm of his expertise, and the details of domestic policy were often managed by Adams or by Hagerty. Vice President Nixon also played an important role in domestic policymaking. Eisenhower particularly shunned the intrigue of domestic party politics, and as a result he was often accused of failing to provide leadership for the Republican Party.[79] Even on critical issues such as civil rights and economic policy, the president tended to follow the lead of his advisors on domestic matters.

In summary, it is fair to say that Eisenhower's advisory groups—as well as his personality—were open. But this characterization is simplistic. Because problems of international politics captivated him, Eisenhower naturally took a greater personal interest in the details of foreign policy than in those of domestic policy.[80] To make foreign policy decisions, he sought out information from many and diverse sources, and this led him to organize his Cabinet, the NSC, and his other groups of advisors to provide a sustained flow of facts and opinions about these kinds of problems. Much decision making in the Eisenhower presidency thus took place under conditions in which the president's personality and the structure of his advisory groups were matched—both were relatively open. This is an arrangement, as argued in chapter 2, that should encourage learning.

To make decisions about less important or (to him) less interesting problems, however, Eisenhower often relied on smaller groups of trusted associates and, in general, made less of an effort to acquaint himself personally with the details of the issues at stake. In such circumstances, substantial and effective information gathering is less likely and groupthink is, correspondingly, more likely. Moreover, the openness of the Eisenhower administration was not entirely under the president's control; Cabinet members, aides, and other advisors come and go in any administration. No president can completely govern their ebb and flow. At times, therefore, Eisenhower was confronted with an even more critical examination of some issues than he may have liked, while on other occasions he might have benefited from a more open and thoughtful discussion of policy alternatives. Despite Eisenhower's general preference for an open advisory system, therefore, it is possible to observe a range of advisory groups in his administration, from the small and insular to the large and contentious.

Ultimately, of course, presidents rather than advisors must bear the responsibility for their decisions. And for all of the importance that Eisenhower placed on advisors, he reserved for himself the right to make the final choices. He summed up this aspect of his decision-making philosophy in *Mandate for Change:*

> On a crucial question during the Civil War, Abraham Lincoln is said to have called for a vote around the Cabinet table. Every member voted no. "The ayes have it," Lincoln announced. The Presidency still works the same way today.[81]

Although the divergence between leader and advisors was rarely quite so sharp in the Eisenhower administration, it nevertheless mattered what Eisenhower, more than anyone else in his administration, thought. Yet precisely for this reason, it also mattered a great deal whether or not he was able to learn from those around him.

THE REAGAN ADMINISTRATION

Some have suggested that it did not matter whether Reagan learned from his advisors or not, because they rather than he made the decisions. As in the case of the Eisenhower administration, such claims have led to a debate over the extent of Reagan's personal detachment from affairs of state. And although such claims ring slightly more true for Reagan, it is easy to overstate the case. Ultimately, even "detached" presidents must make decisions.

According to his critics, Reagan lived in a fantasy world of half-remembered movies and rosy reminisces about small-town America. Rarely, they suggest, did he deign to involve himself in the mundane business of policymaking, and even more rarely was he genuinely interested. Bob Schieffer and Gary Paul Gates write that "just as the star on a movie set would tend to be oblivious of members of the crew who did not directly interact with him or his performance, Reagan evinced almost no curiosity about officials on his team who were not among his inner circle. Beneath the friendly façade was a relentless indifference."[82] And according to Jane Mayer and Doyle McManus, "Reagan was both amiable and friendless, ill informed and incurious, trusting and careless, stubborn and passive."[83] Even members of Reagan's Cabinet and White House staff have remarked on Reagan's apparent detachment and preference for the Hollywood version (or what might now be called the "sound bite" version) of events. Donald Regan maintains, for example, that Reagan's "preoccupation was with what might be called 'the outer Presidency.' He was content to let others cope with the inner details of running the Administration. . . . He listened, acquiesced, played his role, and waited for the next act to be written."[84]

Yet Regan also observed that the president "loved the give-and-take of policy discussions in the Cabinet councils, when he had a chance to pronounce on the broad general principles that primarily interested him."[85] And another of Reagan's economic advisors, Martin Anderson, considered him to be much more active and involved than his critics realized. Anderson vehemently denies the charges that Reagan was "out-of-touch," incompetent, or otherwise unsuited to be president. Indeed, Anderson explicitly draws an analogy to Eisenhower:

> The same kind of lies now being told about the Reagan presidency were once told about the Eisenhower presidency. The last two-term president before Reagan, Eisenhower was widely regarded as an ineffective president, an indecisive man who was a bumbler. . . . [This view] is just as wrong today for President Reagan as it was wrong for twenty years for President Eisenhower.[86]

As with Eisenhower, however, the case of Ronald Reagan is more complex than Anderson suggests. Reagan was a curiously passive individual, but nevertheless an activist—even revolutionary—president. He had very few close personal friends, but almost every acquaintance found him to be warm and congenial. He led an active and apparently fulfilling life, but throughout much of his life he exhibited a preference for fantasy and acting over reality. Even to close associates, Reagan's personality has been enigmatic.

Learning Style

In the case of Eisenhower, a narrower focus on traits relevant to gathering information and learning helped to disentangle some of the debate over his passivity. Beginning in his childhood, a fairly consistent picture of an open and inquisitive learning style emerges for Eisenhower. He was socially outgoing, ready to make decisions when necessary, and prepared to take personal responsibility for them (internal locus of control). Although he may have stuck some observers as a passive politician, he was not generally a "closed" or especially reluctant decision maker. In the case of Reagan, however, a narrower focus on traits related to learning seems at first only to deepen the mystery.

The paradox is that Reagan was both sociable and withdrawn, eloquent and engaged on some matters but utterly disinterested in many others. This was not merely an occasional phenomenon during his adult life, but a consistent pattern beginning in his childhood. Reagan's early family life was complicated by his father's alcoholism. Nelle Reagan may have explained to her children that their father "had no control over those periods when he was drinking" and that it was "'a sickness' which deserved their compassion."[87] Yet on a binge, Jack Reagan was a sufficient embarrassment (and threat) to his family to drive them out of their home entirely. Amid otherwise upbeat reminisces, Reagan himself acknowledges in his second autobiography that his father "could be pretty surly."[88] It is sometimes suggested that children of alcoholics tend toward an external amiability masking an inner detachment, and this is consistent with the paradox of Reagan's personality. By itself, however, his father's alcoholism could hardly be considered decisive. As noted in chapter 2, Saddam Hussein and Bill Clinton are also children of alcoholics, and the similarities among these three are not particularly striking.

Jack Reagan's alcoholism was, however, but one of several factors contributing to Reagan's "agreeable but withdrawn" demeanor. Partly as a result of this drinking problem, and partly as a result of hard economic times, the Reagans rarely stayed long in one place. In fact Ronald Reagan, or "Dutch" as he was then called, was enrolled in a different school every year for five consecutive years beginning at age six.[89] Like his father's alcoholism, these frequent moves left him with little control over important events in his early life, and they encouraged him to pursue solitary activities. His brother Neil remembers that Dutch "was very quiet and he could go for hours all by himself playing with lead soldiers. He was a great collector of lead soldiers in those days. . . . I always sort of ran with gangs. He didn't."[90] These feelings of isolation were also exacerbated by the young Reagan's extremely poor eyesight:

> "Stop that blinking, boy," he'd be scolded at school. Dutch couldn't read the blackboard, even from a front seat, but he was good at bluffing his lessons. It never occurred to him to complain about the faint and fuzzy outlines of what he saw. In his mind, as he described it in his autobiography, *Where's the Rest of Me?,* "the whole world was made up of colored blobs. . . . I was sure it appeared the same way to everyone else."[91]

Because of his nearsightedness, Reagan was also poor at most sports. Together, these difficulties left their mark. As he remembers in his memoirs, "my troubles in sports, along with always having been the new kid in school, left me with some insecurities. . . . For a while it caused me a lot of heartache."[92] According to at least one psychologically minded historian, these problems (and his "fear of his father" in particular) "made young Ronald a 'good' boy" but also a "loner" who suffered "from various phobias."[93] Lou Cannon, perhaps Reagan's most prominent biographer, concurs that he "was a classic adult child of an alcoholic who had learned early in life to retreat from discord and unpleasantness."[94]

If Eisenhower's childhood was a model of the sort likely to encourage a sense of personal efficacy (i.e., an internal locus of control), Reagan's was almost exactly the opposite. That Dutch Reagan should have retreated into a world of fantasy, toy soldiers, and solitary games in which he *could* exert control seems unsurprising. Nowhere is the mark of his childhood more evident than in Reagan's first choice of career. As he put it himself, "I was drawn to the stage . . . as if it were a magnet, astonished by the magic of an ordinary man convincing an audience that he was someone else."[95] Even in his second career as a politician, Reagan relied heavily on techniques of self-presentation he learned as an actor.[96] And more than one political observer has pointed out his occasional tendency to confuse fiction with reality. Not only did Reagan believe in Hollywood, but he also believed in fate, luck, magic, and divine control. He repeatedly referred to fate (or "God's plan") as an important influence in his life: "I was raised," he wrote, "to believe that God has a plan for everyone and that seemingly random twists of fate are all a part of His plan."[97] According to Michael

Deaver, Reagan was "incurably superstitious. If he emptied his pants pocket you would always find about five good-luck charms that people had sent him."[98] Cannon adds that "Reagan knocked on wood, threw salt over his shoulder and carried a good-luck penny."[99] And there is some evidence that he, as well as his wife, believed in astrology.[100]

Ronald Reagan's belief in fate and luck is typical of someone with an external locus of control and, thus, suggests a closed learning style. Being personally well informed is, after all, less compelling a proposition for those who believe that fate determines their prospects. Yet if Reagan was "closed," his apparent social ease and good humor seem incongruous, once again recalling the paradox noted earlier. Cannon, who traveled with Reagan extensively, has observed that Reagan's "unfailing optimism and self-deprecating humor," combined with a disarming friendliness and an ability to find the right words for every situation, endears him to almost everyone he meets.[101] Reagan's social ease was evidently genuine—he seems to have suffered less from stage fright than most actors (or politicians). On one hand, as Nancy Reagan puts it, he "is an affable and gregarious man who enjoys other people," yet at the same time "he doesn't need them for companionship or approval."[102]

This almost schizophrenic orientation toward the world—closed and withdrawn but also cheerful and outgoing—is rendered less puzzling, however, by the realization that it was primarily when he was "on stage" that Reagan was comfortable around others. Despite his geniality and popular image as the "great communicator," many of his adult acquaintances and even close friends and family felt that he maintained a considerable distance between himself and others. Gerald Ford "considered him to be one of the most distant people he had ever met" and once "observed that Reagan was the only politician he knew who told you more about himself in his speeches than he did in conversation."[103] One of his aides perceived "a barrier between him and the rest of the world, a film you can't get through."[104] Even his wife has written that, "although he loves people, he often seems remote, and he doesn't let anybody get too close. There's a wall around him. He lets me come closer than anyone else, but there are times when even I feel that barrier."[105] President Reagan himself cautiously admitted in his memoirs, "Although I always had lots of playmates, during those first years in Dixon I was a little introverted and probably a little slow in making really close friends. In some ways I think this reluctance to get close to people never left me completely. I've never had trouble making friends, but I've been inclined to hold back a little of myself, reserving it for myself."[106]

Reagan was only superficially an extravert. His social ease was genuine but "thin," and his childhood difficulties making close friends never quite left him. He rarely sought out social contact and, though affable, was remarkably passive and content to be left alone.[107] Yet this, rather than mere gregariousness or social ease, is precisely the aspect of extraversion that is most intimately connected to learning. Reagan was not especially inclined to seek out either companionship or information for its own sake. In Cannon's view, he is "uncurious about most aspects of public policy. . . . And he was so quiet at White House briefings that his aides sometimes wondered if he had been paying attention."[108] According to one member of the White House staff, "Reagan did not react to 95 percent of the material that was brought to him."[109]

Although seemingly paradoxical, therefore, Reagan's learning style was consistent throughout his adult life and understandable in light of his childhood experiences. The few quantitative studies on Reagan's personality also support the assessment offered here. Simonton's Adjective Check List study, for example, places Reagan high on "friendliness" (like Eisenhower) but much lower on "flexibility" (unlike Eisenhower).[110] This again suggests a veneer of extraversion laid over an essentially closed (inflexible) personality. My Q-sort survey of experts on the American presidency also places Reagan lower than Eisenhower on openness.[111] Although Reagan may be "more complex than people think," as Nancy Reagan observed, it is thus unlikely that he will one day be revealed as another "hidden-hand Ike."[112] Eisenhower's staff and friends always maintained that he was more active and involved than commonly understood, but Reagan administration insiders make no similar claim. On the contrary, there is overwhelming evidence that his learning style was essentially closed, and this quality shaped the way Reagan gathered and used information during his political career. As Sidney Blumenthal has put it, "with Reagan, facts don't determine the case. Facts don't make his beliefs true. His beliefs give life to the facts, which are parables tailored to have a moral. If one fact doesn't serve, another will."[113] Therefore, as both his aides and many other political observers have noted, Reagan does not concern himself greatly with gathering facts and mastering details. Yet, to quote Blumenthal again, "the central story about Reagan is not that he misses facts. It is that he has a world view in which facts are not important. Facts are pawns of his vision."[114] And it does not necessarily follow that Reagan would have benefited from paying more attention to facts, to details, or to controversies. As chapter 4 will show, Reagan worked best with a small and, more importantly, harmonious group of close advisors: "Heightened tension would not have made of Ronald Reagan a better President, and Reagan knew it. He did not want his personal harmony disturbed."[115]

Advisors

Devising the appropriate staff organization for a president such as Ronald Reagan poses an intriguing problem. Although Reagan was personally closed, his objectives in office were quite activist and ambitious. According to Bert Rockman, "the problem of managing the Reagan Presidency, therefore, can be stated as follows: How can organizational structures, systems, and strategies be developed for a committed Presidency and a detached President?"[116] How, in other words, could a president have remained so aloof from the policy-making process and so detached from policy implementation and yet achieve the successes of the "Reagan Revolution?" How could President Reagan have moved so effectively to restore confidence in the institution of the presidency with so little personal involvement in the daily operations of the White House?[117]

It has become a commonplace among presidential scholars that resolving this apparent dilemma was the key to much of Reagan's success.[118] In marked contrast to President Carter's inclination to "micromanage," President Reagan painted in broad strokes, outlining his policies but leaving the details for his staff to fill in.[119] Whatever their differences of opinion, observers of the Reagan presidency generally agree on this point. According to Cannon, "Reagan simply was not a detail man. Even on issues where he was well informed, Reagan chose consciously to focus on the broad goals of what he intended to accomplish and leave the details to others. . . . He saw himself as a leader, a communicator, an executive decision-maker, a chairman of the board."[120] And Richard Neustadt finds that Reagan thus "stands out as exceptional among his peers for lack of interest in pursuing the details of public policy—not least his own."[121] In Reagan's case, this approach allowed him to exercise his talents of persuasion and leadership unencumbered by problems of policy execution or even by contradictions in the policies themselves. As another presidency-watcher has put it, "the key to the Reagan Presidency was to have the President fuel the policy agenda—to enunciate his goals and sell them rather than watch over operations or intervene obtrusively in the process of decision making and policy formulation at lower levels. Reagan's style has been distinctly that of a 'hands-off' President."[122]

President Reagan's management style has, in fact, been given a variety of labels: *the delegated presidency, the administrative presidency* and even *the disengaged presidency.*[123] Not only was this organizational style, whatever the name, well-suited to a closed learning style, but the very real distance between Reagan and his advisors also yielded political dividends. The president could claim on many occasions, and without guile, that he had been unaware of a problem until it was too late or that he had simply received bad advice. A detached management style made such claims plausible and served to distance the president from the potentially damaging actions of his subordinates when scandals did occur.[124] Perhaps this detachment, more than anything else, helped him to survive the Iran-Contra affair.

Reagan explained his approach to choosing subordinates in an address to the nation in 1987: "The way I work is to identify the problem, find the right individuals to do the job, and then let them go to it. I've found this invariably brings out the best in people."[125] But this approach requires a staff to whom the president can delegate problems with confidence, that is to say, an ideologically and politically homogeneous staff. John Kessel's studies of the Nixon, Carter, and Reagan White House staffs show that the Reagan staff was indeed the most ideologically unified of the three.[126] President Reagan's closest advisors, in particular, knew that "the President expected concord, and the appearance of concord, to prevail among his staff."[127] The inner circle of presidential advisors were perhaps the most careful to bend themselves to the prevailing winds of presidential opinion.[128]

President Reagan's White House staff, then, was organized with these preferences in mind—preferences that required centralization and hierarchy. During Reagan's first term, the trio of

James Baker (chief of staff), Edwin Meese (White House counselor), and Michael Deaver (deputy chief of staff) presided jointly
over the White House staff and, more generally, over administration policy. It is difficult to say which of these three was most
important. As chief of staff, Baker was perhaps nominally superi-
or to the other two, and certainly he played a critical role not only
in the White House but also in overseeing press and congressional liaisons. Meese, however, was the primary conduit for translat-
ing Reagan's ideas and principles into policy.[129] He directed the
NSC and the Office of Policy Development (OPD), the principal foreign and domestic policy councils, earning him the unofficial des-
ignation "prime minister" or even "deputy president." Finally,
although Deaver may have been "the least visible member of the
White House Trio," according to Cannon, he was "the one most
personally valuable to the Reagans."[130] He managed Reagan's
schedule and workload. Perhaps even more than Baker, Deaver
thus played a critical role in regulating access to the president.
Together, this trio—or "troika" as they were sometimes called—
provided "an impregnable center of unity and effectiveness that
was difficult for outsiders to circumvent."[131]

   During Reagan's first term, Donald Regan also played an
undeniably important role. As treasury secretary, he presided—
along with the troika and Office of Management and Budget (OMB)
Director David Stockman—over critical first-term decisions
regarding tax and spending cuts and budget priorities. In February
1985, however, Regan became chief of staff and began a process of
further centralizing authority in the White House. Regan himself
summed up his responsibilities as follows: "All duties formerly
exercised by Baker, Meese, and Deaver devolved on me—personnel, the coordination of information, the choice of issues, the flow
of paper, and the schedule that controlled the President's travel
and other movements and determined who would see him and who
would not."[132] From this point, until his departure in the wake of
the Iran-Contra scandal, Regan exercised unusual control over the
flow of information within the White House. Regan's successors,
Howard Baker and then Kenneth Duberstein, adopted a lower pro-
file. They were more inclined to consult Republican Party officials
and members of Congress before embarking on new policy initiatives, a practice that came as a relief to those who had resented
Regan's control over the presidency. But Baker and Duberstein
also realized that the president had no intention of involving him-

self in policy details. The job of Reagan's chief of staff was to manage these details and to present the president with the fundamental choices of policy—or, when the president's preferences were already well-known, to handle the problem without disturbing the calm of the Oval Office.

Reagan's other advisors generally reported to him through one of the channels already discussed. Even his national security advisors, who in principle had direct access to the president, served more to implement policy than to provide advice.[133] Paradoxically, while the influence of the national security advisors with the president was limited,

> their authority on day-to-day operational decisions was often enormous and unchecked because Reagan provided them with minimal guidance and even less supervision. Reagan did not really know what a national security adviser was supposed to do. What he most often asked his advisers to do was "work things out" by finding a middle ground when none existed between incompatible options advocated by his secretaries of state and defense. Even when a national security adviser was fortunate enough to find such a compromise, he usually lacked the authority to make it stick. In short, it was extraordinarily difficult to be a successful national security adviser to President Reagan.[134]

It was thus another paradox of the Reagan administration that "Reagan's national security advisers wielded insufficient influence and excessive power."[135]

As part of his commitment to delegation, Reagan also gave members of his cabinet considerable discretion in implementing administration policy. In practice, this often produced problems similar to those faced (or created) by the national security advisors. Nevertheless, Reagan relied on his Cabinet and expected them to develop among themselves a consensus about policy choices that he could ratify. Among the most important of these officials, in addition to those already mentioned, were Alexander Haig (secretary of state until 1982); George Shultz (secretary of state thereafter); Caspar Weinberger (secretary of defense); William French Smith (attorney general and a longtime friend of the Reagans); William Casey (director of the CIA and also an old friend of the Reagans); William Clark (deputy secretary of state, then national security advisor, and finally secretary of the interior); and Vice President George Bush.[136]

In addition to these members of Reagan's Cabinet and White House staff, several of President Reagan's other advisors deserve special mention. Richard Darman, assistant to the president and chair of the legislative strategy group, also played a large role in the administration—as an aide both to the president and to Chief of Staff Baker. According to Deaver, Darman was "the fourth most powerful staffer in the White House."[137] Paul Laxalt, the conservative senator from Nevada, was another old friend of the Reagans from California and was particularly valuable as a sounding board for congressional (and conservative) opinion. Finally, Nancy Reagan played a large role in advising the president, although perhaps not quite so large as her detractors sometimes feared. According to Neustadt, Mrs. Reagan was "that rarity, a disinterested adviser" who had primarily the interests of her husband at heart.[138]

Like any president, Reagan relied most heavily on a small group of close, personal advisors. Unlike more open presidents such as Eisenhower, however, Reagan's primary advisors constituted a relatively impermeable barrier between him and administration "outsiders." And unlike Eisenhower, Reagan generally received advice on almost all issues—foreign and domestic, strategic and economic—from roughly the same group of trusted personal associates. Yet this is not to say that President Reagan always presided over a cohesive staff and a "closed" group of advisors. On a number of occasions, including debates over the budget and particularly the Iran-Contra scandal, even Reagan's closest advisors disagreed with each other and brought their disputes to the Oval Office. Rather than producing a solution to the problem, however, such direct appeals to the president caused paralysis or deadlock. Moreover, these disputes opened the gates for outsiders to bring their concerns to the president as well, and this only exacerbated the problem. Ronald Reagan knew that he could not work effectively when surrounded by too much disagreement. He "hated unresolved disputes among his 'fellas.' He had no wish to watch them squirm, and," according to Neustadt, "he was modestly aware that his lack of detail often left him without the wherewithal for resolution."[139]

Reagan's own preferences for small, cohesive advisory groups were reinforced by the preferences of his top advisors themselves.

The fate of two of the president's advisory boards, the President's Foreign Intelligence Advisory Board (PFIAB) and the President's Economic Policy Advisory Board (PEPAB), illustrates this. The PFIAB was created by Eisenhower, eliminated by Carter, and resurrected by Reagan's first national security advisor Richard Allen. It consisted of a group of scholars, military officers, intelligence professionals, and other experts who had access to all of the government's intelligence sources and who reported directly to the president. The PFIAB was charged with oversight of the nation's intelligence-gathering agencies, but CIA Director Casey bitterly resented the PFIAB's intrusion into his domain. In October 1985, he finally succeeded in getting most of its more "inquisitive" members fired.[140] Similarly, Donald Regan resented the PEPAB, which was comprised of a distinguished group of economists chaired (initially) by George Shultz and which, like the PFIAB, enjoyed direct access to the president. According to one of its members, "it would have been very difficult for the Reagan administration to long pursue any important economic policy if it was strenuously opposed by the board."[141] In the same month of the PFIAB purge, the executive order that established the PEPAB was allowed to expire. In this case, however, PEPAB members were able to create enough of a disturbance, once they realized they had been fired (three weeks after the fact), to recover their jobs. The cases of both the PFIAB and the PEPAB illustrate, however, a recurring theme in the Reagan presidency: the tendency not only of Reagan himself but also of his top advisors to seek more rather than less centralization of authority.

These preferences for organizational harmony figured prominently in many of the Reagan administration's most important decisions. In some cases, they enabled Reagan to reach a decision quickly and to act on it effectively. They might even be said to have encouraged a degree of learning. Yet the more controversial and varied the opinions presented to Reagan, the less likely he was to gain anything from the presentation. If the harmony of his administration was sufficiently disturbed, learning became impossible and the decision-making process itself ground to halt.

CONCLUSION

Despite the differences in their learning styles, the similarities between Dwight Eisenhower and Ronald Reagan go far beyond those noted at the beginning of this chapter. Although both were political conservatives, for example, neither was raised in a conservative home. Ida Eisenhower was a committed pacifist, and Jack Reagan was an ardent New Deal liberal. Both grew up in small towns—Eisenhower in Abilene, Kansas, and Reagan in Dixon, Illinois—and both families were poor. Indeed, both men's fathers were occasionally out of work. And yet both claim not to have been aware of their poverty as children. Eisenhower said that he "found out in later years we were very poor, . . . but the glory of America is that we didn't know it then."[142] Reagan put it much the same way: "Later in life I learned that, compared with some of the folks who lived in Dixon, our family was 'poor.' But I didn't know that when I was growing up."[143]

As presidents, both were enormously popular and successful. They were capable, intelligent, and socially graceful individuals who presided over periods of comparative peace and prosperity, of patriotism, and (at least superficially) of national consensus.[144] Reagan, it happens, greatly admired Eisenhower. According to Deaver, it was "the influence of Dwight Eisenhower, rather than Barry Goldwater, as commonly believed, [that] completed his conversion from FDR Democrat to born-again, conservative Republican."[145] At the same time, both were perceived as passive and uninterested in the workings of their own administrations. Each delegated a good deal of authority (Reagan more consistently than Eisenhower), and both preferred relatively formal staff arrangements. A broader study of presidential policymaking might fruitfully inquire into the practices of other more informal (Truman), collegial (Kennedy), or combative (FDR) presidents. Yet Eisenhower and Reagan's similarities help to control for extraneous influences and place the consequences of learning style and staff openness into sharper relief.

By concentrating exclusively on a narrow range of traits related to openness (e.g., extraversion and locus of control), this chapter has sought to untangle some of the apparent puzzles in other studies of presidential character. A strict focus on learning style helps to sidestep a great deal of the confusion and ambiguity in scholarly and journalistic studies of both the Eisenhower and Reagan administrations.[146] The picture that emerges, of a sharp contrast between Eisenhower's open style and staff structure and the much more closed tendencies of the Reagan administration, is substantiated by evidence from many different sources, obtained using a variety of methods. There are lively debates about many aspects of both men's leadership. Yet on the specific question of personal openness to new and challenging information, historians, quantitative social scientists, journalists, and "insiders" converge on roughly the same assessment. By every indication, Eisenhower was comfortable in the presence of large and diverse groups. He sought out divergent opinions, and—despite his popular image as a weekend president—took an active, personal, and detailed interest in his administration's most important decisions. Reagan, on the other hand, preferred to associate with much smaller and more homogeneous groups of advisors. Above all, Reagan demanded consensus.

Both leaders were perfectly capable of learning, but they did so in very different ways, at different times, and in different settings. When they failed to learn, it was for different reasons. The principal danger for Eisenhower was that his customarily open advisory structure might become constricted, as a result either of his own choices or of circumstances beyond his control, resulting in groupthink. On such occasions, Eisenhower failed to get critical advice that might have encouraged him to change policies for which he was subsequently criticized. For Reagan, on the other hand, the greatest danger was that too much advisory openness would produce deadlock. Deadlock did not so much prevent a change in policy as it merely allowed administration policy to drift without presidential supervision. Faced with an excessively open advisory structure, Reagan had nowhere to turn for a decisive solution and, unlike more open leaders, he lacked the personal resources to arrive at one himself.

These are not abstract or purely academic distinctions. In each of the cases described in the following chapters, it mattered a great deal whether or not the president learned. The negative connotations of groupthink and deadlock are implicit counterfactual claims about what might have been different (and presumably better) had learning occurred. Although this book will not enter into a political debate over whether one outcome really would have been better than another, it makes sense to proceed by establishing as a "baseline" that learning was indeed possible for both Eisenhower and Reagan. This is the task of chapter 4.

CHAPTER 4

Learning

Learning is a common enough phenomenon. Not only people, but also animals and computers are capable of it. Even politicians occasionally learn although, as A. J. P. Taylor pointed out, they may well learn the wrong lessons from history.[1] Military leaders are likewise criticized on occasion for having learned the lessons of the last war (and for being unprepared to fight the next war). In its simplest form, *learning* becomes almost a synonym for *perception*—the mere recognition of something in one's environment. Someone who fails to learn, then, is someone who fails to perceive something that is (or should be) obvious. By this definition, all sentient beings are constantly engaged in learning.

Learning is a more useful concept, though, if our definition is slightly more demanding. After all, much knowledge is mundane. One "learns" the time simply by looking at a clock. Learning how to build a clock, on the other hand, involves knowledge of much greater complexity, encompassing not only facts but also causal relationships. Knowledge also differs in the degree to which one is committed to it. It is easy to solicit advice and, thereby, to learn what another person believes. It is much more difficult to re-evaluate one's own cherished beliefs—on the basis of this advice—and to change one's mind about important matters. Yet the latter is a more fundamental kind of learning.

To show that some sort of learning occurred in the Eisenhower and Reagan administrations is a trivial matter. Every

61

important political leader is subjected to a constant flood of information. If he or she pays attention at all, then learning is happening, but this does not mean that the lessons learned were particularly deep or valuable. This chapter will pay special attention, therefore, to the circumstances in which Eisenhower and Reagan acknowledged complexities they previously had ignored and in which they reversed positions to which they previously had been committed. This sets a higher "standard" for learning.

But it will not be useful to set the standard too high. Specifically, as argued in chapter 1, the standard should not require that the "correct" lesson was learned. However tempting it may be to evaluate Eisenhower and Reagan's choices on the basis of my own preferences, others could not be expected to agree. In the absence of a common ethical and political ground, this sort of standard is self-defeating. It would have the effect of making learning a synonym for correctness or rectitude. A useful standard requires more than the animal faculty of sensory perception, but less than godly wisdom. It will suffice to show that on several occasions, at least, Eisenhower and Reagan deepened their own understanding of the complexities of the problems they faced and, on that basis, embraced policies they had previously opposed.[2]

LEARNING IN AN OPEN ADMINISTRATION

Paul S. Holbo and Robert W. Sellen have described the 1950s as the age of consensus.[3] The United States' economy grew steadily and dominated world markets. American military might was unparalleled. College campuses registered comparatively few signs of discontent, even with the Korean War underway. The "silent generation," as it was sometimes called, was seemingly more concerned with material success than with political or moral debate. The American historian Daniel Boorstin concluded at the time that a "pretty good rule-of-thumb for us in the United States is that our national well-being is in inverse proportion to the sharpness and extent of the theoretical differences between our political parties."[4] That Democrats and Republicans alike had courted Eisenhower suggests the absence of entrenched partisan differences among them. John Patrick Diggins chose another term for the era beginning after the war and lasting until the end of Eisenhower's presidency: *the proud decades.*[5]

But the age of consensus was also the age of the Birmingham bus boycotts, of integration at Central High School in Little Rock, and of McCarthyism. It was an era distinguished by John Foster Dulles's gloomy sermons about the United States' global responsibilities and by the first postwar American intervention in Vietnam. And it was a time marked by dramatic and threatening increases in the destructive power of both Soviet and American nuclear arsenals. The nostalgic view of the 1950s as a time of "consensus" and "pride" thus threatens to obscure the many important conflicts and decisions that President Eisenhower confronted.

Chief among these conflicts was the rapidly escalating cold war. Tension between the United States and the Soviet Union fanned the flames of McCarthyism, fueled arms races, and prompted each superpower to intervene in countries on its periphery. If there was widespread consensus on anything in the United States, it was on the threat posed by communism, but there was little agreement on the proper American response.[6] The Eisenhower presidency witnessed important opportunities for change (such as Stalin's death), promising initiatives for peace (such as the "open skies" and nuclear test ban proposals), and disappointing failures (such as the U-2 incident and the subsequent collapse of the Paris summit). In general, East/West rivalry set the tone for American foreign policy throughout the 1950s, and it clearly took an uppermost place among the concerns of President Eisenhower and his advisors.

One of the most significant decisions Eisenhower made about international security is sometimes overlooked. This is understandable, since it led to a non-event: a full-scale American intervention in Vietnam in the 1950s in support of the French, possibly including the use of nuclear weapons, which did not occur. Eisenhower's decision not to intervene militarily is interesting not only in light of the rapid escalation of American involvement in Vietnam during subsequent administrations, but also in consideration of the fact that Eisenhower and Dulles both initially favored military intervention on behalf of the French. Less dramatic than either the French collapse in Vietnam or the problem of McCarthyism at home (discussed in chapter 5), but nevertheless a significant development in American history, was the problem of admitting Alaska and Hawaii into the Union. The latter part of this section focuses on the more difficult case, Alaskan statehood, which not only raised complex problems of domestic party politics but, given its proximity to the Soviet Union, was entangled in the East/West conflict as well. In this case too, Eisenhower's initial position differed sharply from the action he ultimately took.

The Fall of Dien Bien Phu

During the Second World War, Eisenhower urged the French to make plans for the future independence of Vietnam. Yet by 1954, France remained entangled in a costly stalemate. The French presence in Indochina had, of course, taken on broader implications by that time. In a pre-inaugural briefing for President-elect Eisenhower, Dulles set the tone of future American policy by observing, "Korea is important, but the really important spot is Indochina, because we could lose Korea and probably insulate ourselves against the consequences of that loss; but if Indochina goes, and South Asia goes, it is extremely hard to insulate ourselves against the consequences of that."[7] As the "rice bowl of Asia," Indochina was strategically important to the Soviet Union and to the People's Republic of China (PRC) as well as to the United States, and thus almost inevitably the site of superpower conflict. For Eisenhower, the danger was summed up in his famous press conference analogy to "falling dominoes."[8] After a year in office, however, Eisenhower had just succeeded in removing U.S. troops from Korea. To return so quickly to Asia was unthinkable.

Domestic politics placed further limitations on Eisenhower's choices. Having so often criticized Democrats for "losing" China in 1949, Eisenhower's Republicans could ill afford to lose Vietnam. Equally worrisome was the effect a communist victory could be expected to have on French domestic politics. Dulles and Eisenhower saw clearly—and correctly—that the fall of Dien Bien Phu would provoke the fall of the French government and a move to the left in French politics. In February 1954, Dulles reported to Eisenhower that, according to the French foreign minister Georges Bidault, the "bottom will fall out of [the] French home situation unless he (Bidault) does something here to indicate a desire to end [the] Indochina war."[9] Eisenhower and Dulles both understood that the Laniel government was vulnerable, but over the next two months they saw its position deteriorate markedly. By April, during a trip to Paris, Dulles had concluded that the French were "almost visibly collapsing under our eyes. . . . It seems to me that

Dien Bien Phu has become a symbol out of all proportion to its military importance. . . . Probably if Dien Bien Phu falls, the government will be taken over."[10]

The international, strategic significance of the French position in Vietnam and its prominence in both American and French domestic politics all combined to make the prospect of a major French defeat disastrous for President Eisenhower and for U.S. security policy. Eisenhower was convinced that his administration must take some sort of action, and during the first months of 1954 he favored direct intervention if it became necessary to keep the dominoes standing. Like Churchill, Eisenhower also believed that Allied unity was of the utmost importance in the postwar era, and this further disposed him to support the French at Dien Bien Phu. Not only did he share Dulles's convictions about the necessity of containment, but the French implied on several occasions that acceptance of the European Defense Community, which Eisenhower very much wanted, was contingent upon U.S. aid for French troops.[11] Indeed, well before the crisis at Dien Bien Phu, Eisenhower had committed himself to helping the French in Indochina. By the end of 1953 Washington was paying one-third of the war's cost, and the following year Eisenhower offered over $1 billion in additional aid. In 1954, roughly one-third of all U.S. foreign aid went directly to support the French war effort.[12]

The United States actually seemed more determined to win the war, by 1954, than did the French. In Paris popular support had long since vanished, and while continuing to accept American aid, Prime Minister Joseph Laniel had begun to seek a negotiated peace. Eisenhower and Dulles strongly opposed bargaining with the Viet Minh, on the other hand, until French military superiority had been restored. The National Security Council (NSC) likewise concluded that "any negotiated settlement would mean the eventual loss to Communism not only of Indo-China but of the whole of Southeast Asia."[13] Thus, the NSC duly set about evaluating plans for greater U.S. participation in the war, should it become necessary. On January 8, 1954, the council took up a draft policy statement, NSC 177, that included an annex discussing the possibility of direct U.S. intervention.[14] At this meeting, Admiral Radford spoke out strongly in favor of planning for direct U.S. intervention in Indochina and proposed sending an aircraft carrier to relieve the pressure on the French at Dien Bien Phu. Eisenhower himself joined in with the observation that "what you've got here is a leaky dike, and with leaky dikes, it's sometimes better to put a finger in than to let the whole structure be washed away." The president then went on to propose that "a little group of fine and adventurous pilots" might intervene directly using "U.S. planes without insignia . . . from aircraft carriers."[15] Admiral Radford agreed that such a mission was feasible.

A week later, the president directed a special group, composed of Radford, Allen Dulles (CIA director), C. D. Jackson, Walter Bedell Smith, and Deputy Secretary of Defense Roger Kyes, to develop specific contingency plans for action in Indochina. This Special Committee on Indochina was to act independently of the NSC and the Operations Coordinating Board (OCB), and it immediately set about considering a French request for 22 bombers and 400 Air Force mechanics to maintain them.[16] Kyes and Dulles were reluctant to involve U.S. military personnel directly in the conflict at this point, but the other committee members felt so strongly about the strategic importance of the conflict that the two dissenters agreed to a compromise recommendation of sending 200 mechanics.[17] The committee then forwarded its proposal to the president, who approved the French request. Included with the recommendation was an on-the-record statement by Radford and Smith that, if it became necessary, they "personally would favor intervention with United States air and naval—not ground forces."[18]

Despite the infusion of U.S. aid, February and March brought a deterioration of the French position at Dien Bien Phu. By April, Eisenhower could see little alternative to dispatching American forces; indeed, a projected timetable for doing so had already been prepared.[19] During a luncheon with James Hagerty, he mused that the "US might have to make decisions to send in squadrons from 2 aircraft carriers off [the] coast to bomb [the] Reds at Dien bien phu [*sic*]."[20] On April 4, 1954, Eisenhower cabled Churchill to secure the latter's support, warning that "the French cannot alone see this thing through" and that "the future of France as a great power" was at stake. He concluded his letter with the hyperbolic observation that

we failed to halt Hirohito, Mussolini and Hitler by not acting in unity and in time. That marked the beginning of many years of stark tragedy and desperate peril. May it not be that our nations have learned something from that lesson?[21]

The same night, according to Sherman Adams, "in the upstairs study at the White House Eisenhower . . . agreed with Dulles and Radford on a plan to send American forces to Indo-China under certain strict conditions."[22]

Thus poised on the brink of direct intervention in Vietnam, the Eisenhower administration began to prepare the American public for another war in Asia. In a speech at the end of March, Dulles had already warned that "the imposition on Southeast Asia of the political system of Communist Russia and its Chinese Communist ally, *by whatever means,* would be a grave threat to the whole free community" and that it "should not be passively accepted, but should be met by united action."[23] On April 16, in response to a question about U.S. intervention in Vietnam, Vice President Nixon told the American Society of Newspaper Editors, "I believe that the Executive Branch of the government has to take the politically unpopular position of facing up to it and doing it, and I personally would support such a decision."[24] This statement provoked, as Robert Divine put it, "a genuine war scare in the United States."[25] Cyrus Sulzberger, at the time a *New York Times* correspondent in Paris, wrote that "there is considerable fear among the Americans that we are hovering on the verge of World War III."[26]

Through early April, Dulles and Admiral Radford had served as Eisenhower's principle advisors on Indochina. Both of these men supported American intervention if necessary to prevent the fall of Dien Bien Phu. In fact, Radford took a rather free hand in promising the French military assistance. He drew up plans for a series of American aerial bombardments against Viet Minh forces around Dien Bien Phu, possibly using nuclear weapons, and suggested to the French that they would certainly be approved by the president. Indeed, French General Paul Ély returned from a late-March trip to Washington convinced that the plans, named Operation Vulture, *had* been approved.[27] Yet Eisenhower had not yet made a final decision, and when Dulles called him on April 5 "to inform him that the French had told Ambassador Dillon that their impression was that Operation Vulture had been agreed to," Eisenhower was taken aback.[28] Although he agreed in principle with plans for increased U.S. involvement in Indochina, he was not prepared to implement these plans without a more thorough analysis of their virtues. He told Dulles to contact the French and inform them that "such a move is impossible."[29] Dulles then cabled Dillon that "the matter is still under study."[30]

It would have been easy, given the near consensus among his closest advisors on the problem of Dien Bien Phu, for Eisenhower to have given his consent to Operation Vulture. Instead, at just this point, he decided to reopen the general issue of American assistance to the French and, in so doing, significantly enlarged and diversified his group of advisors on the matter. Many of the president's close associates—including Vice President Nixon, NSC Chair Cutler, and Mutual Security Director Harold Stassen—continued to side with Radford in support of an airstrike on Viet Minh forces around Dien Bien Phu. Indeed the air force chief of staff, General Nathan Twining, was prepared to go far beyond what Radford had proposed. As he later put it,

> I still think it would have been a good idea [to have taken] three small tactical A-Bombs—it's a fairly isolated area, Dien Bien Phu—no great town around there, only Communists and their supplies. You could take all day to drop a bomb, make sure you put it in the right place. No opposition. And clean those Commies out of there and the band could play the Marseillaise and the French would come marching out of Dien Bien Phu in fine shape. And those Commies would say, "Well, those guys might do this again to us. We'd better be careful."[31]

Some of Eisenhower's other military advisors, however, were far less sanguine about the prospect of a limited engagement to support the French. Admiral A. C. Davis argued that the United States "should not be self-duped into believing the possibility of partial involvement—such as Naval and Air units only. One cannot go over Niagara Falls in a barrel only slightly."[32] Army Chief of Staff General Matthew Ridgway also vehemently opposed Operation Vulture. He was convinced that it would only lead to another long and costly war of attrition such as that in Korea, and in any case he resented what he saw as Radford's attempt to speak for all of the joint chiefs. Ridgway thus sought a direct meeting with Eisenhower to express his conviction that ground troops would be necessary to save Dien Bien Phu and to warn of "the tremendous costs of intervening in the Indochina War."[33] By Ridgway's estimate, "seven U.S. divisions 'would be required to win a victory in Indochina' and as many as twelve if the French withdrew and the Communist Chinese intervened."[34]

As Eisenhower soon discovered, Ridgway and Davis were not alone in opposing direct U.S. intervention. The other joint chiefs (aside from Radford) also approached the prospect of direct American intervention with caution—or even outright hostility. Marine Corps Commandant Lemuel Shepherd condemned Radford's plan to bomb the jungle around Dien Bien Phu as unlikely to produce results. Jungle warfare was the Marine Corps' specialty, after all, and Shepherd was not ready to concede that an air strike alone could guarantee a French victory.[35] Eisenhower's treasury secretary George Humphrey opposed intervention on the somewhat different grounds that it would be too costly and, if ground troops were indeed required, that it would undo the budgetary achievements of the New Look. In fact, Humphrey was preparing to announce (the following month) a goal of cutting $5 billion from the next fiscal year's budget.[36] He could hardly sanction a new war in Asia. Shepherd and Humphrey's concerns might be dismissed as bureaucratic parochialism, of course, but their objections nonetheless carried weight. As Walter LaFeber has argued, while "Dulles usually carried the Cabinet along with him on his choice of diplomatic moves, . . . his inability and unwillingness to make the Pentagon and Secretary of Treasury George Humphrey subordinate to his own policies drastically cut his options in foreign affairs."[37]

For that matter, Dulles was encountering resistance from other quarters as well. In a meeting with congressional leaders to ask for a resolution supporting the use of American forces in Indochina, he was told in no uncertain terms that Congress wanted "no more Koreas with the United States furnishing 90% of the manpower." Like Ridgway, the congressional leaders strongly suspected that "once the flag was committed the use of land forces would inevitably follow."[38] They concluded their meeting with Dulles by suggesting that a congressional resolution would at the very least require British participation in any military action.

Since his earlier entreaties to Churchill had not yet produced a British promise of assistance, Eisenhower decided to send Dulles to make a personal appeal. On arriving in London, however, Dulles was promptly informed by British Foreign Secretary Anthony Eden that "British opinion, with the Geneva Conference in prospect, would be firmly opposed to any present commitment to become involved in what was already an unpopular war in Indochina."[39] Dulles was unable to counter this sentiment and returned from

Britain having achieved nothing. Yet the situation had become so desperate at Dien Bien Phu (and in France) that Eisenhower did not give up. The secretary of state returned to Europe, and on April 23 Eisenhower instructed him as follows: "I do suggest that you make sure the British Government fully appreciates the gravity of the situation and the great danger of French collapse in that region. The British must not be able merely to shut their eyes and later plead blindness as an alibi for failing to propose a positive program."[40] Meanwhile, Eisenhower discussed the situation with his old friend (and undersecretary of state) Walter Bedell Smith. The two "agreed that there should be no intervention, no air strike, without allies."[41] And Britain, as LaFeber puts it, "never flashed the green light."[42]

On April 29, Eisenhower met with his National Security Council for a final evaluation of U.S. security policy toward Indochina. Stassen made a last-ditch plea for intervention, arguing that the "decision should be to send ground troops if necessary to save Indochina, and to do it on a unilateral basis if that was the only way it could be done."[43] The French, for their part, had kept up the pressure on the Eisenhower administration through a variety of channels. General Henri Navarre met with the U.S. chargé d'affaires in Saigon several days earlier and warned that, without "participation by [the] US in all arms, including infantry," France would seek a political settlement.[44] In Paris, Dulles also confirmed that without U.S. support Bidault would be forced to seek an agreement with the North Vietnamese. The French still believed, however, that American air strikes "would galvanize [the] defenders and dramatically change [the] situation."[45]

Unfortunately for Bidault, it had begun to seem that the French were desperate to end the war regardless of what the United States did. Moreover, it had also become clear that Britain would not join in direct intervention, that American air strikes might well be ineffective without ground support, and that the congressional reaction to any form of intervention would be extremely hostile. In light of these considerations, which became apparent once he broadened his search for advice in April, Eisenhower made his final decision—not to intervene.[46] Eisenhower then saw that his decision stuck. When he received a draft NSC paper the following day outlining plans for an air strike using nuclear weapons, he told his NSC chair Bobby Cutler, "You boys must be crazy. We can't use those awful things against Asians for the second time in less than ten years. My God."[47] Seven days later, the Viet Minh overran Dien Bien Phu.

In light of the later U.S. experience in Vietnam, Eisenhower's decision not to intervene seems prescient, but whether or not it reveals "learning" cannot be determined ex post facto on the basis of subsequent American failures in Vietnam. Rather, one must ask how his decision-making process evolved in March and April 1954. Through March, Eisenhower was clearly predisposed toward military intervention if necessary to save the French and to avoid embarrassing concessions at the Geneva conference. To this point, Dulles and Radford were the principal architects of the administration's Indochina policy. When the matter was discussed in a broader forum—such as the Cabinet—this was not initially done for the purpose of gathering information for the president. Arthur Larson, who was the acting Cabinet secretary during deliberations over Dien Bien Phu, notes in his memoirs that the Cabinet meetings in March and April "were much longer than the usual Cabinet meetings."[48] But Larson may not have been fully aware that the function of these meetings was to gather support, rather than information, for the president. The president's own preparatory notes for a discussion of Indochina during the March 26 Cabinet meeting unmistakably reveal this motive. "The Secretary of State feels," he wrote, "that indoctrination of the Cabinet Members would be a desirable step."[49]

Prior to April 1954, serious analysis of the Indochina problem within the Eisenhower administration took place among a small, inner circle of advisors (Dulles, Radford, and Cutler chief among them). These men shared the president's inclination to intervene in support of the French, and thus gave Eisenhower no reason to examine his own assumptions critically. In a confidential memorandum to Henry Luce summarizing the development of what he called the "U.S.—Indo-China Mess," C. D. Jackson strongly criticizes this "closed" arrangement of advisors. Jackson, one should recall, was himself a member of the OCB that persuaded Eisenhower to send two hundred air force mechanics to assist the French. In retrospect, however, Jackson saw a pattern of closed-door decision making that worked against adequate scrutiny of the repeated proposals for American aid to the French: "a decision on a Navarre Plan, or another $500-million, or the dispatch of six flying boxcars, or what have you."

The line to him always was, "Well, Mr. President, things
don't look too hot, but I think if you will do just this one
more thing, everything will be all right. We can't let the
French down now. We all agree that if Indo-China goes, all
of Southeast Asia goes, and Japan and the Philippines are
outflanked. And this one really looks as though it might
work. . . ." Never until the very end was there genuine realization that the only real pay-off was not dollars, or guns,
or boxcars, but GI's—and the President was inched along
toward the GI climax without being told, or explicitly real-
izing himself, that this would be the inevitable climax.[50]

If this pattern had remained constant, one might expect
groupthink to have prevailed over learning. Beginning in April,
however, the pattern changed dramatically. As it became clear that
Eisenhower would have to make some difficult choices, he made a
final effort to seek out the opinions of a larger and more diverse
group of advisors, including foreign and domestic leaders and both
military and civilian officials. This sudden advisory openness presented Eisenhower with critical views challenging, for the first
time, the cozy consensus that had emerged in favor of supporting
the French. As a result, he gained a greater appreciation for the
uncertainties that were not a part of Radford's optimistic scenar-
ios about the effectiveness of air strikes. He learned that the
British were decidedly unwilling to offer assistance. And he
learned that Congress would not support intensified American
involvement. None of these concerns need have stopped him if he
had been absolutely determined to save Dien Bien Phu. The general who "won World War II" almost certainly could have twisted
British and congressional arms.

But Eisenhower never made this effort because he recognized
in April what he had not appreciated in March: there were simply
too many drawbacks to direct military intervention in Indochina. A
less open leader might have retreated into the security of plans
already made and pressed ahead. Indeed, a number of friends and
close advisors continued to urge an air strike. Eisenhower might
thus have "bolstered" his initial assessment of the situation and
refused to listen to any objections. Or he might have "fled" from the
problem, pretending that it had ceased to exist and hoping that
this would somehow eventually turn out to be the case. Each of
these responses is distressingly common, even from veteran polit-

ical leaders.[51] Yet there is little evidence of either in the Eisenhower administration in April 1954. Eisenhower (and Dulles, for that matter) remained convinced that the fall of Dien Bien Phu, and the subsequent collapse of the French government, were unequivocal disasters. For a time, he went ahead *simultaneously* with plans for intervention and for a message of condolence to the French (in the event Dien Bien Phu fell). Yet the problem did not disappear, and Eisenhower did not define it away. He simply decided, based on what he had learned, that the United States should not become any more involved than it already was.

Alaskan Statehood

An important cause of Eisenhower's change of heart about U.S. intervention during the Dien Bien Phu crisis is that he took control of the decision-making process, widened and diversified his circle of advisors, and brought a difficult problem under much greater scrutiny. Although emotion certainly played a part in Eisenhower's decision about Dien Bien Phu—Eisenhower was furious with the French and almost equally unhappy when advisors such as Ridgway began to challenge his intervention plans—the picture that emerges is nevertheless of an essentially rational learning process.[52] It was also a top-down process, driven by Eisenhower's own desire for more information. Yet not all high-level decisions follow this pattern, even in the Eisenhower administration. Sometimes, advice and conflicting opinions emerge unbidden from lower administrative levels. This was the case as Eisenhower confronted the problem of Alaskan statehood.

During his first term, Eisenhower's rejection of Alaskan statehood was unmistakable. In a January 1954 meeting with his staff and congressional leaders, he exclaimed, "It is one of the great tragedies to make Alaska a state at this time—it's really a national defense area—it's crazy to try to make it a *state*." A few weeks later, he reiterated his position: "Can't understand Alaska statehood. It's an outpost."[53] Consequently, he worked with the Republican leadership in Congress to prevent a move, in the first months of 1954, to join Alaskan statehood to a similar bill for Hawaii. When Senator Eugene Millikan candidly remarked during a strategy meeting, "I can come around to Hawaii after a lot of mental retching and vomiting, but I can't do it for Alaska,"

Eisenhower replied, "Gene, you reflect my sentiments exactly."[54] The president even declared to William Knowland, the Senate Republican leader, "If the bill linking Alaska to Hawaii comes down here, I'll veto it. I just can't see Alaska as a state."[55] Eisenhower's veto was spared, however, by the fact that Congress itself failed to approve statehood for either Alaska or Hawaii during the his first term.

Eisenhower's opposition to Alaskan statehood was sufficiently pronounced that he saw no reason to seek much advice on the matter. When Douglas McKay and Orme Lewis (the secretary and assistant secretary of the interior, respectively) went to see him on one occasion during his first term and tried to raise the topic, he snapped, "Well, it better be goddamn good!"[56] The ensuing meeting was short, and Eisenhower remained unmoved. If anyone learned anything on this occasion, it was probably McKay, who did not press the issue for the remainder of his tenure as secretary of the interior.

From Eisenhower's perspective, Alaskan statehood posed two kinds of difficulties. First, its proximity to the Soviet Union conferred on Alaska considerable strategic value. As a result, Eisenhower sought to maintain as much freedom of action as possible for federal authorities in Alaska, and in this he had the full support of the Pentagon. General Twining in particular, who became the chair of the joint chiefs of staff in August 1957, fought against statehood on the grounds that the military must be free to act in Alaska as it saw fit.[57] Perhaps not coincidentally, Twining had earlier been the commanding general of the armed forces in Alaska.

Eisenhower also feared that Alaska's population was not large enough, and its economy not developed enough, to support statehood. Although Alaska's natural resources were clearly abundant, Eisenhower believed (somewhat uncharacteristically) that federal initiatives would be necessary to develop them. At most—and largely because he could not totally ignore mounting pressure from Democrats, who had made statehood for both Alaska and Hawaii a part of their party platform—he was willing to consider partitioning Alaska. The most heavily populated, southeast region might then become a state, but the remainder would be set aside as a national defense zone under federal control. Indeed, this became the Republican Party platform in 1956. Yet most Alaskans adamantly rejected partition, maintaining that "Alaska was historically and geographically one" and also that partition would deprive the fledgling state of potential revenue from many economically valuable regions.[58] Thus, for a time, the prospect of Alaskan statehood had reached an impasse.

Alaskan (and Hawaiian) statehood was stymied during both the Eighty-third and the Eighty-fourth Congresses, and the stalemate seemed destined to persist throughout the remainder of Eisenhower's term in office. Yet an event unrelated to Alaska, but closely related to Eisenhower's decision making on the statehood problem, finally cleared the way within the administration for a fresh analysis of Alaskan statehood. In March 1956, McKay resigned as secretary of the interior. To the delight of Alaskan statehood supporters, Eisenhower chose Fred Seaton to fill the post. Seaton was a passionate supporter of Alaskan statehood who had an "independent streak."[59] Unlike McKay, he was not particularly inclined to look first to the Oval Office before deciding on his own opinions. To the contrary, Seaton quickly went to work to change Eisenhower's mind.

The new secretary of the interior flooded the president with facts and figures demonstrating that Alaska was economically capable of self-government. Unsurprisingly, given Eisenhower's pessimistic views on the matter, these missives were not always warmly received. When Seaton prepared a report demonstrating that general per capita revenue in Alaska "was higher than 39 of the existing States in 1957," Eisenhower simply rejected it out of hand, writing in its margins, "I don't believe it—unless we take into consideration Fed. expenditures."[60] Seaton also pointed out that among the forty-eight states, Hawaii, Puerto Rico, and Alaska, only the Alaskan government had no outstanding debt at the end of the previous fiscal year. And, were it to become a state, roughly $5 million in new revenues—from oil and gas leases, Pribilof seal hunting, fishing licenses, and other miscellaneous fees—would become available to the new state government.[61] Despite Eisenhower's skepticism, Seaton's economic analysis softened the president's economic objections.

Seaton also devised a face-saving plan to sidestep Eisenhower's concerns about national security. His solution was a compromise somewhere between unqualified statehood and Eisenhower's proposal for partition. Seaton suggested that the federal government retain the authority to make "withdrawals" of land in certain regions of Alaska for reasons of national security, but that Alaska be granted civil and criminal authority in these and all other regions within its borders. This proposal satisfied the Pentagon, yet it allowed the entire territory to be incorporated into the State of Alaska.[62] His basic objections thus met, Eisenhower gradually began to accept if not enthusiastically support the idea of Alaskan statehood. Without great fanfare, Seaton's first two years in office produced a fundamental revision in Eisenhower's thinking.

A final problem, something of a catch-22, nevertheless remained. As in the Dien Bien Phu case, Eisenhower was reluctant to move forward on Alaskan statehood without congressional support. Although the Democrat-controlled House had already voted in favor of statehood, Republicans opposed to statehood were making their stand in the Senate, and Eisenhower was not so enthusiastic about it himself that he personally intended to put much pressure on reluctant members of his own party.[63] Once again Seaton took the lead, arranging meetings between pro-statehood lobbyists and administration officials "from Vice-President Nixon on down."[64] As one of these lobbyists recalled, he "used every resource he had at hand in his position as a cabinet officer and a member of the Administration."[65] Seaton's efforts were so prodigious, in fact, that they provoked an angry protest to Eisenhower from Republican minority leader Joe Martin (who opposed statehood) about the Interior Department's Alaska "blitz."[66] By this point, however, the president was in basic agreement with Seaton's efforts. Soon, enough other Republicans had joined Eisenhower that, on June 30, 1958, the Senate followed the lower house and voted 64 to 20 (with 12 abstentions) to make Alaska the forty-ninth state of the United States. After a popular referendum in which Alaskans voted 40,452 to 7, 010 in favor of statehood, Eisenhower signed the Alaska Statehood Bill into law on January 3, 1959, proclaiming Alaska the forty-ninth state.[67]

Given Seaton's central role in the passage of the statehood bill, one might object that whether or not the president learned was of little consequence in this case. Indeed, Eisenhower never quite overcame his misgivings about statehood for Alaska. Even after signing the statehood bill, he still grumbled that Alaskans were "nuts to want to start paying their own way."[68] But they did, and the president's opinion mattered. Had Eisenhower remained opposed, statehood would have had to wait until Kennedy took office, or it might even have taken a different (partitioned) form. Seaton's arrival was certainly crucial in prompting the president to rethink the issue, but if Eisenhower had refused to listen, or if he had not consequently changed his position, Seaton would never have been allowed to carry on his ultimately successful campaign in Congress. Although lacking tension-filled meetings with the prospect of war hanging in the balance, the decision on Alaska is nevertheless a powerful illustration of the effects of presidential learning. For this reason, as William Ewald has stressed, "the greatest glory must go to Eisenhower" for the passage of the Alaska Statehood Bill—"he chose his lieutenants, gave them freedom to think and to innovate, backed them to the hilt despite his qualms, and thus produced an outcome that in retrospect remains a triumph of his administration."[69]

In both cases discussed so far, Eisenhower had strong initial convictions in favor of courses of action that, ultimately, he did not take. In neither case, moreover, was he compelled to change policies. He could have mobilized opinion in favor of the French at Dien Bien Phu or against Alaskan statehood in the Senate. Yet in each case, based on the information and recommendations offered by his advisors, he changed his mind. Consistent with the argument presented in chapter 2, in each case learning followed a period of increasing advisory "openness." In the case of Dien Bien Phu, Eisenhower opened up his group of advisors as part of a conscious and essentially rational strategy to gather more information before making a decision. In the Alaskan case, on the other hand, there is no evidence at all that Seaton's appointment was part of a clandestine effort to reinvigorate the administration's analysis of Alaskan and Hawaiian statehood. On the contrary, Eisenhower neither sought nor expected further consideration of the issue. Learning was forced on him, in this case, by the emergence of a new voice in the administration that was critical of its earlier policies.

It is in the Alaskan statehood case, therefore, that the effects of learning style are most apparent. Every leader must occasionally call for further study of a problem. Even very closed leaders go through the motions, although they are less likely than open leaders to reassess their own beliefs, as Eisenhower did in April 1954, if new or conflicting perspectives emerge. When critical advice is thrust on a leader, however, the differences between open and closed leaders are likely to be even more pronounced. As the Alaskan statehood case shows, Eisenhower was capable of learning even when he did not want or intend to. The principal danger for such leaders is that, either by design or through socialization over time, their advisors may come to share much the same opinions, leading to groupthink. Ironically, for closed leaders, precisely these conditions of essential agreement are a precondition for learning.

LEARNING IN A CLOSED ADMINISTRATION

The 1980s may be counted as a return to the 1950s in terms of general presidential rhetoric. This is one reason for comparing Eisenhower and Reagan, but it would have seemed an unlikely justification on the eve of Reagan's election. Eisenhower's "proud decade" of peace and prosperity gave way in the 1960s to the Vietnam War and in the 1970s to stagflation, oil embargoes, and finally to the seizure of American hostages in Iran. On the threshold of the 1980s, "proud" was not the first adjective that sprang to mind. Indeed, newspapers were filled with predictions of impending American "collapse." *The New York Times* labeled Carter "the weakest and most incompetent president since Martin Van Buren."[70] With a public approval rating at the end of his presidency among the lowest ever recorded, Carter's ineffectiveness in office evidently struck many voters as symbolic of the United States' general decline.[71]

But it was not pure accident that Ronald Reagan had the good fortune to run against Carter. Reagan, who became the nation's oldest president, struck a responsive chord by promising, ironically, to rejuvenate the national spirit. On the basis of renewed economic and military strength, he declared, America would no longer allow itself to be held hostage. To accomplish this, and to deepen the irony, Reagan further promised to renew the national spirit by returning to "old" values and by restoring a national consensus that Americans seemed to have lost sometime after Eisenhower left office. Robert Dallek, a historian and certainly no apologist for Reagan, describes the latter's two terms in office as "a celebration of old values. Autonomy, self-help, free enterprise, individualism, liberty, hard work, production, morality, religion, and patriotism are as much the identifying symbols of Reagan's administration as the New Deal alphabet agencies were of Franklin Roosevelt's."[72] Reagan took credit for restoring consensus on these values in his farewell address: "They called it the Reagan Revolution, and I'll accept that, but for me it always seemed more like the Great Rediscovery: a rediscovery of our values and our common sense."[73]

Reagan interpreted his election not only as a call for moral leadership, however, but also more concretely as a mandate for a strong national defense, for a tax cut, and for reductions in government spending. On the first two counts, at least, he delivered. Military expenditures rose by 32 percent in real terms during the first four years of the Reagan presidency.[74] And by 1988, the marginal rate of federal income taxation had dropped "from 33 to 15 per cent for most taxpayers and from 70 to 28 per cent for the highest taxpayers."[75] Reagan's admirers can also point to a decrease in inflation and unemployment and to six years of economic expansion, after the recession ended in 1983, as evidence of his accomplishment.

Perhaps even more than during the Eisenhower years, however, the restored pride of the Reagan years was a veneer applied over complex and unresolved social, economic, and political problems.[76] Some of these had been building for years. The international debt crises of the 1980s, for example, had their origins in development policies, international economic trends, and oil price fluctuations that well predated Reagan's presidency. Reagan was not expert in these matters, but it was crucial that his administration take some action to preserve the health of the U.S. banking system and, ultimately, of the American economy. His response to the international debt problem constitutes the first case of learning to be discussed in the next section.[77]

Of course, political debates during the Reagan years extended well beyond economic controversies. Pundits often suggested during the 1980s that the presidency was primarily a foreign policy office, and although Congress undeniably shared responsibility for economic policymaking, Reagan took the lead on matters of strategic policy during the final years of the cold war. While he avoided prolonged foreign military entanglements, Reagan did undertake a series of "limited" military interventions, notably in Lebanon, Libya, and Grenada. The peacekeeping mission in Lebanon was the most costly of these in terms of lost American lives, yet it also reveals much about how learning worked in the Reagan administration.

The International Debt Shock

That government and private investors in developing, semi-industrial countries such as Mexico, Brazil, and Argentina had overbor-

rowed and overextended themselves was not news by the time
Reagan arrived in office. The "shock" that came in the 1980s, however, was twofold. First was the sudden recognition of the magnitude of the problem. After a sustained drop in worldwide oil prices
in 1981, Mexico began to experience serious liquidity problems.
Yet Mexico's problems, it turned out, were also the United States'
problems. As of 1982, "Mexican credits accounted for 44 percent
of the total combined capital of the nine largest U.S. banks."[78]
Moreover, according to Donald Regan's testimony before Congress
the following year, the $10 billion turnaround in the U. S.-Mexican
balance of trade between 1981 and the end of 1982 could be
expected to cause "the loss of a quarter of a million American
jobs."[79] The second part of the shock was the dawning realization
that debtor countries might refuse to make good on their obliga-
tions, perhaps even forming a "debtor's cartel" to coordinate
demands for debt relief. Such action would threaten the survival
of major American banks, and it would directly challenge the liberal principles on which Reagan based his foreign economic policy.

The Reagan administration could hardly fail to take note of
such striking economic and political vulnerability. Its initial
response, however, was to do nothing. This was not mere bureaucratic inertia, as some have suggested, but rather a policy that
flowed from the pronounced market liberalism of the president
and his chief economic advisors.[80] Whatever their differences,
Treasury Secretary Regan, Budget Director David Stockman and
Murray Weidenbaum (chair of the Council of Economic Advisers)
all agreed with the president that such problems were self-
correcting. When a Carter administration official attempted to
warn Beryl Sprinkel (at the time, the undersecretary for monetary
affairs in the Treasury Department) about the debt problems in
Mexico, Argentina, and Poland, his succinct response was that
"the market will take care of them."[81] In principal, the risk associated with growing foreign debts should lead to market pressure in
the form of higher interest rates that would reduce borrowing and
government spending. If "austerity" did not correct the problem,
then inflation would do so by forcing currency devaluation and
thus limiting further borrowing. In the long run, this analysis may
have been sound. Yet since strict austerity was politically too bitter
a pill for the major debtors to swallow, their continued borrowing
at high interest rates and their inflationary fiscal policies led to a
series of international financial crises.

These circumstances forced a 30% depreciation of the Mexican peso in February 1982. The resulting capital flight only intensified Mexico's short-term problems, however, and in April the Mexican Central Bank sought an emergency currency swap from the U.S. Federal Reserve to meet its end-of-the-month legal reserve requirements.[82] On August 4, after yet another currency swap, Mexico entered into discussions with the International Monetary Fund (IMF). Desperate for assistance, Finance Minister Silva Herzog announced a variety of price increases in government-supported commodities: a 30% increase in electricity rates, a 67% increase in domestic oil prices, and even a full 100% increase in bread and tortilla prices.[83] These austerity measures were too little, too late to stop Mexico's capital hemorrhaging, and on August 12, President Lopez Portillo closed Mexico's foreign exchange markets. The same day, Herzog called Regan to say that he would arrive in Washington the following morning.

From this point onward, with the stakes for the U.S. economy so high, the Reagan administration was forced to abandon its hands-off approach to the international debt problem. Its response can be divided into two stages. The final months of 1982 constitute the first stage, during which Reagan's advisors developed an initial plan of action. This plan also established the pattern for subsequent negotiations with Brazil, Argentina, Chile, and several other debtor nations. The beginning of the second period coincides roughly with the beginning of Reagan's second term in office. In October 1985, James Baker (who replaced Regan as treasury secretary) launched a new plan to head off a growing debtor's revolt. Each of these periods saw important adjustments in the Reagan administration's policies.

Herzog's arrival in Washington marks the beginning of the first of these two periods. Although generally aware of the growing crisis in Mexico, President Reagan and his advisors were more preoccupied with other matters, including their internal debate over the growing U.S. budget deficit. Reagan did not want to join in deliberations over Mexico's problems as well, as one might expect in a closed administration, and so he delegated the international debt problem to Donald Regan and the Treasury Department. The president expected to be notified only when consensus had emerged on the proper U.S. response. And given the prior American policy of benign neglect, there was initially no consensus to report. Having underestimated the scope of the problem, Regan was unprepared to offer specific proposals when Herzog arrived. As Benjamin J. Cohen summarizes the situation, in a study commissioned by the Council on Foreign Relations, the Reagan administration "had steadfastly discounted signs of an impending storm in Latin America and had developed no firm game plan for dealing with one. The result may actually have been to add to the sense of urgency, even panic, in many quarters when the tempest finally broke."[84] Cohen also acknowledges, however, that out of this urgency came fairly rapid action: "once they were 'hit over the head,' administration officials together with the Federal Reserve did move quickly to get the crisis under control, and within months a more or less coherent policy program began to crystalize out of their initially hurried, ad hoc efforts."[85]

Regan met with Herzog after lunch on Friday, August 13. By the following Monday, Mexico's currency reserves would be totally exhausted, and Herzog's first concern was to arrange a "bridge loan." For the remainder of the afternoon, Herzog and Regan's deputy, Tim McNamar, worked on a plan for the United States to contribute $2 billion as part of a $3.5 billion bridge loan package. Part of it, they decided, would consist of a $1 billion food credit, which was relatively painless for the United States given its surplus grain reserves. McNamar arranged with the Agriculture Department to extend a $1 billion credit to Mexico to buy surplus American corn. Devising a way to raise the remaining $1 billion, however, proved to be a more tricky political problem.

The second half of the U.S. contribution, they decided, would be repaid in Mexican oil. McNamar and Herzog's plan was for the United States to sell $1 billion of oil from its Strategic Petroleum Reserve and to lend this money to Mexico, which would then repay the loan out of its own oil reserves with interest (also to be paid in oil). The negotiations faltered, however, when Herzog's team began to worry that the deal would undercut Mexico's relations with other oil-producing nations. Herzog was also well aware of how Mexican nationalists would interpret the cut-rate sale of Mexican oil to the "colossus of the North." By proposing an effective interest rate of roughly 30 percent, the U.S. team did little to alleviate such concerns. To obscure the nature of the oil deal (and the amount of the interest charges), however, McNamar finally came up with the device of charging a negotiating fee. Yet this also caused problems. The Americans suggested a $100 million fee, while the Mexican team was willing to offer $50 million at most.

This difference in negotiating fees was the final obstacle to reaching an agreement.

At this point, Regan concluded that the plan should be presented to the president for an indication of whether or not to move ahead and accommodate the Mexican proposal for lower fees. Yet Regan was sensitive to the president's closed decision style. A debate in the Oval Office, he reasoned, would not help Reagan make a decision and would resolve nothing. The treasury secretary thus decided to make the sort of ex parte presentation that Eisenhower abhorred but that Reagan seemed to prefer. When McNamar suggested that the Office of Management and Budget (OMB) should at least be a party to the discussion, Regan curtly rejected the advice.[86] As Regan knew, Stockman was engaged at the time in a hard-fought battle to identify spending cuts and non-tax revenue sources wherever possible. He could be expected to oppose a lower negotiating fee and perhaps to object to the entire plan on the grounds that it was not "a prudent use of taxpayers' dollars" and could not be justified to Congress as such.[87] Indeed, the OMB did later oppose the plan.

On Sunday, therefore, Regan flew to Camp David for a meeting with the president that he deliberately kept small and private. True to Regan's expectations, the president announced that he was in no position "to make a judgment on the details." But Ronald Reagan neither expected nor desired to know the details. His role, as he saw it, was to articulate general principles. And on this occasion, based on Regan's summary of the problem and in a striking reversal of his usual inclination to rely on the market, he decided that "if it was possible to help Mexico he would like it done."[88] Armed with this directive from the president, Regan returned to Washington and approved the lower negotiating fee. On the same evening, U.S. and Mexican negotiators finalized the oil deal and, with it, they temporarily sidestepped a very serious threat to international banking.

Although it was only a stopgap measure, and Mexico still had difficult choices to make, the bridge-loan package set an important precedent. When Mexico announced later the same month that it was suspending payments of principal on its national debt—a development that Morgan Guaranty economist Rimmer de Vries likened to "an atom bomb being dropped on the world financial system"—it nevertheless continued to work with the United States and mainly within the rules of the international financial system.[89]

It continued to pay the interest on its debt, and it continued to cooperate with the IMF on implementing an austerity program while seeking to reschedule its debt. Darrell Delamaide is probably closer to the truth than de Vries in observing that "Mexico shocked the system, but continued to operate within its framework."[90]

Over the next eighteen months, other Latin American countries followed Mexico's example of negotiations with major international lenders. First Brazil, then Argentina, Chile, and others entered into discussions with international banks, the IMF and the Reagan administration.[91] Despite some talk of a debtor's cartel and a moratorium on debt payments, these nations also remained within "the system" throughout 1982 and 1983. By the beginning of 1984, however, the position of many Latin American countries had deteriorated rather than improved.[92] High interest rates on the new bridge loans only aggravated their debt problems, while the anti-inflationary austerity measures imposed by the IMF gave no relief to their already-weak economies. And the poorest citizens of these nations undoubtedly suffered the most from the resulting cutbacks in government services.[93] Although the Reagan administration's initial response had helped to stave off an immediate crisis, it did not solve the underlying problems.

In 1984, the largest Latin American debtors thus stepped up their requests for better deals from the banks and the IMF. In May, the presidents of Mexico, Brazil, Colombia, and Argentina met in Buenos Aires and issued a joint statement condemning the prevailing approaches to reducing their debt burden.[94] Then, the following month, representatives of eleven Latin American nations gathered in Cartagena, Colombia, to discuss their mutual debt problems. Argentina tried for several months, in fact, to defy IMF austerity conditions before finally capitulating. In April of the following year, Alan García won a resounding victory in the Peruvian presidential elections on a "programme of social reform and confrontation with the foreign creditors" in which he "promised not to negotiate any more austerity programmes with the IMF and to limit payments in debt-servicing to 10 per cent of foreign exchange earnings."[95]

To leading international bankers, formation of the Cartagena Group and the developments in Peru seemed like unmistakable signs of "a new degree of militancy and collective action among debtors in the region."[96] The banks hastened to bring their concerns to the attention of the Reagan administration, and thus began the second phase of the U.S. response to the debt shock. James Baker, who had replaced Regan as the secretary of the treasury, concluded that the administration, the banks, and the IMF must make new concessions if they wished to head off any further progress toward a debtor's cartel or outright refusals to make debt payments. The United States' role in this round of renegotiation was all the more important because of the "widespread and growing dissatisfaction with what was viewed as Washington's miserliness and insensitivity."[97]

During the October 1985 Joint IMF/World Bank Annual Meeting in Seoul, Baker presented the Reagan administration's new plan for international debt management. As in the first phase, this new plan was developed primarily within the Treasury Department. Indeed, it came to be known as the "Baker Plan." Yet once again, as Baker himself testified before Congress, the new administration policy had the president's personal approval.[98] It consisted of three proposals. First, debtor nations would undertake "macroeconomic and structural policies to promote growth and balance of payments adjustment, and to reduce inflation"—in short, continued austerity.[99] Second, both the World Bank and multilateral (regional) development banks would play a larger role in overseeing lending to debtor nations. And third, private banks would be encouraged to increase lending to debtor nations. Through the second and third proposals, Baker proposed to make up to $29 billion of new funding available to debtor nations.[100]

The Baker Plan constituted a departure from the Reagan administration's phase one policy in several ways. To begin with, it was a tacit admission that "contrary to numerous previous administration statements, the existing strategy was inadequate."[101] By placing more emphasis on the World Bank and regional development banks, the Baker Plan indicated a more long-term strategy with, correspondingly, less emphasis on the IMF and its austerity requirements (although, to be sure, the United States continued to require "structural adjustment"). Moreover, the Baker Plan indicated a new willingness on the part of the Reagan administration to pressure private banks for additional lending on more lenient terms. As Baker explained the policy to Congress, "a corresponding commitment by the banking community to help support the principal debtor countries" was vital to the administration's new plan.[102]

As with Regan's earlier debt-relief proposals, the Baker Plan had critics even within the White House. Norman Bailey, a member of the National Security Council, went so far as to suggest that the United States should simply impound "a certain percentage of a debtor country's export revenues to retire the debt."[103] Perhaps this was an extreme view, but others shared the sentiment that international debt relief was a waste of government resources and that the United States should take a more uncompromising stance. Many members of Congress opposed the Baker Plan and any other plan to approve additional foreign aid to debtor nations after the Reagan administration itself had asked for cuts in so many domestic programs. As Representative Frank Annunzio pointedly asked during hearings on October 22, how could the administration justify its plan when "the family farmers in Illinois are in desperate straits?"[104] Baker followed Regan's earlier example, however, and shielded the president from much of this controversy by developing new policies first within the Treasury Department and presenting them to him for approval rather than debate.

The Baker Plan also had its share of liberal critics in whose view it did not go far enough. Yet one pragmatic virtue of the plan, from the Reagan administration's perspective, is that it headed off another crisis, forestalling further discussion of a cartel and reducing pleas for a moratorium on debt payments. Debtor nations greeted the infusion of new funds, through the World Bank and regional banks, with general approval. They were well aware, of course, of the dangers of trying to borrow their way out of debt. In February 1986, Mexico sought a third round of debt rescheduling with still easier payment conditions, and a year later Brazil did take the bold step of an outright moratorium on further interest payments. The moratorium did not last, however, and within the year Brazil began new talks with the IMF over yet another round of rescheduling. While President Reagan and his Treasury Department certainly did not resolve the international debt problem—President Bush also found it necessary, for example, to propose additional debt rescheduling—Reagan did at least take the necessary steps during his two terms in office to prevent serious damage to international lending institutions. He avoided an outright explosion of what *Time Magazine* called the "debt bomb" and, by defusing the Mexican debt shock and the subsequent rescheduling crises, bought the major banks valuable time.[105] Indeed, most of the large international banks remained profitable through-out the decade.[106] This was possible because Reagan and his Cabinet (especially his Treasury secretaries) adjusted to the changing international situation at critical junctures in 1982 and 1985.

In some ways, Reagan's decision making on the debt crisis resembles Eisenhower's during debates over Alaskan statehood. In each case, subordinates took upon themselves leading roles in for-mulating new policies. And in each case, these policies were at variance with the president's well-known preferences. Eisenhower's open decision style required, however, that he be convinced through debate and the presentation of evidence. Consequently, Seaton's style was also open; he presented Eisenhower with detailed reasons to change his mind. In contrast, Regan and Baker's style, in successive phases of the debt crisis, was to devel-op a plan on their own and to present Reagan with an opportunity for choice but not for detailed analysis or debate. This style clearly leads to a sharply circumscribed form of presidential learning. But the alternative for Reagan would likely have been, as it was in the cases to be discussed in chapter 6, that no decision at all was made. And this would have had high costs during negotiations over the debt problem. Herzog told a member of his entourage during the flight back to Mexico after negotiating the first loan package with Regan that, if the oil deal had fallen through, he "would have broken" with the United States and allowed Mexico to go into default.[107] This would have been disastrous for both countries. Similarly, if the United States had delayed action in 1985, it is not difficult to imagine the Cartagena group solidifying into a cartel capable of exacting much more from the United States than Reagan actually delivered.

It is an irony typical of a closed administration that President Reagan succeeded in adapting to the international debt problem because he was well-insulated from the important debates. He articulated the general direction of administration policy and then simply ratified the plans of his subordinates. One is tempted to suggest, in fact, that these were not Reagan's policies at all, but rather those of his Treasury secretaries. Certainly, Reagan had little to do with the details of the initial Mexican bailout and the subsequent rescheduling plans. Yet on a basic level, the decisions were Ronald Reagan's. The debt problem was the most serious economic challenge his administration faced other than the recession (in his first term) and the federal budget deficit. Reagan was well aware of the significance of the problem, and he personally approved the direction of Regan's and Baker's efforts. In some cases, he even intervened personally with international bankers to encourage continued lending.[108] On the basis of the available evidence, Reagan cannot be said to have learned a great deal about the international debt problem. But he did learn enough to change the direction of his administration's policy at two critical junctures. This was a case in which President Reagan's advisory structure functioned precisely as he intended it to.

The Withdrawal from Lebanon

It may strike those familiar with the story of the Reagan administration's involvement in Lebanon as implausible to suggest that, in this case as well, Reagan was able to learn from a closed and effectively consensual advisory group. After Israel invaded Lebanon on June 6, 1982, Reagan's principal advisors promptly divided into two rival camps with sharply differing opinions about how the administration should respond. One group, which Raymond Tanter has called the "regionalists," viewed events in Lebanon primarily in terms of local political and socioeconomic problems.[109] The regionalists opposed sending American military forces to Lebanon on the grounds that doing so would not resolve these underlying problems and, likely, would only make them worse. The "globalists" within the Reagan administration, on the other hand, viewed events in Lebanon through the lens of East-West conflict, and they tended to support the use of American force as a counterweight to Soviet influence in the Middle East. Almost from the outset, Reagan's advisors seemed hopelessly divided on whether and, if so, how to intervene in Lebanon. In the critical assessment of a veteran Reagan observer, Lou Cannon, this case more than any other "demonstrates the naïveté, ignorance and undisciplined internal conflict characteristic of the Reagan Presidency."[110]

Both Secretary of Defense Caspar Weinberger and the president's national security advisor during most of the U.S. involvement in Lebanon, William Clark, fell into the regionalist camp. Weinberger compared Israel's actions with Argentina's invasion of the Falklands and publicly declared that the United States should oppose such efforts to "change the status quo by unilateral resort to military forces."[111] Clark and his deputy Robert McFarlane were also critical of Israel's actions and supported delaying or canceling a scheduled sale of U.S. weapons to Israel. Yet none of these men favored direct U.S. intervention or a strong American peacekeeping presence in Lebanon. Secretary of State Alexander Haig, on the other hand, saw in the Israeli invasion an opportunity to drive the Palestine Liberation Organization (PLO) out of Lebanon and thus to secure Israel's northern border, to discredit the Soviet Union's client Syria, and to increase U.S. influence in the region. Ideally, and this required a certain degree of imagination, "Syria might be wooed away from the Soviet sphere of influence, and Israel might be convinced that autonomy for Gaza and the West Bank need no longer be non-negotiable."[112]

President Reagan sought a compromise between his advisors' positions but, as usual, was reluctant to force the issue himself. The dilemma was that "he agreed with Weinberger that Israel should be penalized, and he agreed with Haig that the penalty should be limited."[113] Publicly, Reagan thus reassured Israel of continued U.S. support, particularly against any outside (i.e., Syrian or Soviet) threat. Privately, however, he threatened to cancel arms sales to Israel and personally warned Menachem Begin to end the hostilities in Lebanon. In other words, so long as his advisors were divided, Reagan tried to keep both camps happy by refusing to make a choice.

Despite the prevailing deadlock within the administration, it took less than a month after the Israeli invasion for Reagan to approve U.S. participation in a multinational peacekeeping force. This decision, however, did not signal the emergence of a compromise between regionalists and globalists. Rather it was the product of a unilateral initiative from Philip Habib, the special U.S. envoy in the region, and it followed a pattern similar to that seen in decisions on the debt crisis. Habib was earnestly working to broker a cease-fire in Lebanon. He believed that the fighting in Lebanon would end only when the PLO left, and that the PLO could hardly withdraw under direct Israeli fire. Thus, he sought to interpose a UN force between the combatants. Had this plan been subject to careful scrutiny it might never have been approved, particularly given the regionalists' skepticism about U.S. intervention. General John W. Vessey (the chair of the joint chiefs), for one, felt it would be "very unwise for the U.S. to find itself in a position where it had to put its forces between the Israelis and the Arabs."[114] But the decision was never debated. Habib made a direct appeal to the president, and the decision was "ratified in a brief telephone conversation."[115] Even for a closed president, subjecting a major policy initiative to so little scrutiny is extraordinary. It might be described as groupthink save that most of the relevant groups were barely involved. Nevertheless, this is an extreme instance of the same pattern of learning already noted. It is no accident that Reagan settled on a policy only when the ongoing internal debate was momentarily side-stepped by Habib.

On August 25 the first contingent of U.S. Marines arrived in Lebanon. Far from ratifying the globalist agenda within the administration, however, Reagan's decision to send U.S. troops inaugurated a period of even greater confusion. Shortly after the president approved the first marine deployment to Lebanon, George Shultz replaced Haig as secretary of state. This move initially seemed to signal a reversion to regionalism and, perhaps, a speedy withdrawal from Lebanon. At his confirmation hearings, Shultz argued that "the legitimate needs and problems of the Palestinian people had to be both addressed and resolved."[116] As Tanter puts it, "globalists appeared to be going down and out, and regionalists seemed to be on their way up and in."[117] Even the president "believed that he had taken an important step in achieving cabinet harmony when he agreed to jettison Haig."[118] But Shultz's poor relationship with Weinberger, dating back to the time they spent together at the Bechtel Corporation, brought little peace to White House deliberations on Lebanon, especially after it became apparent that Shultz favored intervention much as his predecessor had. He and Weinberger bickered constantly, reportedly descending even to the level of shouting matches during meetings with the president.[119] Confusion and dissent thus continued to reign over the Reagan administration's Middle East policy-making. Perhaps the only consistent, guiding principle was the president's belief that, having committed U.S. troops, they should remain in Lebanon until their job was done. Their job, unfortunately, was ill-defined.

The initial deployment of Marines succeeded in extricating the PLO from Beirut, but almost immediately afterward Bashir Gemayel, the Phalangist president-elect of Lebanon, was assassinated. For a time thereafter, the marines maintained an uneasy peace—interposing themselves between the Israeli and Syrian armies—and the Lebanese held new elections, selecting Bashir

Gemayel's brother Amin. Yet the U.S. forces came to be viewed as props for the new Gemayel government, and on April 18, 1983, a van full of explosives destroyed much of the U.S. embassy in Beirut, killing sixty-three people including Robert Ames, the chief Middle Eastern affairs analyst for the CIA.[120] This attack strengthened Reagan's resolve to maintain the U.S. presence in Lebanon, and in a speech on April 23 he declared that "the dastardly deed, the act of unparalleled cowardice that took their lives, was an attack on all of us, on our way of life and on the values we hold dear. We would indeed fail them if we let that act deter us from carrying on their mission of brotherhood and peace."[121]

Reagan thus confirmed his commitment to keeping the marines in Beirut, and his advisors remained divided. Weinberger felt that "they're not doing any good over there," whereas Clark had come to agree with Shultz and the president.[122] Lacking consensus, the administration drifted toward greater and greater involvement. On September 11, Reagan authorized the use of naval artillery and air strikes against the Druze militia. When news of this presidential directive appeared in the *Washington Post* the following day, it set off another round of recriminations within the administration over who was responsible for the press leak. Clark, in particular, bitterly complained to the president that the *Post* story had endangered McFarlane, who frequently traveled to the Middle East, by attributing the new policy to his advice.[123] Together with Ed Meese, Clark drafted an executive order empowering the attorney general to investigate the leaks, using polygraphs if necessary. This, in turn, infuriated Chief of Staff Baker, who surmised that Clark suspected him (or someone on his staff) of being the "leaker." Rallying Shultz and Vice President Bush to his side, Baker persuaded the president of the absurdity of subjecting his closest advisors to lie detector tests.

More important than the leak itself or the polygraph issue, however, was the fact that this contest of wills deprived Clark of supporters within the administration, evidently turning even Nancy Reagan against him.[124] Clark was sensitive enough to realize that his future as national security advisor had become limited. On October 9, he asked to be considered for the position of secretary of the interior, a post that James Watt's highly publicized gaffes had made available. This opened the way for yet another important change in Reagan's inner circle of advisors on Lebanon. Robert McFarlane, who succeeded Clark, had spent considerable time in

Lebanon and was perhaps better aware than those who dwelt mainly within the Washington beltway of the difficulties the marines faced.

These difficulties became manifest in another attack on October 23, when a truck carrying 5,000 pounds of explosives crashed into the Beirut airport headquarters of the First Battalion, Eighth Marine Regiment and exploded with the force of 12,000 pounds of TNT. The blast caused the marines' four-story barracks to collapse on itself, killing 241 and wounding over 100 more. As with the earlier attack on the U.S. embassy, however, this escalation of violence against American military personnel in Lebanon only strengthened Reagan's resolve to keep the peacekeeping force in place. In a short and somber speech at the White House, he declared that "these deeds make so evident the bestial nature of those who would assume power if they could have their way and drive us out of that area that we must be more determined than ever."[125] As Reagan later recalled, "in the weeks immediately after the bombing, I believed the last thing we should do was turn tail and leave. If we did that, it would say to the terrorists of the world that all it took to change American foreign policy was to murder some Americans."[126] Ultimately, however, this attack did change U.S. policy: it broke the long-standing deadlock among the president's advisors.

McFarlane had visited the marines personally, and he had called for them to remain in Beirut while others in the administration pressed for their withdrawal. Yet the stunning and brutal effectiveness of the second attack finally convinced him of the futility of their mission. As he later put it himself, "we had to face up to the fact it wasn't working, and we were putting lives at risk."[127] Of course, McFarlane had the full support of Weinberger, who was almost beside himself after the second attack.[128] The president's chief of staff and many Republican congressional leaders had also reached the same conclusion. They felt they had "lined up loyally behind the president on Lebanon," but increasingly they saw in Lebanon "a major Republican political liability" in the upcoming 1984 elections.[129] Even Shultz finally began to question his convictions. At an NSC meeting, he mused ruefully, "If I ever say send in the Marines again, somebody shoot me."[130]

By early 1984, therefore, an extremely unusual situation developed within the Reagan administration: virtually none of the president's close advisors agreed with his views on Lebanon. As late as February 2, Reagan insisted during an interview with the *Wall Street Journal* that "the mission remains the same." Two days later he declared in a radio interview that while "the situation in Lebanon is difficult, . . . that is no reason to turn our backs and to cut and run."[131] Baker spoke with the vice president on February 6, however, and both agreed "it was time for the United States, if not to cut and run, at least to cut its losses in Lebanon."[132] The next morning, while Reagan was away campaigning in Las Vegas, the National Security Planning Group (NSPG) met to discuss Lebanon. At this meeting, Reagan's principal advisors finally reached a consensus that the marines must be withdrawn and, with the internal deadlock broken, they decided to make this recommendation to the president. On February 7, in a phone conversation as short as the one that first sent the marines to Lebanon, Reagan approved the NSPG recommendation to "redeploy" U.S. troops to ships in the Mediterranean.

Even at this point, if one of Reagan's principal advisors had made a strong pitch for remaining in Lebanon, the president would undoubtedly have agreed. To remove the marines was to back down, in his view, and the fiction of "redeploying" them to the Mediterranean was actually as much for Reagan's benefit as for public consumption. Yet a fundamental change had occurred among Reagan's advisors. After almost two years of immobilizing disagreements and infighting, a consensus had emerged that made the president's advisory group effectively closed for the first time on the issue of Lebanon. This was the essential prerequisite for changing the president's mind. Reagan approved the withdrawal not so much because he was convinced that it was desirable or necessary, but because his advisors had finally agreed on it. This is a pure, albeit extreme, example of learning in a closed administration: the critical piece of information for Reagan was not some new development in Lebanon but the simple fact of his own advisors' unanimity. Few other presidents, even relatively closed ones, would give this consideration so much weight. Yet it was characteristic of Reagan's unusually closed learning style that his first instinct in making policy decisions was almost invariably to seek out a consensus recommendation from his closest advisors. Because he did not intend to inquire himself into the details of policy problems, *consensus* was closely tied to *validity*. In the absence of intra-administration agreement, Reagan seemed to conclude that nothing else valid could be learned about a given problem.

CONCLUSION

In each of the cases discussed in this chapter, a U.S. president reversed a policy to which he had been deeply and publicly committed on the basis of recommendations from his advisors. Consistent with the predicted differences between open and closed leaders, Eisenhower learned after new voices of dissent emerged within his administration, whereas Reagan learned either when his advisors presented him with consensus proposals or when they successfully managed to bypass internal controversies. Two heads may be better than one in the abstract, but in practice leaders differ in their ability to learn from conflicting advice. For closed leaders, coherent advice is more important than diverse advice. While Eisenhower often learned from debates, Reagan tended to ignore conflicting signals. New initiatives and changes in policy tended to emerge during the Reagan administration only after consensus proposals—or at least proposals with the appearance of consensus—could be formulated for the president's consideration and approval.

These displays of presidential learning no doubt leave much to be desired. Both presidents relied heavily, after all, on their advisors to filter and organize information. Eisenhower was clearly the more open of the two and, particularly on military-strategic matters, could even resemble such detail-oriented presidents as Carter or Clinton. Congressman Stuyvesant Wainwright recalled of his meetings with Eisenhower that "he knew exactly what he was talking about. I'd read about how he had been out in the morning taking putting practice, but when we went there he knew his business."[133] Yet no president has the time to attend to every policy detail. Although Eisenhower was well-informed about the strategic and political issues raised by the impending French defeat at Dien Bien Phu, for example, his decision ultimately depended a great deal on judgments made by his advisors about support for Operation Vulture at home and abroad. And if Eisenhower needed his advisors, this was all the more true of Reagan.

It would be easy to criticize both, therefore, for not having personally learned even more in these cases than they did. From the altitude afforded by hindsight, both appear somewhat detached from highly consequential decisions. For leaders in government and business, however, learning is not the contemplative personal undertaking that it is in the classroom, the library, or the historical archive. Like all presidents, Eisenhower and Reagan made decisions under the pressure of time constraints with many issues competing for their attention. They had no choice but to depend on others, yet they learned enough in each of these cases to reverse policies that they personally cherished. There were no sudden discoveries of critical, previously overlooked facts. This was not dramatic learning, but the importance of the more routine forms of learning that appear in these cases should not be underestimated.

CHAPTER 5

Groupthink

Warnings against the dangers of groupthink are standard fare in schools of business and government. Excessive concurrence-seeking in policy-making groups has been offered as the chief explanation for poor decision making culminating in disasters ranging from Pearl Harbor and Watergate to the ill-fated *Challenger* space shuttle mission.[1] By one estimate, social scientists now cite Irving Janis's classic work on groupthink in an average of over a hundred publications a year.[2] Groupthink is undoubtedly the most popular theory of how group decision making breaks down and has come to be regarded somewhat uncritically as the prime suspect in a variety of policy-making fiascoes.

Despite its popularity, however, social scientists routinely complain that groupthink is a poorly specified and largely untested theory.[3] Janis's original formulation knits together aspects of group structure such as cohesion and homogeneity with situational factors producing stress or low self-esteem and other variables such as the effects of leadership and group norms. This complex of antecedent conditions for groupthink will generate, he predicts, an equally varied set of negative consequences, including shared (within the group) feelings of invulnerability and self-righteousness, stereotyping of outgroups, self-censorship, and pressure on internal dissenters. Given such a jumble of causes and effects, it is little wonder that efforts to test Janis's argument have often been stymied. Most of these efforts, in fact, have

amounted to little more than the appropriation of Janis's terminology to retell already well-known stories of poor decision
making. In such cases, it is relatively easy to find evidence of many
of the phenomena Janis discusses, but doing so contributes little
to an understanding of the preconditions and consequences of
groupthink.[4] Experimental studies might seem to hold more promise. The few that have been attempted, however, suffer heavily
from the difficulties inherent in reproducing true leadership, group
cohesiveness, and situational stress in a laboratory.[5]

This chapter will examine only two cases, both drawn from
the Eisenhower administration, and thus certainly cannot afford
to make any grand pronouncements about testing Janis's theory
of groupthink. It sets for itself the more limited task of considering only the effects of a mismatch between an open leader (Eisenhower) and a closed group. Yet the predicted result—a deteriorating
ability to learn—is central to groupthink, which Janis originally
defined as a failure "to realistically appraise alternative courses of
action."[6] As in chapter 4, this chapter pays special attention to
occasions when Eisenhower received critical advice intended to
encourage him to reconsider his administration's existing policies. Specifically, at least some administration insiders believed
that Eisenhower's inaction on the mounting balance of payments
problem and his refusal to publicly condemn Senator Joseph
McCarthy would bring, respectively, disastrous economic and
political consequences.

Unlike the cases discussed in chapter 4, however, the groups
responsible for advising Eisenhower on these problems became
more closed over time. These changes create quasi-experimental
opportunities to move beyond mere storytelling and to use historical evidence to explore the causes of at least one specific form of
groupthink. By stating the expected consequences of a more
closed advisory system in advance, it is possible to test a specific
causal chain within the bewildering array of assertions Janis and
others have made about groupthink. These cases hold many of the
variables Janis discusses constant. As Eisenhower's advisors on
these matters become fewer and more homogeneous, other things
being equal, we should expect the president to show less and less
evidence of considering alternative policies. Unlike Reagan, who
might learn and even change policies dramatically in such circumstances, Eisenhower did not critically assess or reconsider

policies when his circle of advisors became closed. The result was groupthink.

BALANCE OF PAYMENTS DEFICITS

The early years of the Eisenhower presidency were a time of economic prosperity. They were the age of the "organization man" in the gray flannel suit; of growing tracts of middle-class suburban homes with television sets, refrigerators and washing machines; and of consumer spending fueled by the growing use of credit cards.[7] Moreover, the organizations filled with these gray-suited worker-consumers enjoyed the benefits of an expanding economy. The first half of the 1950s saw constant economic growth at a rate approaching 5%. Unemployment dropped from over 10% in 1947 to below 5%, and net disposable weekly earnings rose from $48.24 in 1947 to $74.97 in 1957.[8]

By 1957, however, the postwar economic euphoria was over a decade old and beginning to wear thin. In particular, the GNP growth rate dropped from 4.7 percent to 2.25 percent for the second half of the decade.[9] Although American gold holdings had remained essentially constant over most of the decade, short-term liabilities to foreign governments (representing potential demands on U.S. gold reserves) increased from $11.1 billion to $13.6 billion.[10] At the same time, foreign aid payments and other U.S. government expenditures abroad grew in 1958 to almost $6 billion.[11] Other countries were also re-establishing themselves as competitors in export markets that the United States had previously dominated. The result of these trends was a deteriorating U.S. balance of payments position. Balance of payments deficits, as such, were nothing new: the Eisenhower administration recorded deficits in every year of the decade except 1957 (when the Suez crisis boosted U.S. exports). But in 1958 the deficit jumped dramatically to $3.4 billion.[12] What made these deficits particularly noteworthy was the slowly dawning realization that continued American foreign aid payments (and military expenditures abroad) were not temporary burdens created by the Second World War. Rather, they had become a permanent fixture of the postwar world.

Treasury Secretary George Humphrey had begun to recognize the implications of this trend as early as 1955. In a letter to the president that April, Humphrey began with the wry observation that "we no longer need to worry ourselves about an excess of gold."[13] On the contrary, as Humphrey went on to explain, foreign short-term dollar claims had increased to the point that they exceeded actual U.S. gold reserves by $3 billion. Humphrey thus concluded,

> There is nothing to worry about yet, but this illus-
> trates definitely how the monetary reserves of other coun-
> tries have been strengthened and our own weakened to a
> point where we need to give careful thought to making
> sure of continued confidence in the U.S. dollar and safe-
> guarding our remaining reserves.
> We must watch with ever increasing care and vigilance
> our commitments abroad and our expenditures at home to
> get our own financial house in order.[14]

Eisenhower paid more attention to Humphrey's qualifications, however, than to the basic implication of his treasury secretary's letter: that gold convertability and balance of payments problems loomed on the horizon. In a brief response eleven days later, the president surmised that "a lot of bad things would have to happen in a hurry for us to get into real trouble about the matter." He concluded by asking Humphrey to "let me know if anything really serious does come up."[15]

Eisenhower's response to Humphrey's early warning is significant for two reasons. First, it indicates that the president did not yet appreciate the implications of the trend Humphrey had identified. Of course, he might be expected to learn about the problem over time. Second and more significantly, however, Eisenhower's willingness to place all responsibility for overseeing this problem on Humphrey's shoulders stands in marked contrast to his active involvement in all stages of decision making on many other policy problems. His economic decision making in 1955 actually conforms more closely to the conventional image of Eisenhower as an uninformed, part-time president with a penchant for delegation than to the revisionist portrait of an engaged, activist president who was very much the master of his advisors.

Not only did Eisenhower delegate a great deal of responsibility for economic matters to subordinates, but unless an economic problem posed a serious and immediate threat to American interests, he was not especially sensitive to their counsel. This was particularly the case with the balance of payments problem. Over the two years following Humphrey's initial warning, the treasury secretary made several other attempts to bring the drain on U.S. gold reserves to Eisenhower's attention. In a Cabinet meeting on April 20, 1956, Humphrey pointed out "a definite trend over the last six years whereby US gold reserves were being depleted through foreign payments." In the ensuing discussion, he "repeatedly emphasized the necessity of changing the trend." Yet other economic advisors, including Arthur Burns, Gabriel Hauge, and William Martin, did not share Humphrey's sense of urgency. Burns, for example, spoke up to say "that continuation of the trend for another five years would still not make for a situation much different than in the 1920s."[16] Defense Secretary Charles Wilson also warned that cuts in military spending would be dangerous, and when Eisenhower concurred that "the bulk of Government expenditures overseas is for military programs which cannot be touched without great complaints," this effectively closed the subject.[17] The Cabinet then moved on to other matters.

The following May, Humphrey once again raised the issue, this time by forwarding to the president a letter from Russell Leffingwell warning of "the increasing claims of foreigners against the nation's gold reserves and even of the possibility of a flight from the dollar." Along with Leffingwell's letter, Humphrey enclosed a note of his own in which he foresaw "a real danger unless we change the current continuing trend from loss of position to some regular, very moderate gain or at least the maintenance of a balance by reduction of our military forces and expenses abroad."[18] Again, the president paid little attention. As Burton Kaufman points out, Eisenhower simply "ignored Humphrey's warnings about declining gold reserves relative to dollar holdings."[19]

There is a certain irony in Eisenhower's refusing to heed Humphrey's warnings, for the two men were in basic ideological agreement on the subject. Intertwined with the balance of payments problem, as Humphrey was at pains to point out, was the expense of American foreign aid programs and of maintaining a military presence abroad, and Eisenhower took office with the express intention of promoting foreign trade rather than direct foreign grant aid and of reducing overseas military expenditures through the New Look. When he organized the Randall Commission in 1953 to review foreign economic policy, "from the first

. . . [he] intended the study to support the concept of liberalized trade in lieu of expanded aid."[20] And this is precisely what the commission, composed of a carefully selected group of free traders, did. Ultimately, it recommended a foreign economic policy consisting of "aid termination, encouragement of private investment abroad, currency convertibility, and trade liberalization."[21]

The Randall Commission's report, however, was not well-received in Congress. Naturally, the commission's proposals for lower tariff barriers for imports to the United States drew the most opposition. But the perceived threat of international communism, fueled in part by the French collapse in Vietnam, also called into question any proposal to reduce foreign aid to Third World nations or to decrease military commitments. Instead, several of the president's close advisors began to urge him to extend *more* assistance to countries "threatened" by communism. C. D. Jackson, in particular, launched a campaign to persuade Eisenhower to establish a fund for development aid to such countries. Jackson distributed to a number of administration officials a report calling for a "massive loan fund."[22] As the Soviet Union began to expand its own foreign aid programs—in February 1955, for example, it agreed to help India build an immense steel mill—Eisenhower found that he agreed with Jackson. After all, Jackson's advice conformed well to Eisenhower's own convictions about the importance of opposing Soviet communism throughout the world. Once foreign aid became a tool of anticommunist policy, therefore, it was almost a foregone conclusion that Eisenhower would support some form of aid program. At roughly the same time that the balance of payments and gold outflow problems were becoming apparent, therefore, Jackson and many other administration officials concluded that an even bigger menace was at hand. As Jackson put it, "the moment of decision is upon us in a big way on world economic policy. . . . So long as the Soviets had a monopoly on covert subversion and threats of military aggression, and we had a monopoly on Santa Claus, some kind of seesaw game could be played. [Now, they are] muscling in on Santa Claus."[23]

By early 1957, the White House, both houses of Congress, and the International Development Advisory Board had commissioned reports on foreign aid policy. Although the authors of these reports did not agree on every issue, they all pointed to "the changing strategy of the Soviet Union in underdeveloped areas" and suggested that "the United States needed to reconsider old programs and devise new approaches to foreign economic development."[24] In response to this consensus that the United States should pursue new and more aggressive foreign aid programs, the Eisenhower administration unveiled its plans for a development loan fund (DLF) in May 1958. The DLF was to be "capitalized at no less than $500 million for 1958 and an additional $750 million for fiscal 1959 and 1960."[25] At some point between 1953 and 1958, Eisenhower became convinced that the threat of international communism was such that a choice between trade and aid was no longer feasible; both would be essential to his anticommunist strategy.

As with other matters of economic policy, however, Eisenhower delegated most responsibility for formulating and overseeing development assistance programs to his subordinates. In this case Clarence Randall, the chair of the Council on Foreign Economic Policy (CFEP), which Eisenhower created in 1954, played a particularly large role. After Randall reviewed the Fairless report (one of the foreign aid reports commissioned by the White House), Eisenhower simply accepted each of his CFEP chair's twenty-three recommendations.[26] And as with the gold-outflow issue, the president made little effort to involve himself with the details of the relevant economic issues. Occasionally, even proponents of more foreign aid—who, after all, had the president's support—lamented this tendency and the vacuum it created. Jackson made his feelings clear, for example, in a revealing memo to Henry Luce. In February 1957, Jackson met with a number of administration officials to discuss his proposal for a "world economic plan." His description of these meetings to Luce is worth quoting at some length:

> I do not think anyone short of the President, in a command-decision mood, could have made a real dent on that group. Although there were three different types of minds present, they all formed an instinctive alliance.
>
> One type, led by George Humphrey, does not believe that we should do anything beyond strictly military defense unless the proposed recipient country promises to behave like a God-fearing Middle Western businessman.
>
> A second type, led by Foster Dulles, will take no initiative, won't even approve in principle, unless his client, the President of the United States, tells him to damn well pick up the ball and run with it.

The third type, part Hollister, part Hauge, thinks that actually we have not done too badly, and is mildly irritated that someone should suggest something more, given the difficulties on Capitol Hill, the problems of the budget, and the difficulty of coordinating so many divergent and Departmentally protectionist points of view.[27]

As Jackson discovered, it was not easy to get past this group and to bring proposals for new initiatives directly to the president's attention. Eisenhower's familiarity with the nuances of military strategy and international diplomacy may have encouraged him to take an active hand in these domains, but on economic and domestic political matters, he expected to intervene only if a problem was sufficiently and obviously important enough to require presidential action.

Some critical examination of policies was nevertheless made possible by the fact that Eisenhower's economic advisors were far from united in their views. Despite the "instinctive alliance" Jackson describes, these individuals constituted a fairly diverse group with varying opinions on protectionism, foreign aid, gold, and many other issues. Humphrey and Randall—two of the president's main sources of economic advice during his first term—consistently disagreed on economic strategy. Humphrey exuded budgetary conservatism and ultimately viewed most policy initiatives in terms of the fiscal bottom line, while Randall put more emphasis on the United States' global economic role and strongly supported an expansion of foreign aid programs.

The president's other principal economic advisors included Gabriel Hauge, Joseph Dodge, Arthur Burns, Milton Eisenhower, and C. D. Jackson. Hauge, the president's close friend and "assistant on economic matters," was instrumental in the administration's early organizational planning for economic policymaking. One of the most visible results of this organizational planning was the Council on Foreign Economic Policy, of which Dodge (who also directed the Bureau of the Budget) became the first chair.[28] Burns chaired another group during Eisenhower's first term, the Council of Economic Advisors, but this body focused most of its attention on domestic fiscal and monetary policy (rather than on foreign economic policy).[29] Both the president's brother Milton and C. D. Jackson also played important roles as economic advisors and unlike the fiscal conservatives (e.g., Humphrey and Dodge) were strong proponents of expanded foreign aid.[30] Many others played lesser roles in providing economic advice to the president, including Sherman Adams, John Foster Dulles, Herbert Hoover Jr. (the undersecretary of state), William Martin (from the Federal Reserve), Richard Nixon, and Sinclair Weeks (the secretary of commerce).

Although Eisenhower himself was less involved than on military-strategic matters, his group of economic advisors was thus initially fairly large and diverse, containing within it several important divisions. Those supporting expanded foreign aid programs, for example, were more or less balanced by those who stressed budgetary priorities. Jackson often complained about the difficulty of gaining approval for new foreign aid initiatives. Yet when Humphrey made his presentation on the decline in gold reserves at the April 20, 1956 Cabinet meeting, he also faced considerable dissent. The presence of such diversity among the president's advisors contributed to at least one major policy reversal: the administration's increased support for foreign aid and the creation of the DLF.[31] Although Eisenhower had initially opposed such programs, the efforts of Jackson, Randall, and even Dulles ultimately convinced him that extensive foreign aid must become a permanent feature of American foreign policy. If such cases of apparent learning in the domain of economic policy were not particularly common, it is perhaps due more than anything else to Eisenhower's preoccupation with military and diplomatic issues.

The balance of payments deficits in 1958, however, were finally severe enough to attract the president's attention. Eisenhower was forced to confront directly the problem of declining American gold reserves and payments deficits that exceeded $3 billion. By this time, however, the president's economic policy staff had also changed in several important ways. Raymond Saulnier replaced Arthur Burns on the Council of Economic Advisors (CEA), and Clarence Randall replaced Joseph Dodge on the CFEP, both in 1956.[32] The following year, Robert Anderson succeeded Humphrey as treasury secretary, while Christian Herter replaced Hoover as the undersecretary of state. (Later, in 1959, Herter became Eisenhower's new secretary of state, with Douglas Dillon as the undersecretary of state.) With Humphrey's departure, in particular, an important voice of dissent within the administration was removed. In fact, what Walt Rostow has called the "Humphrey-Dodge-Hoover" axis among the president's advisors was entirely eliminated.[33] With it went much of the opposition within the administration to foreign aid programs such as the DLF and, more generally, the Mutual Security program.

Another innovation that helped to foster unanimity at the expense of advisory diversity was the inauguration of a regular series of informal meetings between Eisenhower, Anderson, Hauge, Saulnier, and Federal Reserve Chair Martin. This group, sometimes known as "the financial committee," was "one of the most important forms of inter-agency communication established during the Eisenhower administration" according to Erwin Hargrove and Samuel Morley.[34] It played an important role in addressing the economic problems that began in late 1957. So as the president and his advisors moved toward consensus on issues such as foreign aid, they also moved away from the relative advisory openness that had characterized economic decision making during Eisenhower's first term.

Although the administration's newfound consensus on foreign aid may have partially resolved one issue, it simply ignored others. Increasingly, Eisenhower was trapped between the conflicting imperatives of maintaining foreign aid to combat communism and improving the U.S. balance of payments position to sustain confidence in the American economy. On one hand, foreign aid had never seemed so important as it did in 1958. That year was, as Sherman Adams put it, "a disturbing and unhappy time for Eisenhower and all of us at the White House."[35] Nixon's trip to South America had been a disaster, and the vice president only narrowly escaped injury when his car was attacked in Venezuela. The Soviet Union's successful launch of *Sputnik* also reinforced the administration's fear that Third World countries might not necessarily look first to the United States for leadership. Such events brought the need for American aid to the developing world into clear focus.

At the same time, however, American spending abroad was causing Humphrey's prediction of a balance of payments deficit coupled with larger gold outflows to materialize rapidly. In 1958, gold reserves declined by over $2 billion, the largest single-year drop yet. This was accompanied by increases in both foreign gold and foreign dollar holdings.[36] Moreover, the balance of payments, which had shown a slight surplus in 1957, plummeted to a $3.4 billion deficit in 1958. The following year brought equally dismal news: a balance of payments deficit of $3.7 billion combined with another $1 billion drop in gold reserves.[37] Faced with apparent confirmation of Humphrey's fears, Eisenhower had little choice but to confront the problem.

In August 1959, therefore, Eisenhower established a Cabinet-level group to study the balance of payments deficit and to suggest remedies. At roughly the same time, the National Advisory Council (NAC) directed its Balance of Payments Group (chaired by Alfred Von Klemperer, the assistant treasury secretary) to begin a similar investigation. As part of this effort, Von Klemperer asked the CFEP to coordinate a series of studies with various administration departments to suggest additional means of improving the balance of payments position.[38] Out of these studies emerged two basic strategies for reducing the balance of payments deficits and the gold outflow.

The first approach to the problem, favored particularly by the State Department and the CFEP, was to take steps to increase trade with other countries and to expand U.S. exports—in short, to expand dollar and gold inflows.[39] In September 1959, the United States thus informed its European trading partners (along with Australia, Japan, and South Africa) that the postwar trade preferences they had enjoyed should be dramatically reduced and that "where quantitative restrictions remained, foreign suppliers should have increased access to the market."[40] Eisenhower was even willing to take the somewhat unpopular step of encouraging "peaceful" trade with the Soviet Union, although this effort met with little success.[41] Several of the United States' existing trading partners—notably Austria, France, Italy, and Japan—balked at efforts to liberalize trade relations, but most of the others did make what the CFEP called "significant liberalization moves," and Eisenhower was reluctant to push the remainder too hard for several reasons.[42] First, he wanted to give them no pretext to distance themselves from the United States or to improve their relations with the Soviet Union. Since the Suez crisis, for example, France had pursued a more independent foreign policy, and negotiations to renew the U. S.-Japan security treaty prompted street riots in Japan that ultimately forced the cancellation of Eisenhower's planned visit. Moreover, the United States could only push for trade liberalization to the extent that it was willing to open its own markets. And although Eisenhower had fought a series of battles with Congress to lower tariff barriers, he had himself just authorized, in March 1959, new quota restrictions on foreign oil imports to the United States.

Eisenhower had few other attractive options to promote currency inflows. His new treasury secretary, with the support of the
NAC, proposed that the United States require recipients of its foreign aid to spend the money on goods from the United States.
Unsurprisingly, however, this met with strong opposition from
many quarters. The State Department, in particular, feared that
the new policy would reduce the effectiveness of foreign aid and
produce considerable ill will without many compensating benefits.
Others pointed out that 80 percent of DLF funds were already
spent in the United States.[43] In the end, Eisenhower decided that
DLF aid would be tied to procurement in the United States but
that other International Cooperation Administration (ICA) funds
would not be subject to this restriction—a compromise that generated scant additional income.

The natural complement to the strategy of increasing dollar
and gold inflows was to attempt to reduce corresponding outflows.
One tactic that Eisenhower pursued with diligence (although without real enthusiasm) was to reduce the number of military
dependents and other government personnel stationed abroad.[44] A
second, more far-reaching course of action was to solicit greater
participation from America's allies in development lending. In
December 1959, Eisenhower met with several Western leaders in
Paris to promote a European commitment to long-term development aid. Yet Germany complained that it was already losing
foreign-exchange reserves, Italy was preoccupied with its own
internal development problems (in southern Italy), England
protested that its Commonwealth development responsibilities
precluded any further action, and de Gaulle's France remained
suspicious of any cooperative endeavor with the United States or
Britain.[45] Although the Paris summit did lay the groundwork for
the Organization for Economic Co-operation and Development
(OECD), it produced little near-term relief for the United States'
foreign aid burden.

In fact, none of the Eisenhower administration's strategies for
reducing the balance of payments deficit or for stemming the gold
outflow made much of an impact. Because support within the
administration for the major foreign aid and development programs had solidified with the departure of the "Humphrey-Dodge-
Hoover axis," Eisenhower's advisors offered no major revisions of
any of these policies. Instead, they suggested a series of smaller,
stopgap measures such as the "Buy America" program and the

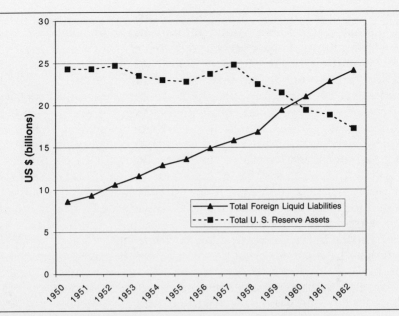

Fig. 5-1. Total U.S. Foreign Liquid Liabilities and Reserve Assets.
Data from *International Economic Report of the President* (Washington,
D.C.: U.S. Government Printing Office, 1973) table 20, p. 86.

repatriation of some American government personnel stationed
abroad. Perhaps these measures helped to avert what Eisenhower's Treasury Department called "a crisis situation."[46] Ultimately, however, they merely postponed the crisis while payments
deficits and the gold outflow persisted.

By the end of Eisenhower's second term in office, it was evident that gold convertibility could not be maintained indefinitely in
the face of the ongoing trends in U.S. gold holdings and foreign
dollar claims. Robert Triffin testified before Congress to this effect
in 1959, observing that "the Bretton Woods system was doomed to
succumb at some point if the United States continued to run
deficits of a magnitude that threatened its ability to convert dollars
into gold."[47] As figure 5-1 shows, foreign liabilities surpassed U.S.
reserve assets (including gold) beginning in 1959.[48] In fact,
Eisenhower left office considering gold outflows and the balance of
payments to be one of the most important problems facing his suc-

cessor. He made a point of stressing these issues to Kennedy and, at one point, had Robert Anderson subject the president-elect to a forty-five-minute lecture on the topic.[49]

Yet although the balance of payments and gold problems clearly ranked among the most serious issues facing Eisenhower during his last years in office, he remained personally aloof from the process of developing solutions for them. In his second term, moreover, he allowed his economic advisors to forge a tightly knit and cohesive group that rapidly reached consensus on a series of stopgap measures to reduce the deficit. This group contemplated no drastic changes in their agencies' programs and policies, Triffin's analysis and the trends shown in figure 5-1 notwithstanding. Typical were CEA Chair Saulnier's views that there was "no reason to doubt that the dollar's strength would in time win the respect in the world that it warranted, and that this would staunch the outflow of gold."[50] They also displayed considerable internal loyalty and a tendency to anticipate each other's needs in a way that worked against dissent and devil's advocacy.[51] When Clarence Randall wrote to Treasury Secretary Anderson regarding several proposals for reducing the payments deficit, for example, he prefaced his comments by stating that Anderson could count on him "to place no obstacles whatever in your path as you face up to the tough decisions on this question. I have too much respect for your own good judgment, and too much awe for the responsibility that you bear in protecting the integrity of our fiscal system." Randall concludes his letter by assuring Anderson that "I shall be a good soldier."[52]

Acting out of some combination of loyalty to each other and bureaucratic self interest, Eisenhower's second-term economic advisors also carefully regulated information on the balance of payments and gold outflow. On March 19, 1959, Anderson moved to tighten his own control on information about gold outflows by requesting at a Cabinet meeting that all outside requests for such information be cleared by him personally. In the name of reducing popular misinformation, the Cabinet approved his request. Because Anderson remained convinced that the gold problem would right itself when the American economy (and foreign confidence in it) improved, he had little interest in publicizing gold outflows that would only increase the apprehension of central bankers abroad.[53] Close teamwork and careful regulation of access to information might have helped the Eisenhower administration function more smoothly, but it did little to encourage critical re-evaluation of policies or to bring in new ideas from the outside.

Instead, bolstered by their emergent consensus on foreign aid and their compromise agreement on the "Buy America" plan, Eisenhower and his advisors moved away from a critical examination of the gold outflow and payments deficit problems. As Kaufman points out, no one in the administration even considered measures such as raising the price of gold (and thus devaluing the dollar), much less abandoning the gold standard.[54] Eisenhower himself was not uninformed on matters of economic policy, but he certainly was not disposed to encourage lengthy discussions of economic theory within the Cabinet or in other meetings with his advisors. In the final years of his administration, in particular, he inclined toward meetings with small groups of economic advisors that approached problems in a pragmatic rather than in an abstract way.[55] Even the reports on foreign economic policy that the president did commission—those of the Randall Commission and the Fairless Committee, for example—were intended more to produce statements that supported the administration's position than to re-evaluate administration policy.[56]

Eisenhower occasionally lamented what he himself perceived as diminishing "openness" within his second-term administration. He complained, for example, that a "lack of communication" had grown up between the White House and the State Department after Herter replaced Dulles.[57] Yet he contributed to this lack of communication, particularly on matters of economic policy, by allowing his circle of economic advisors to contract and to become more homogeneous. Even when he became convinced that the gold outflow and balance of payments problems were serious, he made little effort to solicit the opinions of Congress or of the United States' allies (although the foreign economic problems directly involved both). This stands in sharp contrast to his behavior during the crisis over Dien Bien Phu.

In fact, although the Dien Bien Phu and balance of payments cases involved very different kinds of problems, they began in similar ways. In both cases, a maverick dissenting voice within the administration sounded an initial alarm (Radford called for intervention; Humphrey called for reductions in the gold outflow), and in both cases the president initially temporized, undertaking a review of policy only when the problem became obviously pressing. Ultimately, however, Eisenhower recognized in both cases that vital issues of national security and well-being were at stake. Having reached such a conclusion, one might expect the same leader to engage in much the same process of learning.

The crucial difference between the two cases, however, was in the president's advisory system. Contemplating action in Indochina in 1954, Eisenhower's advisors initially formed a closed group but eventually grew more open. The president also made a considerable effort to solicit information and advice from outside his personal circle of advisors. In consequence, he heard a range of dissenting views about the military situation at Dien Bien Phu, considered a greater number of policy options, and ultimately reversed course and decided not to help the French. In the case of the balance of payments deficits and gold problems, on the other hand, Eisenhower began with a marginally open group of advisors. As the problem became more serious, however, this group simultaneously became much more closed. As a result, although the White House commissioned several studies of the problem for "public consumption," Eisenhower never conducted a serious review of administration policy, nor did he seek out the views of external critics. In short, he gave no evidence of learning in this case beyond the most routine sort of incremental adjustments in policy.

MCCARTHYISM

Perhaps one reason why Eisenhower relied on a much smaller circle of advisors for economic matters than for military-strategic problems is that he was himself a military expert. His own familiarity with diplomatic and strategic problems enhanced his ability to assess the advice he got and freed him from dependence on a small handful of experts within the administration. Occasionally, however, this pattern was reversed. One instance in which Eisenhower moved to close debate within his administration, even though he was well-qualified to pass judgment on many of the relevant issues, involved the problem of how to respond to Senator Joseph McCarthy's quest to uncover communist influence within the U.S. government. Several of Eisenhower's advisors urged him to respond forcefully, particularly after McCarthy accused the administration and even the U.S. Army of harboring communists. Yet Eisenhower steadfastly refused to take a strong public stand, reasoning that McCarthy would eventually destroy himself and that, until then, it was neither appropriate nor necessary for the president to enter the fray personally. Whether or not this was a wise decision is debatable, and depends largely on counterfactual assumptions about how effective a more direct presidential response would have been in bringing McCarthyism's worst abuses to an earlier conclusion. As before, however, this section will leave counterfactual history to others, focusing instead on the more narrow question of whether or not Eisenhower was able to learn from his advisors in considering his response to McCarthy.

Eisenhower's difficulties with McCarthy actually began well before the president took office. In a speech to the Senate on June 14, 1951, McCarthy had blamed General George Marshall for "losing" China and accused him of "a conspiracy so immense and an infamy so black as to dwarf any previous such venture in the history of man."[58] Given his long and close relationship with Marshall, Eisenhower was infuriated. Yet when he had an opportunity to defend Marshall in McCarthy's own home state during a campaign stop in Milwaukee, Eisenhower backed down. Although he was initially eager to speak out on behalf of his friend, he ultimately accepted the recommendation of his advisors (Sherman Adams and Jerry Persons) that such a statement would be unnecessarily divisive and would cost their campaign and the Republican Party the votes of conservatives in a state they needed to win.[59] Unknown to Eisenhower, some members of his campaign staff had already mentioned to reporters the candidate's plan to defend Marshall. That he did not do so was thus interpreted as a signal of deference toward McCarthy and was thus transformed into the opposite of what Eisenhower had intended. Adlai Stevenson subsequently made the most of the incident in a series of speeches questioning his adversary's "backbone."[60]

Emmet Hughes, one of Eisenhower's speechwriters at the time, has echoed Stevenson's criticism and wonders in his memoirs why Eisenhower did not stand up to Adams and Persons—and to McCarthy.[61] Certainly, Eisenhower was perfectly capable of taking unpopular stands when he had strong personal convictions. In this case, however, his personal inclinations dovetailed with those of his political advisors. Although he undoubtedly wanted to come to Marshall's defense, Eisenhower had long since formulated a policy of refusing to "indulge in personalities."[62] His reluctance to criticize McCarthy directly was consistent with this policy. As he explained in a letter to California businessman and friend, Paul Helms, "I [have] developed a practice which, so far as I know, I have never violated. That practice is to avoid public mention of any name *unless it can be done with favorable intent and connotation;* reserve all criticism for the private conference; speak only good in public."[63] Such a pronouncement may seem lofty, but it was an unwritten rule that Eisenhower's speechwriters generally obeyed.[64] Since attacking McCarthy directly might cost votes or undermine the centrist Republican coalition Eisenhower was seeking to fashion, this policy was probably moot so long as McCarthy's behavior was not too destructive. Yet it was not merely an expedient during the campaign. Once Eisenhower was in office, not "indulging in personalities" became a central tenet of his strategy for dealing with McCarthy. As he wrote in his personal diary, "I really believe that nothing will be so effective in combating his particular kind of troublemaking as to ignore him. This he cannot stand."[65]

McCarthy did not wait long after Eisenhower's election, however, to make himself difficult to ignore. With a Republican majority in Congress, Eisenhower expected his appointments for administrative posts to receive *pro forma* congressional approval. But when he submitted Charles Bohlen as his choice for ambassador to the Soviet Union, McCarthy led a group of Republican senators in revolt. Since Bohlen had advised Roosevelt at the Yalta conference, McCarthy viewed him as "one of the 'architects of disaster' who had blindly advanced Soviet power" in Europe.[66] McCarthy went on to brand Bohlen a "security risk" and to imply that the president did not know the background of his own nominee. Only after Eisenhower arranged for two senators (Robert Taft and John Sparkman) to examine Bohlen's loyalty file, which proved to be empty, was Bohlen confirmed. McCarthy next tried his hand at foreign policy, negotiating a pledge from several Greek ship owners that they would not transport goods to mainland China. At the time, Mutual Security Administration Chief Harold Stassen was engaged in talks to obtain assurances from the United States' European allies that they would not do business with China. Stassen might have approved of McCarthy's intentions, but he certainly did not appreciate McCarthy's interference and publicly complained that the senator was undermining the State Department. On this occasion, not only did Eisenhower decline to condemn McCarthy, but he even suggested to reporters that Stassen might have misinterpreted McCarthy's actions.[67]

Further emboldened, McCarthy aides Roy Cohn and G. David Schine then set off in April 1953 for Europe to ferret out subversive books in State Department libraries, where they claimed to discover "books written by 418 Communists or fellow travelers still being circulated."[68] Their investigations prompted a wave of book burnings at some of these facilities and gave rise to much international ridicule.

Eisenhower and his staff had no sympathy for communists and, indeed, implemented a sweeping internal security program to identify and remove subversive elements from the government. It is also worth recalling that, at the time, McCarthy enjoyed a good deal of public support.[69] Yet the book burnings and McCarthy's other antics seemed tenuously connected, if at all, to the problem of communist subversion. Such incidents provoked among several of Eisenhower's advisors the sense that a stronger response from the president would be necessary to prevent an unending series of witch-hunts that interfered with more important matters of foreign and domestic policy. At one White House staff meeting, for example, C. D. Jackson warned that "McCarthy had declared war on the President." Eisenhower, he went on, must step "up to bat on this one soon."[70] Bryce Harlow agreed, but Adams, Persons, and other aides felt that the president should continue to remain aloof from the swirling charges and countercharges of subversion.[71] The vice president, who had benefited politically from anticommunist campaigns himself, was also known to oppose a direct confrontation. Eisenhower made his own position quite clear: he would not, as he put it, become "just another 'whiner and snarler,'" nor would he "get in the gutter with that guy."[72]

In January 1954, McCarthy embarked on his most ambitious anticommunist crusade yet, asserting that communists had infiltrated the U.S. Army itself.[73] The basis for his charge was the army's induction, and subsequent hasty dismissal, of a Camp Kilmer dentist named Irving Peress. Peress received his commission in November 1953 and was automatically promoted to major, under the provisions of the Doctor Draft Law, before the army discovered that he had refused to answer certain questions about his political beliefs. As it happened, he had once been a member of the American Labor Party.[74] On discovering this, the army moved to discharge Peress, but before it could do so McCarthy seized on the matter as evidence of communist subversion. When the army hurriedly granted Peress's request for an immediate discharge,

McCarthy only intensified his attack, demanding to know why the army had given a communist an honorable discharge. The senator called General Ralph Zwicker before his Permanent Subcommittee on Investigations to testify on the matter, and when Zwicker refused to answer certain questions, McCarthy declared that the highly decorated officer "lacked the brains of a five-year-old child" and was "not fit to wear that uniform."[75] In response to what he perceived as "unwarranted abuse," Army Secretary Robert Stevens decided that "under existing conditions no other officers were to honor McCarthy's demands for testimony."[76] McCarthy then subpoenaed Stevens himself, and the Army-McCarthy battle was on.

To this point, as Eisenhower historian Stephen Ambrose points out, "the President's attempt to undercut McCarthy by ignoring him had failed, utterly."[77] Despite Eisenhower's deference to advisors who advocated a "soft" approach to McCarthy, moreover, the president could not be accused convincingly of groupthink in his early deliberations on McCarthy. Although the dominant view among his domestic advisors (notably, Adams, Persons, and Nixon) was clearly that Eisenhower should avoid a direct challenge, Jackson, Harlow, and others had presented an alternative view to the president. As the army was drawn into the fray and as Eisenhower became more personally involved, one might expect a still wider review of options. By this time, however, Eisenhower was convinced as a matter of principle that he should not attack McCarthy publicly. Nor could his advisors have failed to get the message implicit in his tepid support of Marshall and Stassen. There seemed to be little reason for them to persist in trying to change the president's mind, and Eisenhower had no desire to encourage further debate. Even as McCarthy went after the army, therefore, Eisenhower clung to his strategy of aloofness. It is from this point that a diagnosis of groupthink becomes more persuasive.

Seeking to prevent an open rift in the Republican Party, the White House's first maneuver in the battle between McCarthy and the army was yet another effort at conciliation. Vice President Nixon and Jerry Persons arranged a luncheon meeting between Secretary Stevens and the Republican members of the Investigations Subcommittee during which all those present signed a "Memorandum of Understanding." In exchange for a promise that witnesses before the committee would be treated respectfully, Stevens agreed to allow additional testimony from Zwicker and to release information about those involved in promoting Peress.

McCarthy lost no time in declaring a personal victory. Indeed, the headline in the following day's *New York Times* read: "Stevens Bows to McCarthy at Administration Behest. Will Yield Data on Peress."[78] This was hardly the impression Eisenhower hoped to convey. As his press secretary James Hagerty put it, "we were sure dumb. Someone let Stevens walk right into a bear trap."[79]

Privately, Eisenhower fumed at his inability to reign in McCarthy, and the attacks on the army particularly rankled. Hagerty noted in his diary that the president is "very mad and getting fed up—it's his Army and he doesn't like McCarthy's tactics at all."[80] Eisenhower thus intensified his behind-the-scenes efforts to limit McCarthy's influence. In the first two weeks of March, he met personally with Republican congressional leaders to obtain promises that they would attempt to restrain McCarthy. He also issued statements supporting Stevens and General Zwicker and calling for "fair play" in the congressional hearings.[81] He even called the attorney general to inquire about his legal authority, should it become necessary, to "protect people from McCarthy" by ordering them not to testify.[82] Although many Republicans viewed McCarthy as an asset in 1953, in the first half of 1954 an increasing number came to share Eisenhower's view that he was a liability and, perhaps, a serious menace.

Yet Eisenhower still refused to "talk personalities" or to take what Fred Greenstein has called his "covert anti-McCarthy campaign" into the public realm.[83] Even when McCarthy called for federal employees to come directly to him with any evidence of "graft, corruption, Communists, or treason"—a request that Eisenhower viewed as "the most disloyal act we have ever had by anyone in the Government of the United States"—the president held his tongue and issued a statement observing simply that "the executive branch has sole and fundamental responsibility to enforce laws and presidential orders."[84] Eisenhower clung to the hope that Americans would eventually realize that "the public utterances of an individual member of the United States Senate is [sic] strictly not the business of the President."[85] Although some of his advisors were almost frantic about the need for stronger presidential action, Eisenhower cut short their efforts to discuss any such proposal.[86]

Eventually, McCarthy's extremism and bombast, combined perhaps with his growing reliance on alcohol, did lead to his downfall. When the televised Army-McCarthy hearings began, on April 22, Secretary Stevens acquitted himself fairly well in a marathon ten-day appearance before the Investigations Subcommittee. As the hearings stretched into June, McCarthy's bullying and "point of order!" interruptions of witnesses turned even many of his followers against him. By May, one Republican member of Congress summed up prevailing opinion as follows: "'McCarthyism' has become a synonym for witch-hunting, star-chamber methods and the denial of . . . civil liberties."[87] Indeed, while 63 percent of those with opinions had a favorable impression of him in January 1954, 59 percent of this group had an unfavorable opinion of him eight months later.[88] On December 2, 1954, the Senate voted to censure McCarthy for violations of Senate decorum, formally confirming his fall from grace. Two days later, McCarthy noisily "broke" with the president and "apologized" to those he had encouraged to vote for Eisenhower. The White House made it "a point not to have any comment whatsoever."[89] At last, Eisenhower could tell his Cabinet a joke he undoubtedly had held in reserve for some time: "McCarthyism was now 'McCarthywasm.'"[90]

The importance of Joseph McCarthy's decline notwithstanding, the anticommunist movement was larger than the man who gave his name to it in the early 1950s. Well before McCarthy himself seized on the issue, "politicians, plain folk, and many powerful institutions (the Catholic Church, the U.S. Chamber of Commerce, segments of the labor movement, and numerous others) had coalesced in an anti-Communist consensus."[91] The 1946 elections brought a Republican majority to Congress for the first time in sixteen years—Richard Nixon was one of this number, aided in the election by charges that his opponent, Jerry Voorhis, had received support from communist-leaning political action committees—and the new Congress greatly intensified pressure on Truman to implement a stronger governmental "loyalty program." The FBI, under J. Edgar Hoover, and the House Committee on Un-American Activities (HUAC) launched far-ranging inquiries into communist activity in government, labor unions, schools, and the movie industry.[92] Sensational investigations and trials of government officials such as Judith Coplon, Alger Hiss, and Harry Dexter White fanned the flames of suspicion. The Soviet Union's first successful detonation, in September 1949, of an atomic explosive also added to fears (and suspicions of espionage).

If McCarthyism thus preceded its namesake, it also outlasted him. The McCarran Act, which provided a variety of penalties for communist affiliation and granted legal authority to the FBI to maintain a list of potential "subversives," remained on the books. In August 1956, Hoover initiated COINTELPRO, a new program of surveillance and destabilization directed against the U.S. Communist Party. This program was eventually expanded to monitor and interfere with the activities of the Black Panthers and Martin Luther King Jr.'s Southern Christian Leadership Conference as well as the Ku Klux Klan. Later, Vietnam War protesters and even feminists and environmental activists were added to the list.[93] The HUAC also continued to hold hearings. Although its activities met with increasing protest during the 1960s, it persisted until 1975.[94]

The phenomenon of McCarthyism, then, was not restricted to the actions of the junior senator from Wisconsin. Even as they sought to undermine McCarthy, in fact, Eisenhower and Dulles were not above using the anticommunist movement to conduct their own purges of "New Dealers" within the government. Shortly after taking office, Dulles sent a letter to 16,500 State Department employees demanding loyalty to the new administration, and subsequently used new legislation to fire hundreds of them without a hearing.[95] Eisenhower's Executive Order 10450 extended the security program to all departments, expanded the authority of agency heads to fire employees, and reduced avenues of appeal, prompting even the Loyalty Review Board chair himself to worry that it was "not the American way of doing things."[96] Eisenhower's own attorney general, Herbert Brownell, later wondered whether the security program "should have been limited in extent to cover only those employees who actually handled classified information."[97]

Whether or not Eisenhower's strategy of ignoring McCarthy was more effective than attacking him directly is an unanswerable question, and this is no doubt true of efforts to assess the merits of his generally hands-off response to the larger issues at stake as well.[98] Eisenhower himself felt vindicated by the Army-McCarthy hearings, arguing in his memoirs that "it is doubtful that this result would have ever come about had I adopted a habit of referring to McCarthy by name in press conferences, thus making the issue one of Executive versus congressional prestige."[99] As ignoring McCarthy became Eisenhower's idée fixe, however, it signaled a preoccupation with the man more than the broader phenomenon. Not "indulging in personalities" may have been a principled stand, but with his focus thus narrowed, Eisenhower was sometimes willing to abandon other principles.[100] Greatly concerned that McCarthy would exploit questions raised about the nuclear physicist J. Robert Oppenheimer's loyalty, for example, Eisenhower decided to move first, withdrawing Oppenheimer's security clearance and beginning an investigation. Eisenhower personally admired Oppenheimer and shared the physicist's concern with the prospect of an unfettered nuclear arms race. In the climate of the early cold war, however, advocating a halt to the American nuclear weapons program (as Oppenheimer did) was tantamount to treason in the eyes of many conservatives. Fearful that an investigation by McCarthy would wreck the morale of scientists then working on thermonuclear weapons, Eisenhower quietly severed Oppenheimer's contact with the Atomic Energy Commission and, through Nixon, persuaded McCarthy that the matter was resolved.[101]

Eisenhower's own fixation on McCarthy belies the importance of the larger issues of security and civil liberties that were at stake. His hands were not quite so tied by principle as he may himself have sometimes believed: the consequences of his own choices extended well beyond their impact on McCarthy. Eisenhower could very well have embarked on even more sweeping anticommunist programs had the Army-McCarthy hearings not proven so disastrous for McCarthy. Conversely, he could have objected more strongly to the ceaseless loyalty hearings, the book burnings, and the callous association of almost any form of liberalism with communist subversion. Several of his advisors longed for him to examine the choices he did make more carefully, to give them the sort of scrutiny he gave (at roughly the same time) to the problem of Dien Bien Phu.

As Eisenhower's focus narrowed to McCarthy exclusively, however, his willingness to entertain debate on McCarthyism contracted along with it. This constriction of discussion within the administration represents a learning failure, irrespective of whether Eisenhower's decisions were themselves wise. Despite the occasional pleas of Hagerty, Jackson, and several of Eisenhower's other advisors, the president refused to open a general discussion of administration policy on subversion and the red scare. He resisted even broaching the issue in an open forum such as the Cabinet and, when he did so, it was primarily to reiterate his position that the administration should not engage McCarthy directly.[102] Inevitably, the pleas for a new approach became fewer and fainter. On the few occasions when Eisenhower was forced to discuss the problem, he concentrated on specific dilemmas posed by Senator McCarthy's actions, or potential actions, and not on the larger issue of the red scare. At one point, for example, he spent the better part of three days discussing the Oppenheimer case. Yet the issue, as Ambrose points out, "was to keep McCarthy away from Oppenheimer," and not a broader examination of administration policy on subversion and civil liberties.[103]

Eisenhower certainly did not reject a broader debate within his administration because he underestimated McCarthy's importance. On the contrary, precisely because Eisenhower did consider McCarthy important, and because he had long since made up his mind about how to respond, he saw no need for further debate. The contrast between this case and the Alaskan statehood case discussed in chapter 4 is illuminating. As with McCarthy, Eisenhower also quickly made up his mind about Alaskan statehood. In neither case did he desire further debate within his administration. Nevertheless, he repeatedly (though somewhat grudgingly) allowed Fred Seaton to bring up the statehood problem for discussion. In the case of McCarthy, however, not only did Eisenhower have strong personal views, but he made sure that his advisors were well aware of these views and that they were not subject to debate. It was not the mere presence of a strong opinion, therefore, but rather the way it affected the usually open relationship between Eisenhower and his advisors, that was decisive in this case. As Janis has argued, impartial leadership can go some distance toward overcoming the groupthink tendency.[104] In many of the "fiascoes" he examined, as in the case of Eisenhower's response to McCarthy, advisors became reluctant to return to an issue after their leader's views became clear.

Eventually, Eisenhower came to have some regrets about the way he handled McCarthy. He relied heavily on the more conservative members of his administration in formulating responses to McCarthy and the problem of subversion. Bryce Harlow later recalled, of the president's decision not to defend General Marshall in Wisconsin, that Eisenhower "thought he blew that. There is no question that he thought he blew it. He felt he was put upon by aides who induced him to blow it. He gave in to them in a season when he was still getting his sea legs in politics."[105] Yet even if Eisenhower came to see this incident as a personal or political failure, it cannot be considered a *learning* failure. If anything, what Eisenhower learned on the campaign trail was a lesson about the relative importance of friendship and political expediency. The failure to learn came later as, even at the height of the red scare, he put neither his own nor his advisors' decision-making skills to particular use. Having concluded that the problem was McCarthy and that the solution was to ignore him, Eisenhower foreclosed debate within his administration on both McCarthy and on the broader issues his actions raised. Finally, after two difficult years, McCarthy brought about his own downfall with little help from Eisenhower.

CONCLUSION

Chapter 4 described learning primarily in cognitive terms, emphasizing the acquisition of information without dwelling on the political or ethical appropriateness of that information. Although this chapter has examined cases in which Eisenhower's decision making was often criticized, it refrains from offering specific judgments on the positions he ultimately took. It does argue, however, that compared with the cases of learning discussed in chapter 4, Eisenhower made his decisions about the balance of payments problem and McCarthyism on the basis of a less thorough investigation of the relevant issues and of his options for addressing them. This relative failure to learn cannot be explained, moreover, by asserting that there was actually nothing to learn—that the decisions Eisenhower made were foregone conclusions. On the contrary, both the balance of payments problem and McCarthyism involved a number of complex issues, and in each case the president had a range of conceivable choices. He might have expanded his decision making in either case to consider both problems and solutions that, instead, he ignored.

Nor can the differences in Eisenhower's decision making be explained simply by asserting that political passions interfered with a thoughtful evaluation of his advisors' recommendations. It is true that the cases discussed in this chapter stirred strong emotions. Even the seemingly arcane problems of gold outflows and the U.S. balance of payments position were a source of great anxiety to many (including some members of the Eisenhower administration) as they began to call both the gold standard and American competitivity into question. Eisenhower was not made of stone. On occasion, his temper would flare up so impressively that, according to Harlow, "it was like looking into a Bessemer furnace."[106] Yet Eisenhower also had strong convictions about the French collapse in Indochina and the matter of Alaskan statehood. He was infuriated at times by each of these problems, and yet he continued to seek a broad range of advice about how to respond to them.

In each of the two cases discussed in this chapter, however, Eisenhower allowed his group of advisors to become more closed. In the balance of payments case, the group not only became smaller, contracting for practical purposes to his so-called financial committee, but also ceased to represent the broader range of economic views it had when Humphrey, Dodge, and Hoover had been a part of the administration. In the McCarthy case, on the other hand, Eisenhower's principal advisors did not change. The group became more functionally closed, however, after the president made his own position clear and after Nixon, Adams, and Persons, having agreed with him all along, began to dominate his other advisors on the matter. As chapter 4 shows, Eisenhower was certainly capable of changing his mind even when he had strong opinions. In these cases, however, there was no sustained challenge within the administration to Eisenhower's views. Those who might have provided such a challenge had either left the administration or, in the McCarthy case, did not wish to keep returning to a topic that was clearly unpopular with the president.

Eisenhower was not simply, to borrow the title of Janis's original study on the matter, a "victim of groupthink." Although he prided himself on his ability to craft an efficient and smoothly functioning staff, the defects in his advisory system in these cases were partly of his own making. Perhaps because he was less comfortable with economic and political matters than with military and diplomatic ones, he was more willing to rely on a smaller circle of closer advisors. Perhaps idiosyncratic factors, such as his personal distaste for addressing political opponents by name in public, also contributed to this tendency. Perhaps it is simply impossible for any leader to address every issue with an open mind—and with an open advisory staff. Precisely in well-crafted advisory groups, however, leaders must be careful to guard against the overly rapid emergence of consensus on important policy problems.

Failing to incorporate a broader range of social, political, and economic views into the discussions of his inner councils may have spared Eisenhower, on certain occasions, from wrenching debates on matters he was not eager to address. Yet the eight years of the Eisenhower presidency were not, in general, the "age of consensus" they were sometimes alleged to be. Despite the United States' economic prosperity, and despite the "comfort" of having a common enemy in the Soviet Union, Americans passionately disagreed on many political issues. Eisenhower was in an unusual position, even in comparison with other presidents, to provide leadership on these matters when he chose to do so. It therefore mattered that he chose not to lead the United States into Vietnam over the protestations of some of his advisors. It mattered that he would not change his mind about McCarthy, but that he would change it about Alaskan statehood. And it mattered that Eisenhower failed to recognize the contradiction implicit in expanding foreign aid commitments and dwindling gold reserves. In each of these cases, for good or ill, President Eisenhower's propensity to learn made a difference in policies that affected his constituents, the citizens of many other countries, and future generations.

CHAPTER 6

Deadlock

Conventional wisdom has it that Ronald Reagan was poorly informed about many of the major issues of his day. This view was not only held by his political opponents but also encouraged by a spate of critical insider-accounts published by former associates. Accordingly, Reagan seems an obvious choice for a discussion of learning failures. Unlike the Eisenhower revisionists (and administration insiders) who asserted from the beginning that the Eisenhower they knew was very different from his public image as a likable but uninvolved golfer-president, even Reagan's supporters have recognized his tendency to distance himself from the details of policymaking. They do not regard him as particularly reflective or inclined to weigh carefully multiple perspectives on important policy problems.[1] On the contrary, some attribute his successes as president precisely to his reluctance to immerse himself in policy minutia. Reagan articulated a general vision, they argue, and left its implementation to others. By remaining aloof from the details of his policies, Reagan kept both his own attention and that of Congress and many other Americans focused on the broad outlines of his objectives—such as a tax cut and a stronger military—rather than on the trade-offs they entailed.

This distance from his own policies also paid dividends when the policies did not succeed. Sidney Blumenthal was not alone among journalists in grumbling that those "assigned to the White House lock Ronald Reagan in their sights, fire, and believe they've made direct hits. Yet he walks away unscathed. He has survived the assaults of the press better than any president in decades."[2] Reagan defined his job as articulating the ideals of his presidency, not as crafting the methods of attaining them. If a policy was unsuccessful or even counterproductive, this was not the president's fault, but that of whichever agency had implemented it. The president himself remained unassailable.

The Reagan administration thus seems both an easy case and an odd case for the study of learning failures: "easy" because it seems clear that Reagan rarely made an effort to learn a great deal about difficult policy problems, and "odd" because arguably it was not Reagan's learning that mattered, in any event, but that of his subordinates who actually formulated specific policies. As chapter 4 sought to show, the first of these objections is mistaken. It is clear that Reagan did sometimes learn and, as a consequence, change or even reverse his administration's policies. Perhaps another leader would have learned more, or have changed course even more rapidly, but every leader has some capacity to learn. "Did Reagan learn?" is thus a much less interesting question than "When and how did Reagan learn?" Chapter 4 argued that he did so when his supply of information was carefully supervised by his advisory staff and presented to him in manageable form. This chapter takes up the question of what happened in the Reagan administration when the usual orderly arrangements broke down, when the president was given contradictory advice and forced to confront debates even among his closest associates. Although Reagan's customary management style may often have resembled groupthink, the alternative was far worse. The usual platitudes offered by experts on decision making—to promote devil's advocacy and to seek as wide a range of opinions as time permits—are likely to be wrong, and sometimes even catastrophic, for closed leaders.

Whether or not Reagan's decision making was poor is irrelevant, of course, if his subordinates actually made the decisions. It would be naive to assume that the buck always stops in the Oval Office. Yet it would be equally naive to assume that Reagan could (or desired to) simply delegate his job in its entirety to others. In the first case to be discussed in the next section, the debate during Reagan's first term over the growing budget deficit, OMB Director David Stockman and Treasury Secretary Donald Regan undoubtedly played leading roles. Between them, they formulated most of the details of the Reagan administration's fiscal and monetary policies. Yet neither could unilaterally set administration policy. Indeed, they mistrusted each other to such an extent that, at times, only the president's influence prevented a complete breakdown of their working relationship. Although Reagan was hardly an expert on tax policy or on the myriad intricacies of the federal budget, he was nevertheless the only one who could make decisions about his administration's basic policies.

Similarly, after the Iran-Contra affair became public knowledge in November 1986, the scandal came to rest squarely on the president's doorstep. During the earlier phases of planning the arms sales to Iran in an effort to win the release of hostages in Lebanon, and particularly in formulating the plan to divert the proceeds of these sales to the Contra rebels in Nicaragua, it is entirely possible that Reagan was not well informed (or was even misled) by his national security advisor Admiral John Poindexter, by Poindexter's deputy Lieutenant Colonel Oliver North, and by Director of Central Intelligence (DCI) William Casey. After the apparent "arms-for-hostages" deal was revealed, however, control reverted to the president. Whether he would admit the extent of the clandestine operations and, later, whether he would repudiate them were decisions only he could make.

Reagan's public image of serene aloofness is thus somewhat misleading. For major policy decisions, in this administration as in others, there was no substitute for presidential authority. Nor were Reagan's actions in these cases foregone conclusions. He had choices to make, and the choices he did make—or refused to make—had important consequences. That he found it especially difficult to make them in these two cases cannot be explained, moreover, as the result of groupthink. Indeed, the groupthink hypothesis predicts just the reverse: that a leader will too-willingly accept recommendations without a thorough review of alternatives. As these cases wore on, debates over the alternatives overwhelmed Reagan. Deadlock, rather than groupthink, prevented him from learning, making decisions, and moving on.

THE BUDGET DEFICIT

During the final years of the Carter presidency, annual budget deficits ran at approximately $63 billion a year. This amount more than tripled after Reagan took office, averaging over $200 billion a

year between 1982 and 1986.[3] Moreover, whereas the United
States had a current accounts surplus of $141 billion in 1981, its
net foreign debt had surpassed that of either Mexico or Brazil by
1985, making the United States the world's largest debtor nation.
The following year, the interest on the national debt alone amounted to 3.25 percent of the U.S. gross national product (GNP).[4] By
Reagan's final year in office, "relatively optimistic projections saw
the nation becoming a *net* international debtor to the tune of $1
trillion by some time in 1992."[5]

The dramatic escalation of the federal budget deficit during the
1980s stemmed, in good measure, from the Reagan administration's success in achieving two other objectives: increasing U.S.
defense spending and reducing the federal tax burden. A turning
point in planning for the first of these goals occurred ten days after
Reagan took office in January 1981, when David Stockman,
Secretary of Defense Caspar Weinberger, William Schneider (Stockman's deputy for national security matters), and Frank Carlucci
(Weinberger's deputy) met at the Pentagon to begin planning the
administration's first-term defense budget. As a candidate, Reagan
had promised 5% real growth in defense, and the hawks among his
advisors advocated even higher growth. During their meeting,
Stockman and Weinberger agreed on a 7% real growth rate (after
inflation), which was to be implemented in 1982 after a special
increase—a "get-well" package to remedy the presumed deficiencies
of the Carter defense budgets—had already taken effect in 1981.
Because the 7% growth rate was applied to the 1981 budget, and
because Carter had himself included a 5% real growth rate in his
outgoing defense budget, the net effect was over 10% real growth
adding up to "a five-year defense budget of *1.46 trillion dollars.*"[6]

At roughly the same time, Stockman and Regan began to
organize the administration's campaign for tax reduction. The
1981 Tax Reduction Bill, passed by Congress on July 29, 1981,
called for a 25% income tax cut over three years. It also indexed
tax brackets to inflation, which cost the government a source of
automatically increasing revenue through "bracket creep."[7] The
net effect of the bill, according to Stockman himself, was to
"reduce the federal revenue base by *two trillion dollars* over the
course of the decade."[8]

To compensate for the combined effects of a defense spending
increase and a tax cut, Reagan and his economic advisors placed
their faith in part on spending cuts in domestic entitlements and

in part on the projections of a University of Southern California economist, Arthur Laffer, that the tax cut would stimulate the economy, enlarge the tax base, and thus increase federal revenues. Unfortunately, neither compensating factor helped very much. There was a limit even to Reagan's success in pushing cuts in domestic programs through Congress, and although "the California gang . . . seemed to expect that once the supply-side tax cut was in effect, additional revenue would start to fall, manna-like, from the heavens," as Stockman put it, in fact the administration's simultaneous attempts to fight inflation slowed the growth of the money supply and thus decreased federal revenue.[9] Consequently, as Stockman told the president and his Cabinet during a lunchtime budget meeting, "higher real GNP and employment growth will not increase projected revenues by a dime."[10] Moreover, after initial successes in cutting a variety of federal programs, Congress had exhausted both its will and its political ability to absorb additional cuts after the summer of 1981.

Eventually, the contradictions inherent in the simultaneous pursuit of a tax cut, a military buildup, and a balanced budget began to produce discord among Reagan's advisors. During the bulk of Reagan's first year in office, however, the president and his advisors enjoyed a series of legislative successes and serenely anticipated the economic turnaround that they expected would solve the government's fiscal woes. Given the scope of the changes Reagan advocated, in fact, his advisors exhibited remarkably unity. To be sure, the unity was not perfect. Baker and Meese were suspicious of one another, and Regan and Stockman clashed on many occasions—particularly when Stockman ventured into the domain of tax policy (an area Regan wanted to keep under exclusive Treasury Department control).[11] But Reagan's economic advisors agreed, at least initially, on basic principles. Stockman and the OMB worked much more closely with the White House than had been the case during past administrations and, as if to emphasize this, Stockman's position was elevated to Cabinet level.

Such relative harmony was neither an accident nor merely the result of an early string of successes. It was created self-consciously by those who shared a vision of the "Reagan revolution." It was, as we have seen, how the Reagan administration was supposed to work. Martin Anderson (the president's assistant for domestic and economic policy development) even offers a slightly Machiavellian account of attempts to craft this supply-sider consensus: "We all knew that our efforts to control federal spending would be a vital part of the economic program, second in importance only to tax rate reduction. To accomplish that we decided to embrace and co-opt the Office of Management and Budget."[12] Reagan's closest advisors took great care to see that the president's positions were clearly represented in the other major economic policy-making councils and groups as well. Anderson appointed members of his staff to the relevant White House working groups "to make sure President Reagan's views were represented faithfully throughout even the early phases of the analyses, and we were also ensured of being quickly informed if the direction of the analyses began to veer from Reagan's policies."[13]

Not only did Reagan's top aides structure the president's advisory groups to reflect (rather than to evaluate critically) the supply-sider's agenda, but they also took pains to protect the president from any dissenting views on economic policy. Meese, in particular, made a special effort to smooth over intra-administration differences on economic policy: "Whenever there was an argument," as Stockman recalls, "Meese would step in and tell us to take our arguments to some other ad hoc forum. The President would smile and say, 'Okay, you fellas work it out.'"[14] Stockman also claims to have been "a quick learner" in this regard. The OMB director proposed creating a budget working group to deal with budget issues before they reached the president. The budget working group undoubtedly made economic policymaking more efficient, but in so doing it necessarily reduced the flow of information to the president.[15]

None of this is meant to suggest that Reagan faced no dissent and no difficult choices or congressional battles on economic policy early in his first term. On the contrary, Republican leaders in Congress often disagreed with the White House during the Kemp-Roth tax cut campaign in 1981, and both the Treasury Department and Congress disagreed at times with the Federal Reserve's restraint of the money supply.[16] But despite some notable gaffes—such their abortive attempt to cut social security benefits in May 1981—Reagan's White House staff and department heads remained essentially united on the administration's economic blueprint: lower taxes, reduced entitlement programs, and increased defense expenditures.[17]

This consensus began to change during the summer of 1981. Throughout June and July, the Reagan administration focused mainly on the tax cut legislation pending before Congress. When the Conable-Hance Tax Bill passed at the end of July, Stockman returned his attention to the budget. And his forecasts were alarming. On August 3, the president and his Cabinet met for a working luncheon, and Stockman delivered the bad news in a carefully prepared, rather ominous speech. He began his presentation as follows:

> The scent of victory is still in the air, . . . but I'm not going to mince words. We're heading for a crash landing on the budget. We're facing potential deficit numbers so big that they could *wreck* the President's entire economic program. . . . On the margin, every single important number in the budget is going in the wrong direction.[18]

Stockman then proceeded to describe the impact of the tax cut, and of the ongoing recession, on federal revenues. Most of the president's other advisors, however, were unmoved. Meese objected that the tax cut should generate additional revenues (Laffer's prediction) that Stockman had failed to consider. And when Stockman mentioned an increase of oil, alcohol, and tobacco taxes as one means of reducing the deficit, Regan angrily cut him off by objecting that "we've just worked our fanny off to give the American people a *tax cut*."[19] The meeting ended in confusion. As Stockman saw it, "those who already understood (Anderson, Darman, and Weidenbaum) nodded their heads. The others were puzzled, bored, or annoyed."[20]

Shortly after this Cabinet meeting, Stockman turned his attention to the defense budget, reasoning that it—like the other parts of the budget—must absorb some of the necessary cuts. This time, it was Weinberger's turn to object. On August 18, Stockman, Weinberger, and many of the president's other advisors met in California for a planning session on the defense budget. Again, the meeting fell into disarray: Regan objected to the OMB's deficit projections, Weinberger objected to Stockman's conversion of the proposed defense budget into constant 1984 dollars, and predictably the meeting concluded without any firm decisions. A follow-up meeting, a week later, produced a similar lack of results. As the impasse between the Defense Department and the OMB persisted, the president became bored, then angry. On September 11, he called Stockman and Weinberger into the Oval Office for a final attempt at resolving the dispute. It was evident, Stockman recalls, that "Reagan was fed up with this thing."[21] During the meeting, the president followed the strategy he so often used to resolve such disputes: he simply "split the difference" (though somewhat in Weinberger's favor). Stockman had asked for a $25 billion cut in the proposed defense budget, which still allowed a sizable increase over the Carter defense budgets, while Weinberger would accept nothing greater than an $8 billion cut. After an hour-long stand-off between his advisors, Reagan settled on a $13 billion, three-year defense budget cut. Stockman later wrote that the "episode was a critical turning point. If I had to pinpoint the moment when I ceased to believe that the Reagan Revolution was possible, September 11, 1981 . . . would be it."[22]

With deeper cuts in the defense budget eliminated as a source of possible savings, and with further cuts in domestic entitlements very unlikely to pass congressional muster, Stockman turned to the only means left to balance the budget: increasing revenue. In mid-September, both he and Chief of Staff Baker concluded that delaying the hard-won Conable-Hance tax cut was "the only practical option."[23] They decided to bring the proposal to White House Counselor Meese first and then, with his backing, to confront Regan and the president, both of whom were committed to the tax cut. Meese agreed to Stockman and Baker's proposal, but suggested bringing it before the Legislative Strategy Group (LSG) for further discussion. At the LSG meeting, which Regan also attended, Stockman presented a short briefing paper describing the proposed tax cut delay. According to Stockman, the treasury secretary did not take it well:

> "I'm the Secretary of the Treasury!" he roared. "You're not going to make a fool out of me with this plot!" Baker started to say something, but the Secretary of the Treasury was not nearly finished.
> "I'll fight every one of you on this to the last drop of blood!" he shouted, as he furiously shoved . . . [the] briefing paper across the table. . . . "This is the last time anybody is going to make tax policy behind my back."[24]

Eventually Baker mollified Regan, and the group agreed to reconsider its options. Together, Stockman, Baker, and Meese might have ultimately prevailed over Regan, but at this juncture the president's advisory system changed for an unusual reason—Nancy Reagan intervened.

Regan himself explains that "it was Nancy Reagan who brought me into the process—through a back door."[25] Mrs. Reagan strongly agreed with the treasury secretary that the president must deliver on the tax cut, and she evidently urged her husband to seek out Regan's advice directly. This was unusual since, in Reagan's first term, advice and policy proposals alike passed almost exclusively through the "triumvirate" of Meese, Baker, and Deaver. When the president did go directly to his treasury secretary, however, Regan encouraged him not to delay the tax cut or to accept proposals for any new taxes. This advice merely bolstered the president's own views. On January 22, 1982, Reagan wrote in his diary, "I told our guys I couldn't go for tax increases. If I have to be criticized, I'd rather be criticized for a deficit rather than for backing away from our economic program."[26] By circumventing the usual advisory channels and preventing the appearance of a united front among the president's other advisors, Regan helped to eliminate the administration's final clear option for balancing the budget.

The budget deficit problem certainly cannot be blamed, however, on any single administration official. Donald Regan was instrumental in ruling out tax increases, Caspar Weinberger in ruling out meaningful cuts in the defense budget, and both Congress and Jim Baker (the voice of political expediency within the administration) in ruling out additional major cuts in entitlement programs. Reagan's advisors had different interests to protect. The person responsible for shaping differences in interests and opinion into a coherent fiscal policy—the president—was not, by nature, a synthesizer of differing viewpoints. He simply maintained all of his convictions, ignoring the increasingly obvious contradictions, and expected his aides to sort out the details. Reagan himself, as his treasury secretary put it, "sent out no strong signals. He listened, encouraged, deferred. But it was a rare meeting in which he made a decision or issued orders."[27] On this, at least, Regan and Stockman could agree. According to the latter, Reagan was "as far above the detail work of supply side as a ceremonial monarch is above politics."[28]

The president was thus left with the choice either of overruling one of the leading voices in his administration or of allowing unprecedented budget deficits. He had neither the detailed knowledge nor the stomach for the former solution, and so the latter prevailed by default. So long as the other members of his admin-

istration were not also willing to overlook the looming budget problems, however, this "solution" could not prevent Reagan's attention
from being drawn repeatedly to how unsatisfactory a solution
ignoring the deficit was. On these occasions, the president's
response was frustration and anger. During a meeting on the proposed tax cut delay, for example, Stockman remembers that the
president "exploded" and turned on his OMB director: "Well, damn
it, Dave, we came here to attack *deficit spending,* not put more
taxes on the people." Given the apparent contradiction in this
statement, it is little wonder "the two words that were most in use
in the West Wing that afternoon were 'disarray' and 'chaos.'"[29]

Tension within the administration was also ratcheted higher
after William Greider, the national news editor of *The Washington
Post* published an essay entitled "The Education of David
Stockman."[30] Greider had met with Stockman regularly in 1981
and served as a liberal "sounding board" and sparring partner for
the OMB director. In this article, Greider captured Stockman's
increasing disillusionment with the "Reagan Revolution" and his
growing realization that the supply-side tax cut was destined to
produce enormous federal budget deficits. Meese, Deaver, and
most other administration insiders felt betrayed when the article
appeared. Only Baker argued that Stockman's expertise was too
valuable to lose, and for a time Baker prevailed. A much chastened
Stockman was allowed to stay on into the president's second term.
The *Atlantic* article publicly confirmed, however, what Stockman
had known for many months: advancing the "Reagan Revolution"
and balancing the federal budget had become incompatible.

The "disarray" within the Reagan administration is a good
indication of the way advisory openness, and open dissent in particular, affects a president with a closed personality. Reagan bitterly complained, in an April 23, 1982 diary entry, that "the group
debating the budget seems unable to arrive at any consensus."[31]
For their part, his advisors were well aware that the president
desired a consensus recommendation and that the confusion
within the administration over budget policy was only making
matters worse. Collectively, however, they had no consensus to
offer. Regan used the metaphor of overlapping circles of authority
to summarize the situation:

> the whole process (of budget and tax policy-making) pro-
> vided an example of circles within circles, with the Presi-

dent, the First Lady, and the Secretary of the Treasury forming a circle to work within the Chief of Staff's circle, which had been formed to work within the [House] Speaker's circle, which was obliged to work within the circles of the Senate leadership and the Republican leadership of the House. No single, unified circle ever emerged from these separate entities.[32]

Perhaps Regan overestimates his own importance, but his diagnosis of the problem—that "a more orderly process was needed for discussing economic policy"—was essentially correct. Regan believed the solution to be "regular briefings in the Oval Office in the presence of the smallest possible number of people."[33] This might have helped, but even a small circle of advisors was likely to contain divergent viewpoints on this subject. In any event—unlike deliberations over the international debt crisis—the treasury secretary lacked the bureaucratic means to close debate on this issue of the budget deficit.

The mounting tension over the budget problem might have induced a more open leader to take action. With Reagan, however, it had the opposite effect. The subject had become so unpleasant that the president withdrew, insofar as he could, from further consideration of it for the remainder of his presidency. In Stockman's pithy summation, "the President kept hoping, Meese kept deferring, the clock kept running—and the problem kept growing."[34] Finally, Congress took the problem into its own hands in 1985 by proposing legislation, the Gramm-Rudman Act, that would require a balanced budget within five years. The persistence of massive federal budget deficits and the president's inability to suggest an alternative made this act of legislative desperation unavoidable. Although several of its provisions were later declared unconstitutional by the Supreme Court, it nevertheless constituted a dramatic acknowledgment of the deadlock within the Reagan administration on budgetary policy.

THE IRAN-CONTRA AFFAIR

Concern over the mounting budget deficits notwithstanding, Ronald Reagan in 1986 was a very popular president. From January to October 1986, his public support in the Gallup poll

ranged from 61 to 68 percent approval.[35] The "Teflon president"
was evidently immune not only from the budget deficits but also
from a number of scandals involving members of his administration and from such imprudent decisions as his visit in early May
1986 to the Bitburg cemetery in Germany.[36] Despite his considerable popularity, however, Reagan was not able to manage the
public revelation of U.S. arms sales to Iran without serious
damage to his administration. As a former member of the administration put it, "it's like suddenly learning that John Wayne had
secretly been selling liquor and firearms to the Indians."[37] The
result was a twenty-one point drop in Reagan's public approval
rating. Although his public support rebounded somewhat before
he left office, his final two years as president were consumed in
large measure by the Iran-Contra affair.

"Irangate," as it was also called, raised many questions about
the president's management of foreign policy, about the wisdom
and legality of the administration's actions, and indeed about the
extent to which the president was even aware of the plans crafted
and implemented by his subordinates. Several other studies,
mindful of Reagan's preference for small and closed groups of advisors, have explained his decisions as products of groupthink.[38]
This analysis is certainly plausible. Closed leaders are not immune
from groupthink, and indeed, in a sense, it is their standard operating procedure. What groupthink does not explain, however, is
why the Teflon president who had withstood so many other crises
was unable to manage this one. Reagan had endured embarrassing reversals before—in his Lebanon policy discussed in chapter 4,
for example—but nothing affected his presidency as the Iran-
Contra affair did. To explain why, this section begins by describing briefly the decisions that let up to the crisis. Its principal focus,
however, is on the president's management of the crisis during his
final two years in office.

The first months of Reagan's second term brought sweeping
changes in the president's group of advisors. By far the most significant of these was the decision of James Baker and Donald
Regan to switch jobs. Baker evidently felt unappreciated in his role
as chief of staff, and after four years was "looking for the first train
out of the White House."[39] Regan was equally frustrated as treasury secretary (particularly after Stockman's challenges on economic policy), and he considered a move to the White House to be
a step closer to the "real power" in the executive branch. A job

swap would give each man something he wanted. Baker persuaded Michael Deaver to go along with the idea, and Deaver helped to secure Nancy Reagan's approval as well.[40] On January 7, 1985, Baker, Regan, and Deaver met with the president to propose the switch. To Regan's surprise, the president accepted their proposal almost without question.[41] Baker also took Richard Darman with him to the Treasury Department, and shortly thereafter Deaver left the administration to work as a lobbyist. Meanwhile, in February, Edwin Meese was finally confirmed as the new attorney general. Thus, all three members of the triumvirate left the White House early in Reagan's second term.

After Regan's installation as chief of staff, the only other officials with regular unrestricted access to the president were the national security advisor and the vice president.[42] Regan reduced the administration's seven "cabinet councils," which dealt with various aspects of foreign and domestic policy, to only two: a domestic policy council and an economic policy council, chaired by Meese and Baker respectively. These councils, along with the NSC, constituted the president's new, streamlined White House advisory system. Regan also reduced the number of personal assistants to the president from seventeen to eleven.[43] The cumulative effect of these changes was to diminish the president's already-infrequent contact with other advisors. As two journalistic observers summed up these developments with only slight exaggeration, "the White House became a two-level world where conflict went on at a layer the President never saw."[44]

Perhaps unsurprisingly, the Tower Commission investigation into the Iran-Contra affair found that the hierarchy and delegation of the Reagan White House had serious shortcomings. The commission complained that the president "did not force his policy to undergo the most critical review of which the NSC participants and the process were capable. At no time did he insist upon accountability and performance review."[45] In particular, he failed to consult with other high-level advisors and Cabinet officials about his initiative to free the hostages. Only the president, the vice president, Chief of Staff Regan, and Vice Admiral Poindexter regularly met to discuss the sale of weapons to Iran.[46] The Tower Commission also held Regan to blame, finding that "more than almost any Chief of Staff of recent memory, he asserted personal control over the White House staff and sought to extend this control to the national security advisor."[47] Objections to the administration's Middle

East policy were generally kept away from the president, and it was evidently easy for McFarlane, North, and Poindexter to proceed unhindered by critical attention from other administration officials.

It must have been clear even to the president, however, that an arms sale to Iran did not meet with the approval of his entire Cabinet. When, on August 6, 1985, McFarlane and Poindexter proposed that Israel supply TOW missiles to Iran in exchange for efforts to secure the release of U.S. hostages being held in Lebanon, Shultz and Weinberger clearly and strongly opposed the plan.[48] Indeed, as Weinberger put it in a handwritten note in the margin of a proposed National Security Decision Directive concerning the arms sale, "this is almost too absurd to comment on."[49] Nevertheless, shortly after this meeting, the president authorized McFarlane to tell Israel to proceed with the sale.[50] Poindexter replaced McFarlane as national security advisor in December 1985, and a few days later the president once again met with his top advisors to discuss the Iran initiative. Again, Shultz and Weinberger argued that the plan posed practical problems, was politically dangerous, and perhaps even illegal. On this occasion, in fact, even Regan joined with Shultz and Weinberger in opposing arms sales to Iran. Reagan was preoccupied with the fate of the American hostages, however, and insisted that "the American people will never forgive me if I fail to get these hostages out over this legal question."[51] Sensing the president's determination to proceed, Regan quickly retreated from his own objections. By the time the NSC took up the matter again on January 7, 1986, Regan was once more prepared to support arms sales to Iran.[52]

From this point onward, Shultz and Weinberger were increasingly absent from White House decision making about the arms-for-hostages initiative. Since Weinberger continued to balk at plans to arrange a weapons sale to Iran, North and Poindexter went around him, with the assistance of DCI Casey. On January 17, Poindexter asked the president to sign a new finding, authorizing the direct sale of arms to Iran (without Israel as an intermediary), to which Reagan agreed.[53] Weinberger was not consulted, but merely informed of the president's decision. At any rate, having made their objections known, Shultz and Weinberger had both begun to distance themselves from the decision making on the Iran initiative. The Tower Commission Report places special emphasis on this further contraction of Reagan's advisory group:

The NSC principals other than the President may be somewhat excused by the insufficient attention on the part of the National Security Advisor to the need to keep all the principals fully informed. Given the importance of the issue and the sharp policy divergences involved, however, Secretary Shultz and Secretary Weinberger in particular distanced themselves from the march of events. Secretary Shultz specifically requested to be informed only as necessary to perform his job. Secretary Weinberger had access through intelligence to details about the operation. Their obligation was to give the President their full support and continued advice with respect to the program or, if they could not in conscience do that, to so inform the President. Instead, they simply distanced themselves from the program. . . . They were not energetic in attempting to protect the President from the consequences of his personal commitment to freeing the hostages.[54]

CIA counsel Stanley Sporkin summed up the role of Shultz and Weinberger more succinctly: "Weinberger was Dr. No, and Shultz was Dr. I Don't Want to Know."[55] In the absence of sustained objections, and with no coordinated effort by Shultz and Weinberger to oppose the plan after January 17, North and Poindexter proceeded with plans to ship several thousand additional TOW missiles as well as spare parts for Hawk missiles to Iran. Apparently unknown to many of the principals, North also proceeded with a plan to divert profits from the arms sales to the Contra insurgents in Nicaragua.[56]

President Reagan's management of the Iran initiative, until its public revelation in November of the same year, was consistent both with his personality and with his customary way of handling such decisions. Typically, he never directly confronted or resolved the dispute among his advisors. He simply ignored it. As a result of his own strong commitment to freeing the hostages, he was willing to go along with North and Poindexter's plan for arms sales, particularly after North suggested that canceling the initiative might put the hostages at greater risk. The increasing closure of his advisory group gave him little reason to change his mind or to re-evaluate his policies. When Poindexter came to the president on January 17 with the finding authorizing the direct sale of missiles to Iran, Reagan signed it without comment or request for discussion.[57]

The revelation, in the Lebanese magazine *Al-Shiraa* on November 3, 1986, that the United States had shipped arms to Iran set in motion events that fundamentally changed the policy-making process within the Reagan administration. *Al-Shiraa* claimed that Robert McFarlane had made a secret trip to Teheran in October to arrange the arms deal. Two days later, the report appeared in the American press and provoked speculation about an arms-for-hostages bargain with Iran.[58] Reagan's initial response was to deny the operation entirely. On November 6, he told reporters that the story of McFarlane's trip to Iran had "no foundation."[59] At about the same time, Poindexter, North, and McFarlane met to prepare several "chronologies" of the Iran initiative. These accounts contradicted each other and, according to the Tower Commission Report, "suggest an attempt to limit the information that got to the President, the Cabinet, and the American public."[60] As press speculation about an arms-for-hostages trade intensified, Reagan was eventually forced to acknowledge that his administration had been pursuing a secret initiative with Iran for eighteen months. He claimed, however, that "only small amounts of defensive weapons and spare parts" had been sold to Iraq and that his administration "did not—repeat—did not trade weapons or anything else for hostages—nor will we."[61]

While external pressures were forcing Reagan to admit his secret initiative to free the hostages, the internal consensus that had prevailed, at least superficially, within the White House throughout 1986 abruptly dissolved. In a pivotal meeting of the president's advisors on November 10, Shultz gave vent to pressure that had been building up for some time. He had correctly warned that the initiative would be seen as a trade for hostages. After making his objections known, he then looked the other way. Yet when Poindexter explained the full extent of the initiative over the preceding months, Shultz was shocked and lashed out particularly at Poindexter. Weinberger joined in and pointed out, again correctly, that "we had agreed there would be no more shipments after the first 500 TOWs unless we got back all the captives."[62] Shultz and Weinberger's recriminations yielded no clear plan, however, for what to do next.

Several days after the president acknowledged the arms shipments, Shultz made his dissent public during a televised interview on *Face the Nation* by observing, in response to Lesley Stahl's questions about future arms sales to Iran, that he could not speak for the entire administration on this issue. The same day, an interview appeared in the *New York Times* in which Regan explained his efforts at "damage control" to reporter Bernard Weintraub in an equally troubling manner: "Some of us," he said, "are like a shovel brigade that follows a parade down Main Street cleaning up. We took Reykjavik and turned what was really a sour situation into something that turned out pretty well . . . here we go again."[63] Regan, ironically, was unhappy with Shultz's reluctance to back up the president. Shortly after the *Face the Nation* interview, White House officials (presumably encouraged by the chief of staff) began to spread rumors that Nancy Reagan wanted Shultz fired, and Casey even went so far as to write the president directly to urge that Shultz be replaced with former UN ambassador Jeanne Kirkpatrick.[64]

Mrs. Reagan certainly was disturbed by the secretary of state's apparent unwillingness to defend the administration—but she was even more upset with Regan, and not only because of his remark about the shovel brigade.[65] Tension between the president's wife and his chief of staff had grown rapidly after the president's hospitalization in July 1985 to remove a cancerous polyp. Regan met daily with the president after the operation, but Mrs. Reagan sought to limit her husband's contact with visitors and evidently resented the chief of staff's suggestions that the vice president and national security advisor also be allowed to meet with the president.[66] As time went by, their competition to control the president's schedule degenerated into open hostility.[67] After the Iran initiative had been made public, Regan began to make plans to tell the administration's side of the story. He told the president (in a moment of unusual forthrightness), "If these hostages don't materialize soon, you're going to have to speak up. You're going to be ripped apart on the weekend talk shows. The Monday morning papers will pick it up. The American people are going to start demanding to know what's going on here."[68] Nancy Reagan called Regan the same day, however, to countermand the chief of staff's advice, explaining that "it's just *wrong* for him to talk right now." Regan angrily responded: "My God, Nancy . . . He's going to go down in flames if he doesn't speak up."[69] This exchange helped to cement in place a pattern of conflict that immobilized Ronald Reagan in subsequent months.

Although the friction between the president's wife and chief of staff created perhaps the most significant disruption of the harmony that usually characterized Reagan's staff arrangements, it was not an isolated problem. McFarlane believed that he was "being hung out to dry" for his role in the November arms shipment and even threatened a libel suit against Regan unless the public was given a clear account of the Iran initiative. The White House director of communications, Patrick Buchanan, also began to push for speedy statements from the president to head off the growing crisis: "The story will not die," he argued, "until some much fuller explanation—giving our arguments—is provided."[70] Poindexter, on the other hand, still maintained to the president that there had been no arms-for-hostages deal and, incredibly, that any arms shipments prior to January 1986 had been entirely Israel's idea. Further recriminations came from White House legal counsel Peter Wallison and State Department counsel Abraham Sofaer who had so far been kept in the dark and continued to meet with resistance from the NSC staff in their efforts to discover what had taken place. After it became apparent to Sofaer that Casey intended to testify before Congress that the CIA had no idea weapons were shipped to Iran in November (despite the CIA's prominent role in the shipment), Sofaer threatened to resign.[71] With members of Congress clamoring for an explanation, Attorney General Meese began his own investigation to determine what exactly had happened and to disentangle the conflicting stories.

Before he could do so, however, the president gave in to pressure for some sort of public statement. His press conference on November 19 was a disaster by any account. Reagan denied that his administration was aware of arms shipments from other countries (i.e., Israel), and he continued to maintain that the arms shipments he had approved were small and that they were not "a mistake" since they had a noble purpose. He was elusive about what this purpose actually was, variously describing it as the pursuit of an opening with moderates in Iran and as an effort to win the freedom of hostages in Lebanon. Reagan's confusion on this point reflects the confusion among his advisors about the best way to present the arms sales to the public. Poindexter and Casey favored the "diplomatic initiative" cover story whereas Shultz, Weinberger, and Regan urged the president to come clean and admit that the operation had, in effect, become an arms-for-hostages swap. Afterward, opinion polls showed that the public no longer believed that the president "could handle foreign policy well."[72] Theodore Draper's evaluation of the president's dilemma at this point is apt: "In a way, Poindexter had been right. He had fought against divulging anything about the Iran policy and had been overruled. Shultz and Regan had advocated full disclosure. The president's decision had gone in favor of neither one nor the other but something in between."[73] By this point, the overwhelming problem for the White House was to devise a coherent response to the scandal in the face of internal discord. After the November 19 press conference, Secretary of State Shultz fueled the internal debate by arranging another "long, tough discussion" with the president in which he accused the NSC staff of having misled the president.[74] The president's own diary entries indicate that he feared Shultz was about to resign.[75] In Draper's view, Reagan was "losing control of his administration."[76]

At this crucial moment, Meese made the fateful discovery that "residuals" from the arms sales to Iran had been diverted, via a Swiss bank account managed by North, to the Nicaraguan Contras. Meese briefed the president on November 24. The following day, the two held another press conference at which the president read a short statement announcing the discovery of improper activities about which he had not been "fully informed," along with the resignation of Vice Admiral Poindexter, and the reassignment of Lieutenant Colonel North. Without taking questions, Reagan then left Meese to explain the details of the diversion. On November 26, the president announced the formation of a special review board (the Tower Commission). On December 4, the House and Senate agreed to form two select committees that would conduct their own investigations of the affair. And on December 19, Attorney General Meese bowed to congressional pressure to appoint an independent counsel, Lawrence Walsh, to investigate the possibly criminal aspects of the scandal.

Reagan's appearance at the November 25 press conference with Meese was the last time he addressed reporters about the Iran-Contra affair until after the Tower Commission released its report (over three months later). In the meantime, many of the president's staff and Cabinet (including Regan, Shultz, Weinberger, Casey, Poindexter, McFarlane, and North) were called by Congress to testify before the investigating committees. This produced a constant stream of (often contradictory) revelations about the Iran initiative and the Contra diversion—all with no comment from the president. By this point, polls ranked Carter's Iran policy higher than Reagan's, and most of the president's top advisors were anxious for him to speak.[77] The problem was that they continued to disagree about what he should say. Regan, in particular, wanted the president to "go public" with the administration's version of events. Regan's feud with Mrs. Reagan had grown so much worse that they were barely on speaking terms, however, and this made arranging presidential appearances exceptionally difficult. During December, in fact, pressure on the president to replace Regan began to come from several sources—including Congress and Republican Party officials as well as from Mrs. Reagan—and Regan's departure was openly discussed in the press.[78]

The evidence suggests not so much that Reagan made a principled decision to avoid public comment until the investigations were complete, therefore, as that he simply did not know what to say given the complete disarray among his advisors. In this atmosphere, efforts to formulate a coherent policy failed utterly. As a supporter from the Heritage Foundation put it, "We're getting total flip flops from one thing to another. There's schizophrenia across the board."[79] According to John Sears (the president's former campaign manager), "People panicked. . . . They thought, 'Finally we got caught, and now everyone knows that Ronald Reagan doesn't know what he's doing.'"[80] The controversy naturally took a toll on a closed leader who was accustomed to being sheltered from such discord. According to his chief of staff, in January, "he was in grip of lassitude. He seldom, if ever, emerged from his office and wandered down the hallway as he had done before. The quick humor, the curiosity about new subjects, and above all the political combativeness operated at a much lower intensity than usual."[81] Mrs. Reagan herself observed that "in eight years in Sacramento and six more in Washington, we had never experienced anything like this. The entire government seemed to grind to a halt, and only Iran-contra mattered."[82] Lou Cannon sums up the problem expertly: Reagan's "response to conflict had always been withdrawal, but he could now find no haven either in the White House family quarters or the Oval Office."[83]

The result of President Reagan's detachment is that, at the height of the scandal, he offered no substantive public discussion of the Iran-Contra affair between his radio address on December 5 and his State of the Union address almost two months later on January 27. When he did finally prepare to go before the public, moreover, the disorder that immobilized his presidency again intruded. Mrs. Reagan insisted that Kenneth Khachigian, a trusted friend and speechwriter from California, be brought in to write the speech. When he arrived in Washington, Khachigian found that "there was no leadership from the top. . . . No one had talked to the president about any of it."[84] Khachigian consulted with Regan's staff, with Mrs. Reagan, and even with President Nixon before producing a draft of the speech. Yet with no consensus within the administration on what the speech should contain—some felt it must accept blame for the scandal, others (including the president) simply wished to leave the issue behind—Khachigian was unhappy with his efforts and flew back to California to work on another draft. In the meantime, Regan's deputy Dennis Thomas rewrote Khachigian's original draft, emphasizing the points the chief of staff wished to make. And Tony Dolan, a White House staff writer, wrote a third draft. Confronted with three different versions of his speech, the president was at a loss and could only ask in exasperation, "What do the fellas expect me to do?"[85] In the end, Khachigian was brought back from California to produce yet another draft, but by this time the speech had become a patchwork that articulated no clear position on the Iran initiative. With too many speechwriters and not enough guidance, the speech was a flop.

Finally, in February, the ongoing dispute between the president's wife and chief of staff came to a head. By this point, Mrs. Reagan was so upset with the chief of staff's failure to protect the president that she had actually taken to answering Regan's phone calls by asking him "Oh, are you still here, Don?"[86] The two were barely on speaking terms, and the impasse could not last much longer. It had become clear, even to Regan himself, that he would soon have to leave the administration. On Monday, February 23, Vice President Bush suggested that Regan speak with the president. When he did so, the president shocked him by suggesting that he should resign that day. Regan sputtered, "You can't do that to me, Mr. President. If I go before that report (the Tower Commission report) is out, you throw me to the wolves. I deserve better treatment than that."[87] He went on, "I have to tell you, sir, that I'm very bitter about the whole experience. You're allowing the loyal to be punished, and those who have had their own agenda to be rewarded."[88] Amazingly, after this confrontation the president backed down and agreed that his chief of staff could stay on until the Tower Commission released its report, which Regan erroneously believed would exonerate him. They decided that Regan would leave on March 2.

Like almost everything else during this chaotic time, even Regan's departure was poorly managed. On February 26, the Tower Commission presented its findings to the press. The commission described numerous flaws in the policy-making process behind the Iran-Contra affair and found, moreover, that it had been Regan's job to bring these flaws to the president's attention. The commission determined, in fact, that the chief of staff "must bear primary responsibility for the chaos that descended upon the White House."[89] The next day, CNN broadcast a report that Howard Baker had been selected as the new chief of staff. By his own account, Regan was mad and humiliated. He dictated a terse twenty-two-word letter of resignation and then told the president, in a brief telephone call, "I won't be in any more."[90] Shortly thereafter, Meese called Baker to make a request that said a good deal about the preceding months. The attorney general told the new chief of staff, "I think you better get over to the White House. There's no one in charge."[91]

In an administration characterized by strong hierarchical control during its first five years, no one—including the president—was genuinely in control early in 1987. At one point, Reagan himself made this plain while answering the Tower Commission's questions. He stated that he had personally approved the Israeli sale of arms to Iran (corroborating McFarlane's testimony before the commission), but when the question came up again in a later meeting, he contradicted himself (based on an aide-mémoire written for him by Regan) and claimed that the Israelis had decided to sell the arms on their own. The president's confusion on this important point is, in itself, noteworthy. What made it worse is that, during the second meeting, Reagan made the mistake of reading his chief of staff's instructions to him aloud: "If the question comes up at the Tower Board meeting, you might want to say that you were surprised."[92] The commission was stunned that the president would allow himself to be manipulated by his advisors on such a vital point. He appeared to be "a president too feeble to recall his own decisions, and so malleable that he had let others push him into contradicting himself."[93]

The immobilization of the Reagan administration cannot be explained, however, exclusively as the result of the president's decision style, aloofness, or "malleability." The Iran-Contra affair thrust him directly into the sort of controversial situation that his subordinates ordinarily managed. Reagan's customary pattern of delegation is precisely what gave Poindexter and North such unusual freedom of action, of course, and control reverted to the president as this became clear. Yet with his closest advisors at odds and, frequently, paying more attention to their own interests than to the president's, Reagan was ill-equipped to exercise unilateral control. Unable to perceive a consensus within his administration, he was incapable of managing the crisis. Instead, he simply blamed it on the press and waited for it to pass. Reagan refused to acknowledge, even to himself, his own role in producing the chaos that first caused the Iran-Contra scandal and then permitted it to escalate to such a degree that impeachment was a serious possibility.[94] By blaming the press, he found an external explanation for a crisis that was actually a product of his own administration's policies—behavior typical of a leader with a closed learning style.[95]

The combination of Reagan's closed learning style and the collapse of his normal advisory arrangements prevented him from responding to the crisis more actively and constructively. Whereas he had withstood other scandals and responded articulately to his critics on other occasions, he lacked the support and guidance from his own staff to do so in early 1987. By the time the Tower Commission report was released, Reagan had developed such a strong aversion to all aspects of the Iran-Contra affair that he could scarcely bring himself to accept the report. Evidently, he could not bring himself to accept its conclusions. By maintaining his reluctance to look closely at what Poindexter and North had done, Reagan continued to deny the reality of the scandal, and even after it finally subsided he complained that "it was as if Americans were forgiving me for something I hadn't done."[96]

CONCLUSION

From the broader perspective of the public interest, whether or not Reagan learned in these cases is of secondary importance. The underlying issues—the wisdom of persistently large budget deficits, of arms-for-hostages deals, and of covert support for the Nicaraguan Contras—loom larger. But from the perspective of those within the Reagan administration, a partisan struggle to change the president's mind was at the center of each of these crises. The budget deficit and Iran-Contra crises were both, in an important sense, crises of learning. Without presidential approval and action, no progress could be made to resolve either problem. And because Reagan cared deeply both about reducing the federal tax burden and about freeing the American hostages in Lebanon, those who wished to change administration policy inevitably faced a struggle.

In most cases during the Reagan administration, including those discussed in chapter 4, conflicts over policy took place at a level beneath the president. Ordinarily, debates were referred to Reagan only after a consensus had already emerged in favor of a change in policy. By this time, of course, they had ceased to be debates. Instead, the purpose of the meetings with Reagan was to inform him of the new consensus, to change his mind if possible, and to obtain his consent for the proposed new policy. Open disputes in the Oval Office served little purpose and were usually counterproductive.

Donald Regan writes in his memoirs that President Reagan "dislikes confrontations more than any man I have ever known."[97] In an effort to avoid them, Reagan often courted groupthink. In the early phases of decision making in both the budget deficit and Iran-Contra cases, the president's advisors formed cohesive groups, shut out dissenters, and generally presented a united front to the president. This form of decision making weighed heavily against an open and critical review of administration policies. It was precisely this "closedness" that the Tower Commission singled out for criticism. Yet however unfortunate this tendency toward advisory closure, the alternative was likely to be worse and the middle path was difficult to walk. Open debate paralyzed Reagan. Far from encouraging him to consider alternative courses of action, it prompted him to withdraw altogether from the controversy. For leaders like Reagan, deadlock is thus an even greater concern than groupthink.

The cases drawn from the Reagan administration also teach at least two additional lessons about the interaction between leaders and their advisors. First, the "appropriate" level of advisory openness is particularly important for a leader with a closed personality. Whereas an open leader's decision making suffers more often from a deficit than from a surfeit of information and advice, a closed leader may suffer from either, and possibly from both at the same time. Intolerable diversity and lack of consensus may cause the closed decision maker to withdraw from a problem—to exhibit what Irving Janis and Leon Mann call "defensive avoidance"—and thereby to reject any new information out of hand.[98] Such decision makers are confronted with too much information, but they hear too little of it.

During both the Iran-Contra scandal and the budget deficit problems, Reagan suffered from just this difficulty. In each case, his advisors (including informal advisors like Mrs. Reagan) gave him very different, and often conflicting, advice. And in each case, the president reportedly became angry and depressed. Ultimately, he withdrew from the decision-making process as much as he could. He told his "fellas" to work the problem out, and then he waited for the issue to disappear. In the interim, whenever possible, Reagan flatly denied the existence of both of these problems. He managed to convince himself, for example, that the Contra diversion had never been proven. And after Stockman warned of the impending budget deficits, Reagan clung instead to his treasury secretary's prediction that tax cuts would eventually *increase* government revenues. When the problems persisted, Reagan also shifted the blame away from himself: the Iran-Contra affair was the media's fault, and the budget deficits were really Carter's.[99] Such defensive avoidance is the natural response of a leader who has concluded that further efforts to learn are either impossible or useless.

A second implication of these cases is that even leaders with well-formed ideas about how to arrange their advisors cannot always control the way they receive advice in practice. Once again, closed leaders are particularly vulnerable to this problem. While an open decision maker can always seek additional viewpoints from outside sources, it may sometimes be very difficult for a closed leader to avoid controversy. Reagan was certainly able to select his staff and was largely free to consult with whom he pleased. Yet although he paid considerable attention to creating a harmonious staff environment in the White House, he could do little about the bitter disputes that occasionally broke out among his closest advisors. In the cases discussed in this chapter, President Reagan's formally hierarchical and unified staff became, in practice, highly diversified in its advice. In short, this group became more open. Despite the considerable efforts of both Reagan and his staff, the presidency simply is not an office that lends itself to isolation from controversy.

It may be no accident, therefore, that most of the Reagan administration's major policy accomplishments came early on, during the "honeymoon" period, when Reagan's advisors were in substantial agreement on most issues of foreign and domestic economic policy. Although the Mexican bailout and the administration's subsequent management of international debt came later, they were also made possible by the Treasury Department's cultivation of policy consensus within the administration. Reagan's decision to withdraw the marines from Lebanon was similarly made possible by the evolving consensus among his advisors that withdrawal was necessary. Yet when Reagan's advisors disagreed on a problem, as in the cases discussed in this chapter, he typically made little progress toward either learning about or resolving the problem.

In these cases, as in those drawn from the Eisenhower administration, changes in the quality of Reagan's decision making clearly mattered a great deal. Reagan's timely acceptance and approval of his subordinates' advice during the debt crisis and the intervention in Lebanon prevented these problems from becoming worse. His withdrawal from decision making on the budget dilemma and the Iran-Contra affair, on the other hand, allowed crises to develop and persist, tarnishing his presidency. The result of the latter crisis in particular, as Cannon put it, was that "Reagan would never again bask in the unquestioned trust of the American people. . . . He was no longer the magical sun king, no longer the Prospero of American memories who towered above ordinary politicians and could expect always to be believed."[100] Of course, Reagan did not personally control every aspect of these crises. Yet he did control his response to them, and it is on this score that the deadlock in his administration and his resulting failure to learn were particularly damaging.

CHAPTER 7

Conclusion

Five hundred years ago, Niccolò Machiavelli urged princes to pay close attention to their need for advice. Amid the exhortations for which he became famous—that rulers must be cunning, ruthless, and sometimes even cruel—Machiavelli also insists that kings and princes need help. Like modern presidents, however, princes face a dilemma. They must seek counsel, but they must also be prepared to close debate and insist upon a course of action. In Machiavelli's terms, princes must command advice while neither courting flattery *(adulazioni)* nor losing respect *(reverenzia):* "there is no other way of guarding oneself from flatterers except letting men understand that to tell you the truth does not offend you; but when everyone may tell you the truth, respect for you abates." Indeed, he continues, "if a prince . . . should take counsel from more than one he will never get united counsels, nor will he know how to unite them."[1] Here, in pithier form, is the trade-off described in the preceding chapters between openness and learning. A leader surrounded only by flatterers will hear too little useful advice, a condition we might now call "groupthink." A leader unable to regulate the flow of advice, on the other hand, will find it hard to move from debate to decision. In this case, deadlock is the greater danger.

Machiavelli was also well aware that leaders differ in their taste for advice. He cites the case of Emperor Maximilian I:

He consulted with no one, yet never got his own way in anything. This arose because . . . the emperor is a secretive man—he does not communicate his designs to anyone, nor does he receive opinions on them. But as in carrying them into effect they become revealed and known, they are at once obstructed by those men whom he has around him, and he, being pliant, is diverted from them. Hence it follows that those things he does one day he undoes the next, and no one ever understands what he wishes or intends to do, and no one can rely on his resolutions.[2]

It would be hard to devise a more apt description of a closed leader. Since all leaders must not only strike the right balance in seeking advice, but must also take their own need and desire for it into account, Machiavelli insisted that they place high importance on the proper arrangement of counselors.

More recent studies of policymaking sometimes appear to suggest that there is little leaders can do to improve their own use of advice. The original title of Irving Janis's classic study, *Victims of Groupthink*, implies that learning is beyond the control of leaders in high-level policy-making groups. Poor decision making seems to be something that afflicts leaders against their will or, perhaps, without their even being aware of the problem. That Janis's own views were actually more nuanced is suggested both by the second edition's change of title, dropping the term *victims*, and also by the attention he gives to the actions leaders can themselves take to discourage groupthink. They can insist on devil's advocacy, consult outside specialists, and broaden their own inner circle of advisors. They can divide these advisors into multiple working groups in order to reduce pressure toward conformity and to encourage multiple perspectives on problems and solutions. They can reassure their subordinates that voicing criticism will be rewarded rather than punished. Janis suggests that leaders should do all of these things.[3] If they fail to do so, then they contribute directly to their own failure to learn by encouraging groupthink.

Still, there are victims of bad "group dynamics" in a sense Janis does not recognize (but that Machiavelli appears to). For closed leaders like Ronald Reagan, most of Janis's suggestions would be either ineffective or counterproductive. Closed leaders require a more carefully managed flow of information and advice. The openness, heterogeneity, and devil's advocacy that Janis recommends can just as easily cause them to recoil from a problem as to reconsider it. Such leaders find themselves in a catch-22 situation: preferring a more collaborative and harmonious working environment, they may be perfectly aware of the costs of avoiding discord, but unwilling to pay the even larger price of disrupting their standard operating procedures. They must trust their advisors to be aware of important debates and to respect differences of opinion without allowing them to overwhelm the smooth functioning of the decision process. Janis's choice of the term *victims* seems apt to describe the fate of closed leaders whose subordinates fail to walk the sometimes thin line between fairly representing diverse points of view and preserving staff harmony. They may become victims, in fact, of both groupthink and of deadlock.

Open leaders are at a relative advantage. They are probably less likely to succumb to either problem, and particularly to the latter. They are simultaneously capable of considering and integrating more diverse points of view than are closed leaders and, not coincidentally, more inclined to seek out such advice. Not even open leaders can be sure, however, of receiving counsel representing a sufficiently wide range of perspectives. A leader's openness offers no guarantee of immunity to advisors should they repeatedly take unpopular positions. Nor can leaders prevent the occasional departure of important, critical voices among their advisors.

Open and closed leaders alike can thus become "victims" of poor group decision making. At the same time, both kinds of leaders can take steps to improve their ability to learn before making consequential decisions. This final chapter outlines several strategies for doing so, but it does not share the common assumption that everyone can benefit from pretty much the same strategies. Taking the difference between open and closed learning styles as a starting point, it reviews and explores additional implications of this distinction. It pays special attention to specifically political considerations that were often hinted at in the preceding chapters but that, surprisingly, have received little attention from political psychologists. The chapter concludes by returning to a broader issue raised in chapter 1: the political value of learning itself.

THE POLITICS OF ADVICE

It did not take Machiavelli's treatise to let kings know how dependent they are on good counsel. It has always been obvious that leaders need advice. Yet not all kings (and not all politicians) view its provision with equanimity. The *Milinda-pa-ha*, a Theravada Buddhist collection of "questions" posed to King Milinda (Menendes) by a monk named Nagasena in the late second century B.C., recounts the following conversation:

> The King said: "Venerable Nagasena, will you converse with me?"
> Nagasena: "If your Majesty will speak with me as wise men converse, I will; but if your Majesty speaks with me as kings converse, I will not."
> "How then converse the wise, venerable Nagasena?"
> "The wise do not get angry when they are driven into a corner, kings do."[4]

Nagasena recognizes, first, that not everyone reacts the same way to advice. His reluctance to speak freely to the king also shows his political awareness. No advisor can afford to imagine, when "speaking to power," that advice is a neutral thing or that all leaders will treat it dispassionately.

Even the most basic prescriptions about getting (and giving) advice must therefore be tailored to the needs of the person seeking it and to the relationship between this person and those who provide the advice. This conclusion challenges the dominant refrain from specialists in staff organization and policymaking who tend to emphasize only the problem of too little advice and who suggest devil's advocacy as a general remedy. Few scholars have been willing to introduce complications of either leadership style or political context into their theories of group decision making. This is not to say that they have eagerly or recklessly embraced simplistic approaches. On the contrary, there has been widespread recognition that the most popular models of advisory groups are very crude.[5] But this recognition is usually given only lip service; it has produced few systematic efforts to understand the relationship between individual differences and group effectiveness.

The preceding chapters have explored the way in which individual differences affect learning. They show that closed leaders require different staff arrangements than do open leaders.[6] The remainder of this chapter considers the specifically political dynamics of decision making in what are often, after all, highly politicized groups. Every leader—not only in government, but in business as well—knows that assembling advisors is also a political task, with political implications. Senior advisors have their own ambitions, interests, and loyalties. This is no less true of junior advisors, and in addition the perceived (or real) political costs of speaking honestly may be even greater for this latter group than for their superiors. Gathering together individuals of different rank, loyalty, and interests into a functional group capable of formulating useful recommendations and facilitating (rather than hindering) learning is a difficult problem of small-scale governance. Political psychologists rely heavily on theories from the domain of psychology to study this problem, yet they rarely integrate expressly political theories of balance of power, coalition politics, or voting behavior into their arguments. A smattering of examples to the contrary notwithstanding, few studies of advisory groups treat the group itself as an entity whose behavior must be understood in political, as well as in psychological, terms.[7]

The problem is for a leader to distribute power among advisors in a way that optimizes the upward flow of useful advice. As we have seen, *optimize* does not necessarily mean *maximize*, since some leaders will require a greater diversity of advice than others. To accomplish their purpose in a way that also suits their learning style, therefore, leaders may opt for a variety of political arrangements. Richard Tanner Johnson describes three common approaches as *formal, competitive,* and *collegial*.[8] Although he treats these organizational forms categorically, they can also be understood as points on a scale describing the devolution or distribution of power within the leadership circle. *Formal* arrangements place the leader at greatest remove from subordinates.[9] They provide (and require) specific channels of communication and, in consequence, reserve most power for those at the organization's pinnacle. In *competitive* groups, the leader is more intimately involved in internal disputes, and representatives with competing constituencies have greater access. Information is less filtered as it makes its way toward the top, and this is another source of power for those at other levels. Finally, the most open and *collegial* arrangements place the leader at the center of a web of information and advice. In the extreme, they may be completely informal and nonhierarchical, allowing anyone who wishes unimpeded access to the leader. As with learning style, however, it is difficult to find examples of truly extreme cases when considering prominent leaders. In practice, no leader has the time or patience to grant unlimited access, and at the other extreme, no

leader would be well-served by a hierarchy of advisors so attenu-
ated that all debates were reduced to a single point of view.

A leader's decision about how to distribute power among advisors, then, will represent an effort to manage the trade-offs
between the competing objectives of learning and control. To
recast the argument once again in Machiavelli's terminology,
excessively centralized authority will not do if it produces only flattery, and excessive decentralization of power is dangerous if it
undermines respect and the ability to reach a decision. Figure 7-1
illustrates these trade-offs and shows a region of possible advisory structures that avoid either danger. Smaller and more cohesive
(i.e., closed) groups can afford to distribute power more evenly.
Failing to do so would limit internal debate (already "externally"
limited by the group's closure) and would court groupthink. Large
and divided (e.g., open) groups, on the other hand, require more
directed management. If some hierarchy is not imposed on such
groups, debate is likely to lead nowhere, and the result would be
deadlock.

These trade-offs would be fairly straightforward were it not for
one other consideration: not every leader can manage them in the
same way. Open groups provide more information and alternatives to leaders but, in consequence, produce a more stressful
environment. If closed leaders cannot escape the stress by partially foreclosing debate, then they must take steps to manage it
by imposing a political solution on the group, asserting greater
control over deliberations or formalizing channels of communication. Open leaders, on the other hand, can afford to allow less
formal, less coercive arrangements in open groups. When groups
are already closed, the supply of information rather than stress is
the chief concern. Open leaders, in these circumstances, should
take special care that collegiality or respect for their authority
does not prevent critical thinking and dissent. At intermediate
levels of group openness (point B in figure 7-1), a relatively wide
range of political arrangements within the group might be effective, depending on the leader's learning style. As the group moves
toward intellectual closure, diffusion of power (point A) will help
to encourage critical evaluation. As a group becomes more open,
conversely, authority must gradually be centralized (point C) to
guide debate. As groups move toward either extreme (A or C),
therefore, there is less room for leaders to maneuver. Still, in all
cases, leaders must take their own learning style into account.

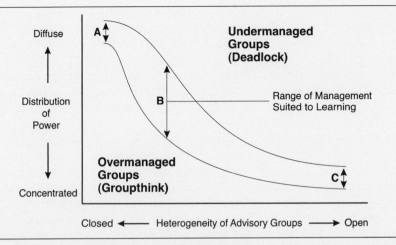

Fig. 7-1. Regions of Optimum Trade-offs between Advisory Openness and Power Distribution in Policy-making Groups.

Typically, closed leaders adopt advisory structures that concentrate power in fewer hands. Although their intent may be simply to manage information effectively, they must also remember that deciding with whom (and with how many) to consult in itself confers power. Donald Regan's considerable influence during Reagan's second term, Henry Kissinger's dominance of foreign policy decision making in the Nixon administration, and Colonel Edward House's close relationship to President Wilson all provoked resentment from other presidential advisors. Of these three examples, Kissinger's rise to prominence is especially noteworthy in that, even more than the others, he was himself able to wield a great deal of power that was formally the president's. Although Nixon approved a plan to resupply Israel during the October War, for example, the evidence suggests that Kissinger delayed implementation of this directive because of his own strategic designs for a Middle East peace settlement. Even more striking, Kissinger evidently ordered U.S. strategic forces to DEFCON 3 alert status later during the same crisis without prior presidential approval, increasing the tension in what was already one of the most dangerous episodes of the cold war. Nixon was asleep during the all night meeting when U.S. forces were placed on heightened alert.[10]

A commitment to advisory openness also has political consequences. It entails the diffusion of power among individuals who
might prefer, given the opportunity, to seize more of it for themselves. If hierarchy and authority are sufficiently unclear, protract-
ed power struggles are likely. These rivalries may have their uses.
Franklin Roosevelt encouraged rivalries among his advisors precisely to be assured of hearing different perspectives before making
up his own mind about policy matters.[11] Carter evidently attempted a similar arrangement, though with less success, by refusing
early in his administration to draw clear lines of authority among
his principal advisors. By doing so, he sought to encourage freer
and more open policy debates (and to avoid the stigma attached to
Nixon's hierarchical system). So strong was his aversion to administrative hierarchy, in fact, that he initially dispensed altogether
with the position of chief of staff. Yet the ensuing power struggles—
particularly between Zbigniew Brzezenski and Cyrus Vance, but
also involving Hamilton Jordan, Jody Powell, Bert Lance, and
Joseph Califano among others—and the resultant lack of policy
coordination eventually forced him to elevate Jordan to the position
of de facto chief of staff.[12] Unfortunately, as his chief speechwriter
James Fallows put it, "a year was wasted as we blindly groped for
answers and did for ourselves what a staff coordinator could have
done."[13] Carter may have learned from his subordinates' frequent
clashes, but his decision making did not benefit in a broader sense.
His personal openness led him to adopt an advisory system that
lacked procedures of governance adequate to the tasks it was
charged with performing.

As for the two presidents on which this book focuses, neither
Eisenhower nor Reagan appears to have spent much time dwelling
on these trade-offs or compensating for them. In opting for an
open staff, open leaders such as Eisenhower are likely to be criticized for providing inadequate guidance and leadership, or for
reacting too slowly to crises. Eisenhower was widely reproached for
just these failings. His wait-and-see attitude toward McCarthyism
and toward the civil rights movement may have given him a broader perspective that partisans lacked. But his policies in these
arenas satisfied almost no one. Even in making decisions that
have since been praised, such as his refusal to enter the war in
Vietnam on behalf of the French, it is worth keeping in mind that
his efforts to learn had costs as well. Suppose, for example, that
Eisenhower had discovered wide support for a more active

American role in Indochina after having consulted his chief military advisors, members of Congress, and allies overseas. By the time he actually finished these consultations, it was unlikely that U.S. intervention could have changed the outcome at Dien Bien Phu. It remains fair to say that Eisenhower learned in this case. Yet, while he was doing so, the passage of time helped to make the decision for him. Bearing the disadvantages of openness in mind, open leaders would thus do well to formally charge one or more of their subordinates with the task of monitoring and reporting on the urgency of the decision at hand. Ultimately, however, leaders cannot delegate this responsibility to others. Eisenhower was not without associates eager to impress on him the importance of active leadership on McCarthyism, civil rights, the balance of payments problem, or even Indochina. Open leaders must be sensitive to how easy it is for learning to become delay and avoidance.

Relatively closed leaders may actually be more likely to take decisive action than open leaders (despite the stereotypical association of introversion with timidity and caution). Reagan, far more than Eisenhower, was prepared to order sudden, bold changes in policy: the airstrike against Libya, the invasion of Grenada, and the development of a space-based missile defense system, to name a few. The dramatic foreign policy initiatives of Richard Nixon, another closed leader, are also consistent with this observation.[14] Typically relying on closed and hierarchical advisory systems, closed leaders can more easily marshall internal acceptance of controversial policies; indeed, this internal harmony is built into their advisory structure. Moreover, they are less likely to second-guess their initial decisions. Their "overmanagement" thus leaves them vulnerable to enacting poorly thought-out plans. Several of these examples, as well as the Iran-Contra affair, suggest themselves as illustrations of this danger. Yet, for reasons already elaborated in detail, the solution for closed leaders cannot be simply to throw open their advisory groups. To avoid deadlock, they must preserve a relatively closed advisory structure.

One is tempted to suggest that closed leaders use their tendency toward formality and hierarchy to their own advantage and designate devil's advocates whose duty it is, within the confines of a hierarchical and relatively closed system, to ensure that opposing viewpoints are nevertheless presented. Yet it is all too easy to imagine what would become of such arrangements. The unfortunate individual occupying this role would be deprived of real power in an organization that values consensus. As a result, any efforts to advocate contrary positions would also lack force. Such superficial devil's advocacy recalls George Ball's role in the Johnson administration during the Vietnam War. Every week, in the "Tuesday lunch group," Ball would voice his concern with the administration's assumptions about Vietnam. The others would listen politely then proceed to ignore him, all the while feeling good that a critical perspective had been taken into account.[15] Ultimately, the only solution to this dilemma—as in the case of open leaders facing the problem of procrastination—is for leaders themselves to remain alert to the dangers inherent in the advisory system they implement. Closed leaders must occasionally prompt their trusted advisors to reconsider assumptions and to explore the claims of their critics. Sometimes, even closed leaders must also go outside of their customary, comfortable channels of information to seek fresh perspectives. This does not mean abandoning a relatively closed system but, rather, subjecting it to occasional external checks to ensure that it is working properly.

The dilemmas faced by devil's advocates highlight the political character of staff organization. Those who seek closure in an open administration are likely to be considered reckless, impetuous, or self-serving, whereas dissenters in a closed administration will not be seen as team players and will soon find themselves treated as "outsiders" (in an effort by "insiders" to preserve harmony). In either case, those who try to act as counterweights to the dominant tendencies within a group of advisors will likely find themselves deprived of the very power they seek: the ability to influence others. Leaders must take not only their own learning style into account when providing for devil's advocacy, but they must also ensure that the political structure of their staff encourages and rewards appropriate dissent.

The implications of this discussion can be reduced, therefore, to several key points. *First,* more even distribution of power among members of a high-level policy-making group will encourage consideration of a broader range of alternatives and more extensive debate on their merits. So long as the members of a group are relatively secure in their positions, they will find it easier to voice critical or unpopular opinions. When power is unevenly distributed, however, the group's junior members are particularly likely to hesitate before voicing unpopular opinions. And senior members may find it more expedient to defer to one another so long as their own vital interests are not at stake. To put this another way, concentration of power may encourage a form of procedural logrolling in which senior group members hesitate to challenge each other's pet projects and junior members are expected to toe the "party line" of their superiors.[16] These groups tend toward the lower-left quadrant of figure 7-1. Even when debates do occur in such overmanaged groups, dissenters are unlikely to press the issue. Thus, after Shultz and Weinberger perceived that Reagan's chief of staff and national security advisors had decided to move ahead with the sale of arms to Iran, they simply distanced themselves from discussions of the matter rather than continuing to make the same objections.

Second, although a more even distribution of power may encourage realistic debate and facilitate learning, it is also likely to hinder efforts to reach firm decisions and to implement policies. Such groups are "undermanaged" and tend toward the top right quadrant of figure 7-1. Open leaders who permit diffusion of power within their staff have often been criticized, as just noted, for failing to provide leadership. One reason for this is that open staff arrangements may lack the governmental apparatus to provide clear recommendations and to enact policies readily. Precisely because the diffusion of power encourages debate, it hinders efforts to move beyond debate to decision and implementation. Eisenhower, Carter and Clinton all adopted relatively open advisory staffs, availing themselves of far-ranging debates on policy matters, and each has been accused of vacillating between policies and providing weak leadership. Kennedy, on the other hand, seems to be an exception: an open leader with open advisory groups (notably excepting the group that planned for the Bay of Pigs invasion) but who was nevertheless seen by most as providing strong leadership. Perhaps this is simply due to the force of his personality, but it also implies a distinction between hierarchy and formality.

As just suggested, both terms describe ways in which power can be concentrated. Yet there are important differences between them. *Hierarchy* expresses differences in position, whereas *formality* refers to differences in procedure. Typically, one accompanies the other. Subordinates are expected to follow specific procedures and to obey certain lines of authority in reporting to superiors—but this is not inevitable. In the Kennedy administration, there was a conscious effort to decrease some of the organizational formalism that was perceived as a weakness of Eisenhower's system. This would seem to leave Kennedy with an even more open advisory structure than Eisenhower and, consequently, at even greater risk of policy drift due to lack of leadership. Kennedy compensated, however, by maintaining a hierarchy in the form of an "inner club" of close advisors including McGeorge Bundy, Robert McNamara, Theodore Sorensen, and his brother Robert. As Roger Hilsman explains, this inner circle was ultimately responsible for the "pulling and hauling, debating and discussing for no other purpose than to keep the government together, to get all the others to come around."[17] Of course every leader has an inner circle of advisors. But Eisenhower tended to rely on different advisors for different problems, trusting in his somewhat formalistic procedures to keep these typically open groups manageable. Kennedy's procedures may have been more flexible, but his inner circle was also more constant, providing a different mechanism of governance and, perhaps, thereby facilitating leadership. Particularly during his first years in office, Carter lacked both formality and hierarchy, and thus suffered more acutely than other recent, open presidents from problems of internal governance.

A *third* point, suggested by the distinction between Kennedy's inner club and larger arenas such as the Cabinet or the NSC, is that larger groups require more directive forms of governance than do smaller groups. Because big groups intrinsically pose greater problems of coordination, power must be distributed more unevenly within them. Large groups also encourage the illusion that one's own contribution is relatively less important, leading to free riding or what social psychologists call "social loafing."[18] Both formal procedures and hierarchy can partly compensate for these tendencies in large groups, whereas in smaller groups the same forms of governance would seem ponderous and overbearing. What distinguishes a big group from a small one is, unfortunately, impossible to specify in the abstract. Depending on the nature of the problem a group faces or on the decision rules it must employ (e.g., unanimity or majority vote), the same number of group members might seem either unwieldy or inadequate to the task. Groups intended for debate, for example, are typically larger than groups in which decisions must be made.[19] Consistent with the general argument of this book, moreover, the definition of a large group is also likely to depend on the learning style of the group's leader.

A *fourth* point, finally, is that some leaders require more hierarchical forms of governance than others, depending on their individual needs for cohesion and consensus. Whereas closed leaders must concentrate power sufficiently to produce a manageable flow of advice, open leaders are themselves able to provide governance and guidance that permit larger and more egalitarian groups of advisors. In any event, though, all leaders must take into account the trade-off between comprehensiveness and variety, on one hand, and problems of coordination, on the other. In compensating for their own learning style, moreover, they must be careful not to overcompensate. Typically, closed leaders prefer groups that are both small and hierarchical, while open leaders are comfortable in groups that are both larger and in which power is more evenly dispersed. Closed leaders are thus vulnerable to the overmanagement of their subordinates, whereas the staffs of open leaders are more likely to be undermanaged.

At first glance, this final assertion seems at variance with the main argument of this book: that the primary danger for closed leaders is deadlock resulting from excessively open advisory groups whereas, for open leaders, it is groupthink resulting from insufficient openness. In fact, leaders can err in either direction. They must be aware of the dangers of overcompensating, as well as the dangers of failing to compensate, for their own learning style. As Stephen Hess writes of Richard Nixon, for example, "a president so given to isolation should have guarded against choosing a system that permitted him to become remote from the people and forces that a president must be in continuous contact with to govern effectively." Hess is mistaken, however, is asserting that "the problem of the Nixon White House was not so much that it had a structured staff system, which had served Eisenhower well, but that this was the wrong system for Richard Nixon."[20] It was no accident that Nixon chose the system he did: it was the right system for him. He could not have governed effectively within an open system. Yet Nixon failed to guard against the predictable shortcomings of a hierarchical, closed advisory system. Having opted for a closed system, he allowed power to become too concentrated, and he emphasized loyalty at the expense of occasional, external "reality checks" on his advisors' positions. Reagan suffered a similar problem prior to the Iran-Contra affair, replacing a system with some built-in checks (the triumvirate of Baker, Meese, and Deaver) with an even more hierarchical system under

Regan. Evidently lacking an awareness of the implications of further advisory closure, President Reagan failed to ensure that his
top aides continued to listen to dissenters. They did not, and the
result was the most serious crisis of his presidency.

Leaders who concentrate power among a select few of their
subordinates to create an orderly and efficient advisory system
must take steps to ensure that these lieutenants remain open to
the lower levels of their advisory hierarchy. The more hierarchical a
leader's staff, the more essential it is that those in the top positions
be "honest brokers" of information from lower ranks, with sufficient
stature to present unpopular positions and to speak candidly when
the need arises. Hess argues that presidents tend to choose
younger, ideologically similar activists for key White House staff
positions, whereas they select more experienced individuals of
higher stature for Cabinet and other departmental posts. The
result, he contends, is that "presidents often have had the wrong
people in the wrong types of jobs at both ends, White House and
departments."[21] Where closed presidents, in particular, can least
afford unseasoned but ambitious ideologues is at the heart of their
own staff. The three most closed modern presidents—Nixon,
Johnson, and Reagan—all suffered a great deal politically from pursuing policies endorsed by ideologically unified top advisors but not
subjected to wider scrutiny.[22] The Watergate scandal, the futile
escalation of the Vietnam War, and the Iran-Contra scandal ought
to serve notice to closed leaders that loyalty and cohesion are not
enough. If they choose their top aides carefully and ensure that the
lower levels of their hierarchy are sufficiently broad, on the other
hand, closed leaders need not be at any particular disadvantage.
They can take advantage of the filtering effects of hierarchy to
ensure that a wide variety of perspectives and opinions are presented, but in an orderly and manageable way.

Leaders who opt for larger and more open groups should also
be aware of the potential dangers of openness. They should not
forget that such groups, far more than small and cohesive ones,
need some structure to work effectively. Truman and Eisenhower
both handled this problem through formalism, whereas Roosevelt
and Kennedy relied instead on "inner circles" to maintain order in
otherwise more freewheeling administrations. Carter and Clinton
were both disinclined to adopt either solution, and the result, particularly during their first year in office, was a higher degree of disarray in their decision making. Without allowing their advisory

groups to become closed, therefore, open leaders must take steps to insure that they have some assistance in setting priorities and organizing their approach to major decisions. They cannot afford to serve, as Carter appeared to want to, as their own chiefs of staff.[23] Even the most open leader can easily become overwhelmed at the head of a large organization, and particularly by the demands of the Oval Office. Openness carries with it the price of having to ensure that there is sufficient concentration of power and authority among top aides to provide some administrative guidance.

In general, leaders must remember that monitoring the structure of their advisory group is a permanent and ongoing task. Typically, leaders pay special attention to the selection and organization of advisors only on assuming a new office. Having then done so, they may be reluctant to revisit these decisions for many reasons. They may develop personal bonds with some of their staff, and they may fear the signal it would send if they replace others (particularly those advisors who have attained public stature in their own right). Inertia is also a powerful force. It is often easier to stay with a "known quantity" than to face the upheaval of replacing an important aide. Leaders should cultivate an awareness, however, that some of the advisors they appoint will not work out. Others, while initially successful, may lose their effectiveness over time. Bitter rivalries may develop or, conversely, an unhealthy collegiality tending toward sycophancy that prevents critical assessment of policies. Monitoring these developments is not a job that can be delegated. It is one of the most critical tasks of effective leadership. Unfortunately, the longer a leader remains in power, the less attention he or she typically gives to this problem. Familiar faces and familiar routines sooner or later grow to dominate decision making. It is a certainty, however, that some changes will be necessary as time passes to maintain a proper balance of advisors consistent with a leader's learning and decision style. All leaders, regardless of learning style, should approach their job with this in mind.

WHY LEARN?

Implicit all along in this book has been the assumption that learning is a valuable activity so long as it can accommodate the requirements of a leader's learning style. To this, the present chapter adds the further caveat that efforts to learn must respect political necessity and the organizational needs of the leader's staff. Against the basic assumption that learning is important, however, stands the claim that political learning and adaptation are overrated. One might argue that Reagan's ideological intransigence served him better, on balance, than Carter's ability to master complexities. Learning did not pay the dividends that Carter expected it to, and a preoccupation with it may on occasion have limited his ability to take in the larger political picture. After all, learning is only a beginning in the process of decision making. It is no substitute for good judgment, and it can serve as a convenient excuse for avoiding decisions. A preoccupation with fact-finding, for example, or excessive mulling over alternatives can lead to lost opportunities. Most studies of learning and policymaking, including this one, thus typically offer caveats such as Alexander George's warning that "the search for a higher-quality decision cannot or should not be prolonged insofar as the failure to make a timely decision may itself reduce the likelihood of achieving a successful outcome."[24] A priori, of course, it is difficult to distinguish clearly between prudent deliberation and unnecessary delay.

In any event, it is sobering to realize that neither Eisenhower nor Reagan got what he wanted in any of the four cases of learning discussed in chapter 4. The outcome at Dien Bien Phu, for example, was far from what Eisenhower hoped to achieve. Communists won a victory in Vietnam and, adding insult to injury, a liberal government also came to power in France. As for Alaskan statehood, although he grudgingly came to support it, Eisenhower continued to believe that the federal government should have retained greater authority and, at any rate, he believed that Hawaii deserved statehood first. Reagan similarly came to support Regan's and Baker's bailout plans for Mexico, but he did not particularly approve of them and would have preferred instead to let the market solve such problems. He liked withdrawing the marines from Lebanon even less. Despite efforts at "spin control," it was a retreat that Reagan had vowed never to make. In none of these cases of learning, then, did the president achieve his initial objectives.

Of course every leader who rises to a position of prominence is intellectually aware that the most diligent efforts to address a policy problem rationally can fail, and all leaders at this level have some experience with failure as well as success. For elected politicians—particularly in the afterglow of electoral victory—it is nevertheless tempting to believe that even the thorniest problems must give way to one's mandate, expertise, and commitment. Perhaps this is one reason why many presidents stumble early in their first terms, as Kennedy did with the Bay of Pigs crisis and as Clinton did with his unsuccessful proposals for health care reform.[25] A well-structured decision-making process may help, but learning does not inevitably lead to good political judgment. Leaders should resist the comfortable illusion that it will.

Still, on balance, leaders generally benefit from more learning rather than less. The "underlying causes of erroneous beliefs will never simply disappear," as Thomas Gilovich has observed in a study of how popular myths become resistant to disconfirming evidence. Our only recourse, he argues, is a persistent effort to hold them "in check by compensatory mental habits that promote more sound reasoning."[26] Stephen Jay Gould puts it more forcefully: "when people learn no tools of judgment and merely follow their hopes, the seeds of political manipulation are sown."[27] That political history consists in such strong measure of the repetition of past mistakes cannot be purely a coincidence. It suggests that the "tools of judgment" are not used often enough.

Perhaps it is ironic to begin with praise of Machiavelli's insight and to conclude by expressing hope that "political manipulation" can somehow be avoided. Certainly, he did not think it could. It is also clear enough that learning cannot guarantee good judgment, much less moral judgment. Moral capacity must rest within leaders (and within advisors) themselves. Writing in the age of Cesare Borgia gave Machiavelli no grounds for optimism. Even leaders who do aspire to higher purposes can fall well short. For them, learning is no guarantee of achieving noble goals, but it is the only available remedy for bad judgment.

Notes

CHAPTER 1. INTRODUCTION

1. Yasuo Kuwahara, *Decision-making Structures and Processes in Multinationals in Japan* (Geneva: International Labour Office, 1985); and Ezra F. Vogel, ed., *Modern Japanese Organization and Decision-making* (Berkeley: University of California Press, 1975).

2. Charles R. Evans and Kenneth L. Dion, "Group Cohesion and Performance: A Meta-Analysis," *Small Group Research* 22 (1991), pp. 175–186; Henry Kellerman, *Group Cohesion: Theoretical and Clinical Perspectives* (New York: Grune & Stratton, 1981); and Stephen J. Zaccaro and Charles A. Lowe, "Cohesiveness and Performance on an Additive Task: Evidence for Multidimensionality," *Journal of Social Psychology* 128 (1988), pp. 547–558.

3. Henk A. M. Wilke and Roel W. Meertens, *Group Performance* (London: Routledge, 1994); and Alvin Zander, *Making Groups Effective* (San Francsico: Jossey-Bass, 1994).

4. Irving Janis, *Groupthink: Psychological Studies of Policy Decisions and Fiascoes* (Boston: Houghton Mifflin, 1982); rev. ed. of *Victims of Groupthink: A Psychological Study of Foreign-Policy Decisions and Fiascoes* (Boston: Houghton Mifflin, 1972). All page references are to the 1982 edition.

5. Aristotle, *Rhetoric,* book 1, ch. 6.

6. See Gustave Le Bon's classic study, *The Crowd* (London: T. Fisher Unwin, 1896).

7. Dean A. Minix, *Small Groups and Foreign Policy Decision-making* (Washington, D.C.: University Press of America, 1982); and Dean G. Pruitt, "Choice Shifts in Group Discussion: An Introductory Review," *Journal of Personality and Social Psychology* 20 (1971), pp. 339–360.

8. See Stephen Krasner, "Are Bureaucracies Important? (Or Allison Wonderland)," *Foreign Policy* 7 (1971), pp. 159–179.

9. Christian J. Buys recently prompted a humorous exchange among social psychologists by asserting precisely this. See Buys, "Humans Would Do Better Without Groups," *Personality and Social Psychology Bulletin* 4 (1978), pp. 123–125; Lynn R. Anderson, "Groups Would Do Better Without Humans," *Personality and Social Psychology Bulletin* 4 (1978), pp. 557–558; David Kravitz et al., "Humans Would Do Better Without Other Humans," *Personality and Social Psychology Bulletin* 4 (1978), pp. 559–560; Richard Green and Jonathan Mack, "Would Groups Do Better Without Social Psychologists? A Response to Buys," *Personality and Social Psychology Bulletin* 4 (1978), pp. 561–563; and Leigh Shaffer, "On the Current Confusion of Group-Related Behavior and Collective Behavior: A Reaction to Buys," *Personality and Social Psychology Bulletin* 4 (1978), pp. 564–567.

10. Classic statements of this argument include Leon Festinger, *A Theory of Cognitive Dissonance* (Stanford: Stanford University Press, 1966); and Fritz Heider, *The Psychology of Interpersonal Relations* (New York: Wiley, 1958). See also Robert P. Abelson, "Whatever Became of Consistency Theory?" *Personality and Social Psychology Bulletin* 9 (1983), pp. 37–54.

11. Janis, *Crucial Decisions: Leadership in Policymaking and Crisis Management* (New York: Free Press, 1989); Janis and Leon Mann, *Decision Making: A Psychological Analysis of Conflict, Choice, and Commitment* (New York: Free Press, 1977); Rossall J. Johnson, "Conflict Avoidance Through Acceptable Decisions," *Human Relations* 27 (1974), pp. 71–82; and David W. Miller and Martin K. Starr, *The Structure of Human Decisions* (Englewood Cliffs, New Jersey: Prentice-Hall, 1967).

12. It is usually suggested, therefore, that a curvilinear relationship exists between stress or arousal and performance. A moderate amount of anxiety is helpful. Too little arousal causes attention to wander, and too much produces panicky responses that interfere with reasoning and appropriate action. See Richard S. Lazarus, James Deese, and Sonia F. Osler, "The Effects of Psycho-

logical Stress upon Performance," *Psychological Bulletin* 49 (1952), pp. 293–317; and Herbert A. Simon, "Motivational and Emotional Controls of Cognition," *Annual Review of Psychology* 30 (1979), pp. 29–39.

13. Margaret S. Clark and Alice M. Isen, "Toward Understanding the Relationship Between Feeling States, Judgments, and Behavior," in Albert Hastorf and Alice Isen, eds., *Cognitive Social Psychology* (New York: Elsevier North-Holland, 1982), pp. 73–108.

14. Susan Fiske and Shelley Taylor, *Social Cognition* (New York: Random House, 1984), pp. 326–333.

15. Important discussions of the way leaders organize advisory staffs include John P. Burke and Fred I. Greenstein, *How Presidents Test Reality: Decisions on Vietnam, 1954 and 1965* (New York: Russell Sage Foundation, 1989); Alexander George, *Presidential Decisionmaking in Foreign Policy: The Effective Use of Information and Advice* (Boulder, Colorado: Westview, 1980); Margaret G. Hermann and Thomas Preston, "Presidents, Advisers, and Foreign Policy: The Effects of Leadership Style on Executive Arrangements," *Political Psychology* 15 (1994), pp. 75–96; and Richard Tanner Johnson, *Managing the White House: An Intimate Study of the Presidency* (New York: Harper & Row, 1974).

16. Theodore J. Lowi, *The Personal President: Power Invested, Promise Unfulfilled* (Ithaca: Cornell University Press, 1985), p. 136.

17. For a discussion of the difficulties inherent in developing causal explanations for human behavior, see Peter D. McClelland, *Causal Explanation and Model Building in History, Economics, and the New Economic History* (Ithaca: Cornell University Press, 1975), esp. pp. 65–104. This problem has re-emerged with new vigor in the writings of both postmodern and constructivist theorists. See David Dessler, "What's at Stake in the Agent-Structure Debate?" *International Organization* 43, 3 (1989), pp. 441–473; Nicholas Onuf, *World of Our Making: Rules and Rule in Social Theory and International Relations* (Columbia: University of South Carolina Press, 1989); Michael Shapiro, *Language and Poltical Understanding: The Politics of Discursive Practices* (New Haven: Yale University Press, 1981); and Alexander E. Wendt, "The Agent-Structure Problem in International Relations Theory," *International Organization* 41, 3 (1987), pp. 335–370.

18. Stephen Skowronek, "Presidential Leadership in Political Time," in Michael Nelson, ed., *The Presidency and the Political System* (Washington, D.C.: Congressional Quarterly, 1990), pp.

117–161; and Skowronek, "Notes on the Presidency in the Political Order," *Studies in American Political Development,* vol. 1 (New Haven: Yale University Press, 1986), pp. 286–302. For another good discussion of cycles in political movements, see Sidney Tarrow, *Democracy and Disorder: Protest and Politics in Italy 1965–1975* (Oxford: Clarendon Press, 1989); and Tarrow, *Struggle, Politics, and Reform: Collective Action, Social Movements, and Cycles of Protest,* Occasional Paper no. 21 (Ithaca: Center for International Studies, Western Societies Program, Cornell University, 1989).

19. For a related argument, see Robert Jervis, *Perception and Misperception in International Politics* (Princeton: Princeton University Press, 1976), ch. 1. I do not mean to imply, certainly, that enduring political institutions are completely unrelated to abrupt political changes. Some destabilizing institutions may even encourage rapid change. The combination of international alliances and offense-minded military bureaucracies in pre-World War I Europe, for example, was highly destabilizing once mobilization began and contributed to the rapid onset of a war that no one really wanted. See Barbara Tuchman, *The Guns of August* (New York: Dell, 1962); and Jack Snyder, *The Ideology of the Offensive: Military Decision Making and the Disasters of 1914* (Ithaca: Cornell University Press, 1984). But such cases do not change the basic point about institutional inertia: deeply imbedded bureaucratic, national, or international institutions change slowly and do not account—at least, by themselves—for fundamental discontinuities.

20. See Sidney Hook, *The Hero in History* (New York: John Day, 1943).

21. Exceptions to this tendency are the essays contained in George W. Breslauer and Philip E. Tetlock, eds., *Learning in U.S. and Soviet Foreign Policy* (Boulder, Colorado: Westview, 1991). Also see Jervis, *Perception and Misperception in International Politics,* pp. 217–287; Janis and Mann, *Decision Making,* pp. 81–133; and Yaacov Y. I. Vertzberger, "Foreign Policy Decisionmakers as Practical-intuitive Historians: Applied History and Its Shortcomings," *International Studies Quarterly* 30 (1986), pp. 223–247.

22. Janis, *Groupthink,* p. 9. Janis uses the more general term *vigilance* to denote "high-quality" decision making that clearly includes *learning.*

23. Richard Ned Lebow, *Between Peace and War: The Nature of International Crisis* (Baltimore: Johns Hopkins University Press, 1981), pp. 309–333.

24. For good overviews of *learning* as information acquisition, see William K. Estes, *Models of Learning, Memory, and Choice* (New York: Praeger, 1982), pp. 79–106; Douglas Medin, "Theories of Discrimination Learning and Learning Set," in William K. Estes, ed., *Handbook of Learning and Cognitive Processes: Approaches to Human Learning and Motivation,* vol. 3 (Hillsdale, New Jersey: Lawrence Erlbaum, 1976), pp. 131–169; and John R. Anderson, *Cognitive Psychology and Its Implications,* parts 3 and 4 (San Francisco: W. H. Freeman & Co., 1980).

For further discussion of different types of learning and learning theories, see Gordon H. Bower and Ernest R. Hilgard, *Theories of Learning* (Englewood Cliffs, New Jersey: Prentice-Hall, 1981); Estes, *Models of Learning,* pp. 1–21; Leo Postman, "Methodology of Human Learning," in Estes, ed., *Handbook of Learning,* pp. 11–69; Thomas H. Leahey and Richard J. Harris, *Human Learning* (Englewood Cliffs, New Jersey: Prentice-Hall, 1985); and esp., T. A. Ryan, "Intention and Kinds of Learning," in Gery d'Ydewalle and Willy Lens, eds., *Cognition in Human Motivation and Learning* (Hillsdale, New Jersey: Lawrence Erlbaum, 1981), pp. 59–85.

25. Philip E. Tetlock, "Learning in U.S. and Soviet Foreign Policy: In Search of an Elusive Concept," in Breslauer and Tetlock, *Learning in U.S. and Soviet Foreign Policy,* pp. 20–61.

26. This is Max Weber's well-worn distinction between instrumental rationality (Zweckrationalität) and value rationality (Wertrationalität) in another guise. See Weber, *Economy and Society,* edited by Guenther Roth and Claus Wittich (Berkeley: University of California Press, 1978), pp. 24–26, 85–86, and 107–109; and also Herbert A. Simon, "Rationality as Process and as Product of Thought," *American Economic Review,* (*Papers and Proceedings*) 68 (1978), pp. 1–16.

Stimulus-response psychologists and evolutionary biologists also use the term *learning* in an evaluative sense. When they speak of adaptive learning, they mean by learning that a person (or another organism) is better suited to a particular environment. See Joseph Nuttin and Anthony G. Greenwald, *Reward and Punishment in Human Learning* (New York: Academic, 1968); and Estes, *Models of Learning,* pp. 63–78.

27. "Fundamental" learning may appear more important because it is more difficult. As Ernst B. Haas observes, "[a]daptive behavior is common whereas true learning (i.e., reassessing fundamental beliefs) is very rare" (p. 80). See Haas, "Collective Learning: Some Theoretical Speculations," in Breslauer and Tetlock,

Learning in U.S. and Soviet Foreign Policy, pp. 62–99. Yet leaders who continuously question their fundamental beliefs will appear vacuous or inconstant, and those who are unable to adapt to "minor" challenges will likely be removed much more quickly than those who have difficulty responding to fundamental challenges.

28. William Osler, quoted in Raymond B. Cattell, *Personality and Learning Theory: The Structure of Personality in Its Environment,* vol. 1 (New York: Springer, 1979), p. 29.

CHAPTER 2. WHO LEARNS, AND WHEN?

1. Jerrold M. Post, "The Defining Moment of Saddam's Life: A Political Psychology Perspective on the Leadership and Decision Making of Saddam Hussein During the Gulf Crisis," in Stanley A. Renshon, ed., *The Political Psychology of the Persian Gulf War: Leaders, Publics, and the Process of Conflict* (Pittsburgh: University of Pittsburgh Press, 1993), pp. 49–66.

2. Fred I. Greenstein, "Political Style and Political Leadership: The Case of Bill Clinton," in Stanley A. Renshon, ed., *The Clinton Presidency: Campaigning, Governing, and the Psychology of Leadership* (Boulder, Colorado: Westview, 1995), p. 144. See also David Maraniss, *First in His Class: A Biography of Bill Clinton* (New York: Simon & Schuster, 1995).

3. Alexander George and Juliette George, *Woodrow Wilson and Colonel House: A Personality Study* (New York: John Day, 1956; reprint, New York: Dover, 1964, subsequent page references are to the reprint edition); see also Bernard Brodie, "A Psychoanalytic Interpretation of Woodrow Wilson," *World Politics* 9 (1957), pp. 413–422; and Greenstein, *Personality and Politics: Problems of Evidence, Inference, and Conceptualization* (Chicago: Markham, 1969; reprint, Princeton: Princeton University Press, 1987), pp. 68–93 (page references are to the reprint edition). One of the most controversial studies of Wilson is Sigmund Freud and William C. Bullitt's *Thomas Woodrow Wilson, Twenty-Eighth President of the United States: A Psychological Study* (Boston: Houghton Mifflin, 1967), which was originally written in the 1930s. The Freud-Bullitt volume lacks the Georges' tone of impartiality; for a good critique, see Erik Erikson and Richard Hofstadter, "The Strange Case of Freud, Bullitt, and Wilson," *New York Review of Books* (February 9, 1967), pp. 3–8.

4. George and George, *Woodrow Wilson and Colonel House*, p. 116.

5. In the decade following World War II, studies of personality and politics flourished. Harold D. Lasswell investigated the relationship between education, personality, and democracy. And, as a natural counterpoint, Theodore W. Adorno and several collaborators produced a pioneering study of the psychological susceptibility of Germans, in the interwar period, to fascism. See Lasswell, *Power and Personality* (New York: Norton, 1948); Adorno, et al., *The Authoritarian Personality* (New York: Harper, 1950); and also Gordon W. Allport, *The Nature of Prejudice* (Boston: Addison-Wesley, 1954).

6. Bernard J. Baars, *The Cognitive Revolution in Psychology* (New York: Guilford, 1986).

7. The most important such criticism was voiced by Walter Mischel in *Personality and Assessment* (New York: Wiley, 1968). Mischel complained that existing research rarely found a correlation between behaviors that should follow from the same underlying trait, that redundant methods inflated the correlations that were obtained, and that individuals are often situated (or situate themselves) in fairly consistent environments, further diluting the contribution of personality to any observed consistencies in behavior.

8. Important statements in this debate include Gunnar Backteman and David Magnusson, "Longitudinal Stability of Personality Characteristics," *Journal of Personality* 49, 2 (June 1981), pp. 148–160; Daryl J. Bem and A. Allen, "On Predicting Some of the People Some of the Time," *Psychological Review* 81 (1974), pp. 88–104; Bruce A. Campbell, "On the Utility of Trait Theory in Political Science," *Micropolitics* 1, 2 (1981), pp. 177–190; James J. Conley, "Longitudinal Stability of Personality Traits: A Multitrait-Multimethod-Multioccasion Analysis," *Journal of Personality and Social Psychology* 49, 5 (1985), pp. 1266–1282; and Arthur C. Houts, Thomas D. Cook, and William R. Shadish, "The Person-Situation Debate: A Critical Multiplist Perspective," *Journal of Personality* 54, 1 (March 1986), pp. 52–105.

9. Good discussions of methodological advances in research on personality include S. L. Golding, "Flies in the Ointment: Methodological Problems in the Analysis of Percentage of Variance Due to Persons and Situations," *Psychological Bulletin* 82 (1975), pp. 278–288; S. E. Hormuth, "The Sampling of Experiences *in situ*," *Journal of Personality* 54 (1986), pp. 262–293; D. S.

Moskowitz, "Comparison of Self-Reports, Reports by Knowledgeable Informants, and Behavioral Observation Data," *Journal of Personality* 54 (1986), pp. 294–317; and Paul D. Werner and Lawrence A. Pervin, "The Content of Personality Inventory Items," *Journal of Personality and Social Psychology* 51, 3 (1986), pp. 622–628.

10. Among the most important of these studies are Jack Block, *Lives Through Time* (Berkeley: Bancroft, 1971); Paul T. Costa and Robert R. McCrae, "Still Stable After All These Years," in P. B. Baltes and O. G. Brim, eds., *Life Span Development and Behavior*, vol. 3 (New York: Academic, 1980), pp. 65–102; Robert McCrae and Paul T. Costa, *Emerging Lives, Enduring Dispositions: Personality in Adulthood* (Boston: Little, Brown, 1984); McCrae and Costa, *Personality in Adulthood* (New York: Guilford, 1990); and Mischel and P. K. Peake, "Beyond Déjà Vu in the Search for Cross-Situational Consistency," *Psychological Review* 89 (1982), pp. 730–755.

11. Janis, *Groupthink*.

12. Alexander George, *Presidential Decisionmaking in Foreign Policy*, pp. 149–150; Stephen Hess, *Organizing the Presidency* (Washington, D.C.: Brookings, 1976), 2d ed., pp. 27–43.

13. James David Barber does, in fact, characterize FDR in these terms. See Barber, *The Presidential Character: Predicting Performance in the White House* (Englewood Cliffs, New Jersey: Prentice-Hall, 1972), pp. 209–246.

14. Carl G. Jung, *Psychological Types* (London: Routledge and Kegan Paul, 1923).

15. Research on personality traits has converged on a fivefold taxonomy of basic personality traits, commonly called the "five-factor model" (FFM) or "big five." For a good account of the FFM and the research sustaining it, see John M. Digman, "Personality Structure: Emergence of the Five-Factor Model," *Annual Review of Psychology* 41 (1990), pp. 417–440; Lewis R. Goldberg, "The Structure of Phenotypic Personality Traits," *American Psychologist* 48 (1993), pp. 26–34; McCrae and Costa, *Personality in Adulthood* (Boston: Little, Brown, 1984) and McCrae and Oliver P. John, "An Introduction to the Five Factor Model and Its Applications," *Journal of Personality* 60 (1992), pp. 175–215. Extraversion is, in fact, generally the first "trait" to emerge in factor analyses of personality inventories and is thus conventionally labeled *Factor I;* see Digman, "Personality Structure." The other four traits are agree-

ableness, conscientiousness, emotional stability (or neuroticism), and culture (or intellect, or openness).

16. The reticular brain stem formation acts as an amplifier for sensory stimuli. See Hans J. Eysenck, *The Biological Basis of Personality* (Springfield, Illinois: Charles C. Thomas, 1967); and Eysenck and S. B. G. Eysenck, "On the Unitary Nature of Extraversion," in Eysenck, *Eysenck on Extraversion* (New York: Wiley, 1973), p. 42. According to Eysenck, "introversion is a product of cortical arousal, mediated by the reticular formation; introverts are habitually in a state of greater arousal than extraverts, and consequently they show lower sensory thresholds, and greater reactions to sensory stimulation" (Eysenck and Eysenck, "On the Unitary Nature of Extraversion," p. 42). See also Jeffrey A. Gray, "The Psychophysiological Basis of Introversion-Extraversion," *Behavior Research and Therapy* 8 (1970), pp. 249–266; and Marvin Zuckerman, ed., *Biological Bases of Sensation Seeking, Impulsivity, and Anxiety* (Hillsdale, New Jersey: Lawrence Erlbaum, 1983). Gray proposes that, in addition to the reticular brain stem, the orbital frontal cortex and the hippocampus may also affect extraversion by rendering some individuals more sensitive to punishment and reward than others.

17. See Isabel Briggs Myers, *Gifts Differing: Understanding Personality Type* (Palo Alto, California: Consulting Psychologists Press, 1980; reprint, 1993), esp. pp. 115–164, for a discussion of practical applications of the MBTI.

18. Ronald Reagan's learning and decision style will be discussed at length in chapter 3. On Lyndon Johnson's "closed" style, see Robert Caro, *The Years of Lyndon Johnson: Means of Ascent* (New York: Knopf, 1990).

19. Julian B. Rotter, *Social Learning and Clinical Psychology* (Englewood Cliffs, New Jersey: Prentice-Hall, 1954); Rotter, "Generalized Expectancies for Internal Control of Reinforcement," *Psychological Monographs* 80, 1 (1966), whole no. 609. Good overviews of locus of control include Herbert M. Lefcourt, *Locus of Control: Current Trends in Theory and Research* (Hillsdale, New Jersey: Lawrence Erlbaum, 1982); and E. Jerry Phares, *Locus of Control in Personality* (Morristown, New Jersey: General Learning Press, 1976).

20. See Jo Ann Basgall and C. R. Snyder, "Excuses in Waiting: External Locus of Control and Reactions to Success-Failure Feedback," *Journal of Personality and Social Psychology* 54 (April 1988),

pp. 656–662; William L. Davis and E. Jerry Phares, "Internal-External Control as a Determinant of Information-Seeking in a Social Influence Situation," *Journal of Personality* 35, 4 (1967), pp. 547–561; Charles H. Ingold, "Locus of Control and Use of Public Information," *Psychological Reports* 64 (April 1989), pp. 603–607; Phares, "Differential Utilization of Information as a Function of Internal-External Control," *Journal of Personality* 36 (1968), pp. 649–662; Ashton D. Trice and Judith Price-Greathouse, "Locus of Control and AIDS Information-Seeking in College Women," *Psychological Reports* 60 (April 1987), pp. 665–666.

An internal locus of control may also enhance the retention and processing of information. See Henry C. Ellis and James B. Franklin, "Memory and Personality: External versus Internal Locus of Control and Superficial Organization in Free Recall," *Journal of Verbal Learning and Verbal Behavior* 22 (1983), pp. 61–74; Thane S. Pittman and Paul R. D'Agostino, "Motivation and Cognition: Control Deprivation and the Nature of Subsequent Information Processing," *Journal of Experimental Social Psychology* 25 (1989), pp. 465–480; and Nicholas A. Vacc and Nancy Nesbitt Vacc, "Cognitive Complexity-Simplicity as a Determinant of Internal-External Locus of Control," *Psychological Reports* 52 (January 1983), pp. 913–914.

21. Lefcourt, *Locus of Control*, p. 69.

22. See Betty Glad, *Jimmy Carter: In Search of the Great White House* (New York: Norton, 1980); Paul A. Kowert, "Where *Does* the Buck Stop?: Assessing the Impact of Presidential Personality," *Political Psychology* 17 (1996), pp. 421–452; and Bruce Mazlish and E. Diamond, *Jimmy Carter: A Character Portrait* (New York: Simon & Schuster, 1979).

23. Individuals might be arrayed, more properly, on a continuum from open to closed, but to simplify matters, I will simply refer to open and closed types. For further discussion of this distinction, see also Russell G. Geen, "Preferred Stimulation Levels in Introverts and Extraverts: Effects on Arousal and Performance," *Journal of Personality and Social Psychology* 46 (June 1984), pp. 1303–1312; Michael S. Humphreys and William Revelle, "Personality, Motivation, and Performance: A Theory of the Relationship Between Individual Differences and Information Processing," *Psychological Review* 91 (April 1984), pp. 153–184; and Milton Rokeach, *The Open and Closed Mind* (New York: Basic, 1960).

24. Robert M. Yerkes and J. D. Dodson, "The Relation of Strength of Stimulus to Rapidity of Habit Formation," *Journal of Comparative Neurology and Psychology* 18 (1908), pp. 459–482.

25. See Rolf Bronner, *Decision Making Under Time Pressure* (Lexington, Massachusetts: Heath, 1982); Ole R. Holsti, *Crisis Escalation War* (Montreal: McGill-Queen's University Press, 1972), pp. 11–25; and Janice Gross Stein and Raymond Tanter, *Rational Decision Making: Israel's Security Choices, 1967* (Columbus: Ohio State University Press, 1980), pp. 57–62. Two good reviews of the relationship between stress and performance are Lazarus, Deese, and Osler, "Effects of Psychological Stress upon Performance" and F. E. Horvath, "Psychological Stress: A Review of Definitions and Experimental Research," in L. von Bertalanffy and Anatol Rapoport, *General Systems Yearbook* 4 (Ann Arbor, Michigan: Society for General Systems Research, 1959).

26. Johnson, *Managing the White House*.

27. In recent studies, Margaret G. Hermann and Thomas Preston explore two similar dimensions of group structure, which they distinguish as formal/informal and "process focus"/"problem focus." The latter dimension somewhat resembles collegiality/competition. See Hermann and Preston, "Presidents, Advisers, and Foreign Policy"; and Hermann and Preston, "Presidents and Their Advisers: Leadership Style, Advisory Systems, and Foreign Policy Making," in Eugene Wittkopf, ed., *Domestic Sources of American Foreign Policy* (New York: St. Martin's, 1988). Also see Burke, *The Institutional Presidency: Organizing and Managing the White House from FDR to Clinton* (Baltimore: Johns Hopkins University Press, 2000); and Charles E. Walcott and Karen M. Hult, *Governing the White House: From Hoover through LBJ* (Lawrence: University Press of Kansas, 1995).

28. Alexander George, *Presidential Decisionmaking in Foreign Policy*, p. 164. See also Patrick Haney, *Organizing for Foreign Policy Crises* (Ann Arbor: University of Michigan Press, 1997).

29. Alexander George, *Presidential Decisionmaking in Foreign Policy*, p. 166; and Burke and Greenstein, *How Presidents Test Reality*, p. 21.

30. Alexander George, *Presidential Decisionmaking in Foreign Policy*. See also Alexander George, "The Case for Multiple Advocacy in Making Foreign Policy," *American Political Science Review* 66 (1972), pp. 751–785.

31. Janis, *Groupthink*. Two excellent, recent efforts to refine the groupthink model are Paul 't Hart, *Groupthink in Government: A Study of Small Groups and Policy Failures* (Amsterdam: Swets and Zeitlinger, 1990; reprint, Baltimore: Johns Hopkins University Press, 1994) page references are to the reprint edition; and 't Hart, Eric Stern, and Bengt Sundelius, *Beyond Groupthink: Political Group Dynamics and Foreign Policymaking* (Ann Arbor: University of Michigan Press, 1997). Another useful and "state-of-the-art" collection of essays on groupthink can be found in a special issue of *Organizational Behavior and Human Decision Processes* 73, 2/3 (February/March 1998), pp. 103–374, entitled "Theoretical Perspectives on Groupthink: A Twenty-Fifth Anniversary Appraisal." In this volume, see esp. Marlene E. Turner and Anthony R. Pratkanis, "Twenty-Five Years of Groupthink Theory and Research: Lessons from the Evaluation of a Theory" (pp. 105–115), and James K. Esser, "Alive and Well after 25 Years: A Review of Groupthink Research" (pp. 116–141). Telling criticisms of Janis's original hypotheses are offered in each of these works and in J. Longley and Dean G. Pruitt, "Groupthink: A Critique of Janis' Theory," *Review of Personality and Social Psychology* 1 (1980), pp. 74–93.

32. See Janis, *Groupthink*, pp. 260–276. On the virtues and dangers of group cohesiveness, in particular, see also Kellerman, *Group Cohesion;* and Zander, *Making Groups Effective*.

33. Alexander George, *Presidential Decisionmaking in Foreign Policy*, p. 203.

34. Eysenck, *Biological Basis of Personality*, p. 95.

35. W. P. Colquhoun and D. W. J. Corcoran, "The Effects of Time of Day and Social Isolation on the Relationship Between Temperament and Performance," *British Journal of Social and Clinical Psychology* 3 (1964), pp. 226–231; Geen, "Preferred Stimulation Levels in Introverts and Extraverts"; and Geen, Eugene McCown, and James Broyles, "Effects of Noise on Sensitivity of Introverts and Extraverts to Signals in a Vigilance Task," *Personality and Individual Differences* 6, 2 (1985), pp. 237–241. Also see H. W. Riecken, "The Effect of Talkativeness on Ability to Influence Group Solutions of Problems," *Sociometry* 2 (1958), pp. 309–321.

36. Jerry Burger, "Desire for Control and Achievement-Related Behavior," *Journal of Personality and Social Psychology* 48 (1985), pp. 1520–1533; and Burger, "Desire for Control and Conformity to a Perceived Norm," *Journal of Personality and Social Psychology* 53 (1987), pp. 355–360. See also Stephen J. Dollinger, Leilani Green-

ing, and Barbara Tylenda, "Psychological-Mindedness as 'Reading Between the Lines': Vigilance, Locus of Control, and Sagacious Judgment," *Journal of Personality* 53 (1985), pp. 603–625.

37. Cecil Crabb and Kevin Mulcahy, *Presidents and Foreign Policy Making: From FDR to Reagan* (Baton Rouge: Louisiana State University Press, 1986), p. 317.

38. Hermann and Preston, "Presidents, Advisers, and Foreign Policy"; and Hermann and Preston, "Presidents and Their Advisers."

39. Alexander George, *Presidential Decisionmaking in Foreign Policy*, ch. 8.

40. The structure of advisory groups often differs from one issue to another. Eisenhower, for example, seemed to have only a few close advisors for most domestic issues (e.g., Sherman Adams and Bryce Harlow); for international policy, however, he relied first on Dulles and then on a wide range of experts and analysts including members of the NSC and old military acquaintances.

41. On the comparative analysis of case studies, see Harry Eckstein, "Case Study and Theory in Political Science," in Fred Greenstein and Nelson Polsby, eds., *Handbook of Political Science* (Reading, Massachusetts: Addison-Wesley, 1975), vol. 7, pp. 79–138; and Alexander George, "Case Studies and Theory Development: The Method of Structured, Focused Comparison," in Paul G. Lauren, *Diplomacy: New Approaches in History, Theory and Policy* (New York: Free Press, 1979), pp. 43–68. On the case study as a tool for research on decision making in particular, see also Haney, *Organizing for Foreign Policy Crises*.

42. John Odell, *U.S. International Monetary Policy: Markets, Power, and Ideas as Sources of Change* (Princeton: Princeton University Press, 1982). Other studies that demonstrate the decisive influence of leaders, their beliefs, and their decisions on markets include Peter Hall, *The Political Power of Economic Ideas: Keynesianism across Nations* (Princeton: Princeton University Press, 1989); Judith Goldstein, *Ideas, Interests, and American Trade Policy* (Ithaca: Cornell University Press, 1993); and Henry R. Nau, *The Myth of America's Decline: Leading the World Economy into the 1990s* (New York: Oxford University Press, 1990).

43. Some recent examples include R. N. Anthony, *The Management Control Function* (Boston: Harvard Business School Press, 1988); Colin Eden and Jim Radford, *Tackling Strategic Problems: The Role of Group Decision Support* (London: Sage, 1990); William

Fox, *Effective Group Problem Solving* (San Francisco: Jossey-Bass, 1988); Carl E. Larson and Frank M. J. LaFasto, *Teamwork: What Must Go Right, What Can Go Wrong* (Newbury Park, California: Sage, 1989); Lloyd Williams, *The Congruence of People and Organizations* (Westport, Connecticut: Quorum Books, 1993); and Zander, *Making Groups Effective*.

44. Lasswell, *Politics: Who Gets What, When, How* (New York: Meridian, 1958), pp. 131–132.

CHAPTER 3. EISENHOWER AND REAGAN:
COMPARING LEARNING STYLES

1. Greenstein, "Ronald Reagan—Another Hidden-Hand Ike?" *PS: Political Science and Politics* 23, 1 (1990), pp. 7–13. Greenstein concludes, for some of the reasons discussed in this chapter, that Reagan is *not* another "hidden-hand Ike." See also Greenstein, *The Hidden-Hand Presidency: Eisenhower as Leader* (New York: Basic, 1982).

2. Dwight D. Eisenhower, *Mandate for Change: The White House Years, 1953–1956* (Garden City, New York: Doubleday, 1963), pp. 120 and 121.

3. Ronald W. Reagan, *An American Life* (New York: Simon & Schuster, 1990), p. 207.

4. Lowi, *Personal President*, ch. 1.

5. Reagan, *American Life*, p. 219.

6. The public mood, to which Eisenhower and Reagan responded so effectively, was at least partly the product of similar events in each case. Both Truman and Carter suffered from overseas entanglements (in Korea and in the Middle East, respectively) which contributed to a sense of American impotence and irresoluteness. Eisenhower and Reagan promised to do much more than replace inaction with action: they promised to restore American superiority. They promised unequivocal American leadership abroad and political, social, and even moral consensus at home. For a provocative statement of these points, grounded in a psychological interpretation of the "American psyche," see Lloyd deMause and Henry Ebel, eds., *Jimmy Carter and American Fantasy: Psychohistorical Explorations* (New York: Two Continents, 1977); and deMause, *Reagan's America* (New York: Creative Roots, 1984). See also Skowronek's discussion of cycles in political time

(Skowronek, "Presidential Leadership in Political Time") for analogous, but more modest claims, about Eisenhower's and Reagan's relationships with the American public.

7. Richard H. Immerman, Introduction, in Immerman, ed., *John Foster Dulles and the Diplomacy of the Cold War* (Princeton: Princeton University Press, 1990), p. 5.

8. Greenstein says that "Adams reputation as 'abominable no man' helped preserve Eisenhower's image as a benevolent national and international leader" (Greenstein, *Hidden-Hand Presidency*, p. 147).

9. The *lightning-rod effect* is Greenstein's term (see *Hidden-Hand Presidency*, p. 147).

10. Ibid., p. 53.

11. Quoted in Kenneth Thompson, "The Strengths and Weaknesses of Eisenhower's Leadership," in Richard Melanson and David Mayers, *Reevaluating Eisenhower: American Foreign Policy in the 1950s* (Urbana: University of Illinois Press, 1987), pp. 17 and 19.

12. Barber, *Presidential Character*, pp. 156–173. One wonders why such an individual would persist in a political career. Barber explains that the passive negative personality acts out of a sense of duty rather than out of genuine desire or inspiration. In Barber's view, Eisenhower thus "felt that he ought to serve, ought to contribute, ought to do what he could to make things better for America. But one senses in their (the passive-negative type's) attitude an assumption that merely occupying the office of President provided justification enough, and that all expenditures of energy beyond that point were extra, not required" (p. 172).

13. Peter Lyon, *Eisenhower: Portrait of the Hero* (Boston: Little, Brown, 1974), p. 40.

14. Quoted in Thompson, "Strengths and Weaknesses of Eisenhower's Leadership," p. 16; see also Arthur Larson, "Eisenhower's World View," in Kenneth Thompson, ed., *The Eisenhower Presidency: Eleven Intimate Perspectives of Dwight D. Eisenhower* (Lanham, Maryland: University Press of America, 1984), pp. 42–44.

15. Paul S. Holbo and Robert W. Sellen, eds., *The Eisenhower Era: The Age of Consensus* (Hinsdale, Illinois: Dryden Press, 1974), p. 1.

16. Holbo and Sellen, *Eisenhower Era*, p. 2. See also Patrick Anderson, *The President's Men* (Garden City, New York: Doubleday, 1968). From Anderson's perspective, Eisenhower's inatten-

tiveness to the important social problems of the 1950s was tragic. As he puts it, "the misfortune of Eisenhower's Presidency is that a man of such immense popularity and good will did not accomplish more. All the domestic problems which confronted the nation in the 1960s—the unrest of the Negro, the decay of the cities, the mediocrity of the schools, the permanence of poverty—were bubbling beneath the surface in the 1950s, but the President never seemed quite sure that they existed or, if they did, that they were problems with which he should not concern himself" (quoted in Barber, *Presidential Character*, p. 140).

17. See Stephen E. Ambrose, *Eisenhower: The President*, vol. 2 (New York: Simon & Schuster, 1984), pp. 55–76, 152–153, 160–168, 487–488, and 644–645.

18. Max Lerner, "The Big Mangling Machine," *Chicago Sun-Times*, June 26, 1971, quoted in Holbo and Sellen, *Eisenhower Era*, p. 10.

19. As Barber puts it, "to [Eisenhower's] natural disinclination to be 'bothered' was added, as a result of extreme delegations, his staff's disinclination to 'bother' him. 'But the less he was bothered,' as Richard Neustadt noted, 'the less he knew, and the less he knew, the less confidence he felt in his own judgment. He let himself grow stale'—and thus all the more dependent on his advisors" (Barber, *Presidential Character*, p. 140). See also William B. Ewald's account of Eisenhower's student exchange plan (which Dulles opposed) in Ewald, *Eisenhower the President: Crucial Days, 1951–1960* (Englewood Cliffs, New Jersey: Prentice-Hall, 1981), pp. 213–216.

20. Dwight D. Eisenhower, *At Ease: Stories I Tell to Friends* (Garden City, New York: Doubleday, 1967), p. 168.

21. In a March 16, 1955 press conference, Eisenhower responded to a question about whether the United States would use nuclear weapons in the Far East by saying: "In any combat where those things can be used on strictly military targets and for strictly military purposes, I see no reason why they shouldn't be used just exactly as you would use a bullet or anything else" (quoted in Ambrose, *Eisenhower*, vol. 2, p. 239).

22. Robert A. Divine, *Eisenhower and the Cold War* (New York: Oxford University Press, 1981), pp. 65–66.

23. Ambrose, *Eisenhower*, vol. 2, p. 245.

24. Barber, *Presidential Character*, p. 157.

25. Eisenhower, *At Ease*, pp. 37–38.

26. Ibid., p. 39.

27. Ambrose, *Eisenhower: Soldier, General of the Army, President-Elect, 1890–1952* (New York: Simon & Schuster, 1983), vol. 1, p. 22. Ambrose cites Kenneth S. Davis, *Soldier of Democracy: A Biography of Dwight Eisenhower* (Garden City, New York: Doubleday, Doran, 1945), pp. 67–68.

28. Eisenhower, *At Ease*, p. 39.

29. Ambrose writes,

the central importance of sports, hunting, and fishing to young Eisenhower cannot be overemphasized. He literally could not imagine life without them, as shown by the most dramatic incident of his childhood. During his freshman year, he fell and scraped his knee. . . . Infection set in, . . . [and eventually the] doctors agreed that only amputation would save his life. During one of his conscious moments, Dwight heard his parents discussing amputation. They distrusted surgery, but the doctors insisted on it. Fourteen-year-old Dwight listened, then said, quietly but firmly, "You are never going to cut that leg off." By this time the infection had reached his groin and his periods of consciousness were few and short. He called in Edgar and said, "Look, Ed, they are talking about taking my leg off. I want you to see that they do not do it, because I would rather die than to lose my leg. . . ." At the end of the second week, the poison began to recede. (Ambrose, *Eisenhower,* vol. 1, pp. 35–36)

30. Ibid., p. 49.

31. Ibid.

32. Ibid., p. 50. Ambrose cites Lyon, *Eisenhower,* p. 45; Eisenhower, *At Ease*, p. 16; and Davis, *Soldier of Democracy*, p. 140.

33. See, inter alia, Ambrose's extensive work, including *Eisenhower* (vols. 1 and 2), and *The Supreme Commander: The War Years of General Dwight D. Eisenhower* (New York: Doubleday, 1970); also Greenstein, *Hidden-Hand Presidency;* and Lyon, *Eisenhower.* As Lyon puts it, "Growing up in this small town (Abilene), in this farming country, had bred in him an ample self confidence and a readiness to assume responsibility. He was sure of himself and of what he could do" (p. 41).

34. Eisenhower learned this lesson so well, as Ambrose notes, that during his career in high school and college athletics, he routinely blamed himself for his team's defeats; see Ambrose, *Eisenhower,* vol. 1, p. 34.

35. See Rotter, "Generalized Expectancies for Internal versus External Control of Reinforcement," p. 24.

36. Chapter 4 will provide further evidence for this assertion. See also Greenstein, "Eisenhower as an Activist President: A Look at New Evidence," *Political Science Quarterly* 94 (1979–1980), pp. 575–599; and Immerman, "Eisenhower and Dulles: Who Made the Decisions?" *Political Psychology* 1, 2 (1979), pp. 21–38.

37. Lyon, *Eisenhower*, p. 38.

38. Ambrose, *Eisenhower*, vol. 1, p. 42.

39. Hazlett, quoted in ibid., p. 51.

40. Ambrose, *Eisenhower*, vol. 1, p. 57.

41. Divine, *Eisenhower and the Cold War*, p. 10.

42. Ambrose, *Eisenhower*, vol. 1, p. 539.

43. See Greenstein, *Hidden-Hand Presidency*; Greenstein, "Eisenhower as an Activist President"; Immerman, "Eisenhower and Dulles"; and Kenneth Kitts and Betty Glad, "Presidential Personality and Improvisational Decision Making: Eisenhower and the 1956 Hungarian Crisis," in Shirley Anne Warshaw, ed., *Reexamining the Eisenhower Presidency* (Westport, Connecticut: Greenwood, 1993), pp. 183–208.

44. Dean Keith Simonton, "Presidential Personality: Biographical Use of the Gough Adjective Check List," *Journal of Personality and Social Psychology* 51 (1986), pp. 149–160. More precisely, Eisenhower's scores were high on "friendliness" and low on "*inflexibility*."

45. Lloyd S. Etheredge, "Personality Effects on American Foreign Policy, 1898 1968: A Test of Interpersonal Generalization Theory," *American Political Science Review* 72 (1978), pp. 434–451.

46. Kowert, "Where *Does* the Buck Stop?"; Kowert, "Between Reason and Passion: A Systems Theory of Foreign Policy Learning" (Ph. D. diss., Cornell University, 1992); and Kowert and Daryl J. Bem, "Assessing the Personality of Public Figures: Profiles of Six Postwar American Presidents," forthcoming.

47. Smith, quoted in Greenstein, *Hidden-Hand Presidency*, p. 34.

48. Ambrose, *Eisenhower*, vol. 1, p. 29.

49. Ewald, *Eisenhower the President*, p. 73.

50. Ewald, *Eisenhower the President*, p. 63.

51. Eisenhower, *Mandate for Change*, p. 114.

52. On the military value of an efficient organization, Eisenhower once remarked that "no man can be a Napoleon in modern

war" (Ambrose, *Eisenhower*, vol. 2, p. 19). In another of his memoirs, *Crusade in Europe* (Garden City, New York: Doubleday, 1948), Eisenhower added that "the teams and staff through which the modern commander absorbs information and exercises his authority must be a beautifully, interlocked, smooth working mechanism *[sic],*" quoted by Bradley H. Patterson, "An Overview of the White House," in Thompson, *Eisenhower Presidency*, p. 122.

53. Truman, quoted in Richard Neustadt, *Presidential Power: The Politics of Leadership* (New York: Wiley, 1960), p. 9, emphasis in original. For his part, Eisenhower did not hold Truman's leadership style in particularly high regard either. "It was inconceivable to me," Eisenhower wrote, "that the work of the White House could not be better systemized" (Eisenhower, *Mandate for Change*, p. 87).

54. Letter to Swede Hazlett, July 21, 1953, in Dwight D. Eisenhower Presidential Library, Dwight D. Eisenhower's Papers as President (Ann Whitman File), DDE Diary Series, Box 3. Henceforth cited as "Whitman File."

Ann Whitman records in her diary that Eisenhower "used to correspond with him (Hazlett) more frankly than any other individual." See Whitman's diary entry for November 5, 1958, Whitman File, Ann C. Whitman Diary Series, Box 10.

55. Letter to Swede Hazlett, July 21, 1953, Whitman File, DDE Diary Series, Box 3.

56. Ambrose, *Eisenhower*, vol. 2, pp. 79–80; Ambrose cites Arthur Minnich's (administrative assistant for general correspondence) handwritten Cabinet notes for May 29, 1953. For another example of Eisenhower's deference to his aides, see Ewald's account (Ewald, *Eisenhower the President*, pp. 60–63) of the decision to delete a politically charged paragraph about George Marshall from a campaign speech to be delivered in Milwaukee in 1952. Eisenhower's inclination was to leave the paragraph in, but he accepted Sherman Adams's advice that the paragraph was "out of place." The paragraph was leaked to the press, however, and proved an embarrassment.

57. Ewald, *Eisenhower the President*, p. 219, see also pp. 63–73.

58. Immerman, ed., *John Foster Dulles and the Diplomacy of the Cold War*, p. 17. For an extended discussion of Dulles's background and his preparation for the office of secretary of state, see Ronald Pruessen, *John Foster Dulles: The Road to Power* (New York: Free Press, 1982).

59. Eisenhower diary entry for January 10, 1956, Whitman File, DDE Diary Series, Box 9. This diary entry is reproduced in Robert H. Ferrell, *The Eisenhower Diaries* (New York: Norton, 1981), pp. 305–307. Also see Ewald's account ("A Biographer's Perspective," in Thompson, *Eisenhower Presidency*, pp. 33–34) of Eisenhower's respect for Dulles.

60. Eisenhower, *Mandate for Change*, p. 142.

61. Greenstein, *Hidden-Hand Presidency*, p. 120.

62. Eisenhower diary entry for May 14, 1953, Whitman File, DDE Diary Series, Box 9; also Ferrell, *Eisenhower Diaries*, pp. 236–240.

63. Karl G. Harr, "Eisenhower's Approach to National Security Decisionmaking," in Thompson, *Eisenhower Presidency*, p. 105.

64. Hess, *Organizing the Presidency*, p. 60.

65. Eisenhower diary entry for May 14, 1953, Whitman File, DDE Diary Series, Box 9; also Ferrell, *Eisenhower Diaries*, pp. 236–240.

66. For other general discussions of President Eisenhower's advisors, see Andrew Goodpaster, "Organizing the White House," in Thompson, *Eisenhower Presidency*, pp. 63–87; Greenstein, *Hidden-Hand Presidency*, pp. 100–151; and Bradley H. Patterson, "Eisenhower's Innovations in White House Staff Structure and Operations," in Warshaw, *Reexamining the Eisenhower Presidency*, pp. 33–56.

67. Adams was commonly perceived, during the years Eisenhower was in office, as "an all-powerful gatekeeper who controlled the flow of information and recommendations to the president, and forwarded to him merely for ratification, consensus policy recommendations" (Greenstein, *Hidden-Hand Presidency*, p. 144). See also Marian D. Irish, "The Organizational Man in the Presidency," *Journal of Politics* 20 (1958), p. 269; and "O.K., S.A.," *Time*, January 9, 1956, pp. 18–22.

68. See, for example, Hess, *Organizing the Presidency*, pp. 65–67; and Patterson, "Overview of the White House."

69. Patterson, "Overview of the White House," p. 129. From the beginning of his presidency, Eisenhower used the Cabinet as an arena for debate. To this end, he held an average of thirty-four Cabinet meetings each year (Greenstein, *Hidden Hand Presidency*, p. 113).

70. Patterson, "Overview of the White House," pp. 127–128.

71. Ibid., p. 123.

72. Hess, *Organizing the Presidency*, p. 68.

73. Ibid., p. 68. Kennedy was evidently unmoved by this statement and, after becoming president, moved to strip away much of what he regarded as the excessively rigid bureaucratic structure Eisenhower had imposed on the White House. Kennedy thus relied far less on formal advisory arrangements such as the NSC.

74. NSC meetings were often attended by more than thirty individuals, including both statutory NSC members and others present to discuss particular items on the agenda (see Hess, *Organizing the Presidency*, pp. 68–69).

75. Goodpaster, "Organizing the White House," in Thompson, *Eisenhower Presidency*, pp. 78 and 80.

76. Hess, *Organizing the Presidency*, p. 56.

77. Ewald, *Eisenhower the President*, p. 65.

78. Ibid.

79. The third chapter of Arthur Larson's White House memoirs, entitled "Eisenhower and Politics," gives a good account of the president's views on party politics; see Larson, *Eisenhower*, pp. 34–53.

80. On Eisenhower's assessment of his own foreign policy expertise, see Emmet John Hughes, *The Ordeal of Power: A Political Memoir of the Eisenhower Years* (New York: Atheneum, 1963), p. 251.

81. Eisenhower, *Mandate for Change*, p . 115.

82. Bob Schieffer and Gary Paul Gates, *The Acting President* (New York: Dutton, 1989), p. 169.

83. Jane Mayer and Doyle McManus, *Landslide: The Unmaking of the President, 1984–1988* (New York: Houghton Mifflin, 1988), p. 27.

84. Donald T. Regan, *For the Record: From Wall Street to Washington* (New York: St. Martin's, 1988), p. 299.

85. Ibid., p. 305.

86. Martin Anderson, *Revolution: The Reagan Legacy* (Stanford, Connecticut: Hoover Institution Press, 1990), pp. xl and xli.

87. Lou Cannon, *Reagan* (New York: Perigee, 1982), p. 26.

88. Reagan, *American Life*, p. 34, see also p. 25. And see Reagan, *Where's the Rest of Me?* (New York: Karz Publishers, 1981), pp. 9 and 11.

89. Gail Sheehy, *Character: America's Search for Leadership* (New York: Bantam, 1990), p. 238.

90. Cannon, *Reagan*, p. 28.

91. Sheehy, *Character*, p. 238.

92. Reagan, *American Life*, p. 35.

93. DeMause, *Reagan's America*, p. 39. See also Frank van der Linden, *The Real Reagan* (New York: William, Morrow, 1981), p. 38.

94. Cannon, *President Reagan: The Role of a Lifetime* (New York: Simon & Schuster, 1991), p. 401. Cannon also notes that "relatively few studies have focused on the experiences of successful children of alcoholics" (p. 210). But at least one which does finds, among other things, that such children tend to have an internal locus of control. See Emmy E. Werner, "Resilient Offspring of Alcoholics: A Longitudinal Study from Birth to Age 18," *Journal of Studies on Alcohol* 44 (1986), pp. 34–40.

95. Reagan, *American Life*, p. 57. At the risk of engaging in "armchair psychoanalysis," it is difficult to ignore Reagan's apparent desire, expressed in this statement, to be "someone else."

96. In two chapters of *President Reagan*, entitled "The Acting Politician" and "The Acting President," Cannon offers an extended discussion of Reagan's reliance on Hollywood "scripts," even as president. See Cannon, *President Reagan*, pp. 37–64. See also Schieffer and Gates, *Acting President*.

97. Reagan, *American Life*, p. 28, see also pp. 57 and 123.

98. Michael K. Deaver, with Mickey Herskowitz, *Behind the Scenes* (New York: Morrow, 1987), p. 35. Deaver goes on to say that Reagan believed in ghosts and that "he reads his horoscope every day" (pp. 35 and 106). On Reagan's belief in fate and luck, see also Bill Boyarsky, *The Rise of Ronald Reagan* (New York: Random House, 1968), pp. 13–14; and Francis FitzGerald, "A Critic at Large: Memoirs of the Reagan Era," *New Yorker*, January 16, 1989, p. 91.

99. Cannon, *President Reagan*, p. 593. Cannon (pp. 287–293) also describes Reagan's interest in mysticism and Armageddon.

100. Boyarsky, *Rise of Ronald Reagan*, p. 14; and Cannon, *President Reagan*, pp. 583–584. On Reagan and magic, see Sidney Blumenthal, *Our Long National Daydream: A Political Pageant of the Reagan Era* (New York: Harper & Row, 1988), pp. 307–310. Even "Reagan's view of history," according to Clifford Geertz, "was mythological from day one" (Geertz, quoted in Blumenthal, *Our Long National Daydream*, p. 307). Nancy Reagan's consultations with an astrologer (Joan Quigley) were revealed by Donald Regan in his memoirs; see Regan, *For the Record*, esp. pp. 81–83, 400, and 409–410.

101. Cannon, *President Reagan*, pp. 32 and 33, see also pp. 172–174.

102. Nancy Reagan, with William Novak, *My Turn: The Memoirs of Nancy Reagan* (New York: Random House, 1989), p. 106.

103. Schieffer and Gates, *Acting President*, p. 59.

104. Cannon, *President Reagan*, p. 172. Cannon also points out that "Reagan's children are unanimous in testifying to their father's difficulty in dealing with closeness" (p. 229).

105. Nancy Reagan, *My Turn*, p. 106.

106. Reagan, *American Life,* p. 31.

107. See, for example, chs. 10 and 11 of Cannon's *President Reagan,* pp. 172 and 231, entitled "Passive President" and "The Loner," respectively.

108. Ibid., p. 135.

109. Ibid., p. 181.

110. Simonton, "Presidential Personality," p. 154.

111. Kowert, "Where *Does* the Buck Stop?"; see table 11. The Q-sort is a method of observer rating widely used in the study of personality trait psychology.

112. Cannon, *President Reagan,* p. 32.

113. Blumenthal, *Our Long National Daydream,* p. 5.

114. Ibid., p. 7.

115. Cannon, *Reagan*, p. 376.

116. Bert A. Rockman, "The Style and Organization of the Reagan Presidency," in Charles O. Jones, ed., *The Reagan Legacy: Promise and Performance* (Chatham, New Jersey: Chatham House, 1988), p. 8.

117. See also Richard Neustadt, *Presidential Power and the Modern Presidents* (New York: Free Press, 1990), pp. 269–294. Neustadt finds Reagan's combination of personal withdrawal and political activism unique and observes that "he seems to have combined less intellectual curiosity, less interest in detail, than any President at least since Calvin Coolidge—about whom I remain unsure—with more initial and sustained commitments, more convictions independent of events or evidence, than any President at least since Woodrow Wilson championed the League. And if those separate attributes are each unusual, their combination seems to be unique" (p. 270).

118. See Richard P. Nathan, *The Administrative Presidency* (New York: Macmillan, 1986), pp. 69–93. This view was common in the popular press—at least until the Iran-Contra affair—as well.

See, for example, George J. Church, "The President's Men," *Time*, December 14, 1981, pp. 16–22; interview with Erwin C. Hargrove, "Reagan Understands How to Be President," *U.S. News & World Report*, April 27, 1981, pp. 23–24; and Robert A. Kittle, "After 3 Months: Report Card on Reagan," *U.S. News & World Report*, April 27, 1981, pp. 20–22.

119. On Carter's penchant for detail, see inter alia Colin Campbell, *Managing the Presidency: Carter, Reagan, and the Search for Executive Harmony* (Pittsburgh: University of Pittsburgh Press, 1986), pp. 58–67; and Neustadt, *Presidential Power and the Modern Presidents*, pp. 230–243. For a critical discussion of Carter's decision making process and his ability to seek out and benefit from diverse opinions, see Alexander Moens, *Foreign Policy Under Carter: Testing Multiple Advocacy Decision Making* (Boulder, Colorado: Westview, 1990).

120. Cannon, *Reagan*, p. 375.

121. Neustadt, *Presidential Power and the Modern Presidents*, p. 276.

122. Rockman, "Style and Organization of the Reagan Presidency," p. 9.

123. Cannon, *Reagan*, pp. 371–401; Nathan, *Administrative Presidency*; and "A Disengaged Presidency," *Newsweek*, September 7, 1981, pp. 21–23.

124. Whereas revelations about the banking practices of Carter's budget director, Bert Lance, did considerable damage to the Carter presidency, a long series of similar scandals seemed to have little impact on public perceptions of the Reagan administration. Among those who faced ethics charges were Lyn Nofziger (assistant to the president for political affairs), who was convicted in 1988 of illegal lobbying on behalf of defense contractors (including the Wedtech Corporation); Michael Deaver (White House deputy chief of staff), who was convicted in 1987 of lying to Congress and to a federal grand jury about his own lobbying activities; Paul Thayer (deputy secretary of defense), who was found guilty of obstructing justice by giving false testimony about insider trading; Rita Lavell (assistant administrator of the Environmental Protection Agency), who was convicted in 1984 of lying to Congress; Richard Allen (national security advisor), who left the administration amid allegations he had illegally accepted one thousand dollars from Japanese businessmen; and, finally, Ed Meese (counselor to the president and, later, attorney general), who was inves-

tigated but never convicted for several cases of ethics violations, including the Wedtech scandal. For a discussion of these cases and several others, see Ronnie Dugger, *On Reagan: The Man & His Presidency* (New York: McGraw-Hill, 1983), pp. 25–42.

125. Ronald Reagan, televised address, March 4, 1987; for transcript, see the *Los Angeles Times*, March 5, 1987.

126. John H. Kessel, "The Structures of the Reagan White House," *American Journal of Political Science* 28 (1984), pp. 231–258; and Kessel, "The Structures of the Carter White House," *American Journal of Political Science* 27 (1983), pp. 431–463. For a similar conclusion, see Dugger, *On Reagan*, esp. the chapter entitled "The Board of Directors of the United States," pp. 25–42; and Rockman, "Style and Organization of the Reagan Presidency," pp. 9–10.

127. Cannon, *Reagan,* p. 376. Or, as Rockman has put it, "more than any other administration, . . . many individuals who composed this one were loyal to the ideas for which Ronald Reagan stood" (Rockman, "Style and Organization of the Reagan Presidency," p. 24).

128. Reagan's closed advisors internalized his perspective to a remarkable extent. According to Cannon, for example, "over the years [Michael] Deaver had come to think in terms of the Reagans rather than in terms of Mike Deaver" (Cannon, *Reagan,* p. 378). Similarly, rather than acting as the independent critic and "counselor" that his job title implied, Edwin Meese "was Reagan's geographer. He drew maps to accomplish Reagan's purposes rather than his own and knew how to chart a course to reach the President's destination" (p. 381).

129. See Schieffer and Gates, *Acting President* (p. 83), for a reproduction of the one-page document, dated November 13, 1980, in which Baker outlined his own duties and those of Meese.

130. Cannon, *Reagan,* p. 376.

131. Ibid., p. 382. Of course, one can overstate the degree of unanimity among Reagan's advisors. Even the triumvirate occasionally disagreed, despite the efforts of all three men to achieve consensus (efforts that included a regularly scheduled breakfast together every working day). Deaver evidently had a low opinion of Meese; and Meese, in turn, resented Baker's appointment as chief of staff, the job he expected to receive. See Schieffer and Gates, *Acting President,* pp. 77–86.

132. Regan, *For the Record,* p. 262.

133. Perhaps Reagan's national security advisors played such a limited advisory role because none of them remained in office for very long. Altogether, Reagan had six national security advisors: Richard Allen, William Clark, Robert McFarlane, John Poindexter, Frank Carlucci, and Colin Powell.

134. Cannon, *President Reagan,* p. 341.

135. Ibid., p. 340.

136. During the Reagan administration, the position of director of the CIA was elevated to Cabinet rank.

137. Dugger, *On Reagan,* p. 35.

138. Neustadt, *Presidential Power and the Modern Presidents,* p. 313.

139. Ibid., p. 273. See also Cannon's discussion of Reagan's reaction to dissent among his advisors during his presidential campaign in November 1979 (Cannon, *Reagan,* pp. 237–240).

140. For a good account of the purge of the PFIAB, see Martin Anderson, *Revolution,* pp. 352–369.

141. Ibid., p. 268. According to Anderson, Regan "brooded about those private economic advisers poaching on his policy turf. Even though he admitted that they were useful, that they provided a fresh point of view, he now seemed to feel they were no longer needed. . . . Regan evidently decided to tidy up the policy advisory structure" (pp. 269–270).

142. Dwight D. Eisenhower, June 4, 1952, from a speech marking the laying of the cornerstone for the Eisenhower Museum in Abilene, Kansas; quoted in Ambrose, *Eisenhower,* vol. 1, p. 19.

143. Reagan, *American Life,* p. 28.

144. The originally low estimates of Eisenhower's intelligence were perhaps unduly biased by his notoriously sloppy syntax during press conferences. Yet even a passing acquaintance with the archival record of his personal correspondence, and the minutes of White House meetings, makes a low estimate difficult to credit. Some close associates make similar claims about President Reagan. For a good extended discussion of Reagan's intelligence, see Cannon, *President Reagan,* pp. 131–140.

145. Deaver, *Behind the Scenes,* p. 44.

146. It also helps to avoid confusion stemming from the multiplicity of approaches to studying personality. Gordon Allport once counted no fewer than fifty different *types* of personality definitions. No doubt, among them is something for everyone. But the more expansive a given approach—the wider the array of charac-

ter traits it examines—the more likely it is to encounter both similarities and differences in every comparison of subjects, and thus to fail at explanation or prediction. See Gordon Allport, *Personality: A Psychological Interpretation* (New York: Holt, 1937), pp. 24–54.

CHAPTER 4. LEARNING

1. A. J. P. Taylor, *From Napoleon to Lenin* (New York: Harper & Row, 1966), p. 64; cited in Jervis, *Perception and Misperception in International Politics*, p. 217. See also Vertzberger, "Foreign Policy Decisionmakers as Practical-intuitive Historians."

2. Studies of the "cognitive complexity" of national leaders' spoken and written statements suggest that these pronouncements are rarely complex. Evidence of presidential learning that deepens cognitive complexity is thus a significant finding. See Peter Suedfeld and Philip Tetlock, "Integrative Complexity of Communications in International Crises," *Journal of Conflict Resolution* 21 (1977), pp. 169–184; Tetlock, "Integrative Complexity of American and Soviet Foreign Policy Rhetoric: A Time-Series Analysis," *Journal of Personality and Social Psychology* 49, 6 (1985), pp. 1565–1585; and Tetlock, "Monitoring the Integrative Complexity of American and Soviet Policy Rhetoric: What Can Be Learned?" *Journal of Social Issues* 44, 2 (1988), pp. 101–131. Suedfeld and Tetlock's definition of integrative complexity requires evidence both of *distinction* or nuance (as opposed to black-and-white thinking) and also of *integration*—that is, the recognition of complex relationships among mental distinctions.

3. Holbo and Sellen, *Eisenhower Era*.

4. Daniel Boorstin, *The Genius of American Politics* (Chicago: University of Chicago Press, 1953), p. 3; quoted in Holbo and Sellen, *Eisenhower Era*, p. 9.

5. John Patrick Diggins, *The Proud Decades: America in War and in Peace, 1941–1960* (New York: Norton, 1988).

6. A good account of the Eisenhower administration's anti-communist activities in Central America is Richard Immerman's *The CIA in Guatemala: The Foreign Policy of Intervention* (Austin: University of Texas Press, 1982). For a discussion of foreign aid policies designed to limit the spread of communism, see Burton Kaufman, *Trade and Aid: Eisenhower's Foreign Economic Policy*

1953–1961 (Baltimore: Johns Hopkins University Press, 1982); and on the contributions of ideology to the cold war, see Deborah Larson, *Origins of Containment* (Princeton: Princeton University Press, 1985).

7. John Foster Dulles, notes from a meeting on board the *U.S.S. Helena,* December 10, 1952, quoted in Ambrose, *Eisenhower,* vol. 2, p. 173.

8. For a good summary of American interests in Indochina at the time, see Immerman, "Prologue: Perceptions by the United States of its Interests in Indochina," in Lawrence S. Kaplan, Denise Artaud, and Mark R. Rubin, *Dien Bien Phu and the Crisis of Franco-American Relations, 1954–1955* (Wilmington, Delaware: Scholarly Resources Books, 1990), pp. 1–26.

9. Telegram from Dulles to Eisenhower, February 6, 1954, Whitman File, Dulles-Herter Series, Box 2.

10. Message from Dulles to Eisenhower, April 23, 1954, Whitman File, DDE Diary Series, Box 6.

11. Denise Artaud, "France Between the Indochina War and the European Defense Community," in Kaplan, Artaud, and Rubin, *Dien Bien Phu and the Crisis of Franco-American Relations,* pp. 251–268.

12. George McT. Kahin, *Intervention: How America Became Involved in Vietnam* (New York: Knopf, 1986), p. 42.

13. Divine, *Eisenhower and the Cold War,* p. 39.

14. See memorandum of discussion, 179th meeting of the National Security Council, January 8, 1954, in *Foreign Relations of the United States, 1952–1954,* vol. 13, pt. 1 (Washington, D.C.: U.S. Government Printing Office, 1982), pp. 947–954; henceforth referred to as "*FRUS 1952–1954.*"

15. Memorandum of discussion, 179th meeting of the National Security Council, January 8, 1954, in *FRUS 1952–1954,* vol. 13, pt. 1, pp. 952 and 953. Earlier in the same meeting, Eisenhower observed "that if any of our people were to get into this jungle fighting, they should certainly be given the proximity fuse or VT fuse bombs, not just ordinary bombs" (p. 952). Although he was hesitant on this point, Eisenhower thus considered even the possibility of using ground troops to assist the French.

16. The prospect of this "limited intervention"—and, indeed, the existence of the Special Committee—produced a storm of controversy among those members of Congress who felt the president was secretly planning for war and that he had exceeded his authority in not consulting them *before* arranging to send Ameri-

can military personnel to Indochina. Eisenhower attempted to mollify congressional leaders during a series of February meetings in which he defended his actions but assured them that he would not commit the United States to war without congressional approval. At one of these meetings, he nevertheless asserted, "Don't think I like to send them there, but . . . we can't get anywhere in Asia by just sitting here in Washington and doing nothing—My God, we must not lose Asia—we've got to look the thing right in the face" (notes from Legislative Leaders meeting, February 8, 1954, James C. Hagerty Papers, 1953–61, Diary Entries Series, Box 1, Eisenhower Presidential Library; henceforth referred to as "Hagerty Papers").

17. Dulles was not opposed to intervention in principal. As Melanie Billings-Yun explains,

> the secretary of state thought that the situation and mood [of despair in France] actually might act to Washington's advantage. Navarre's and Laniel's deep desire to avoid a humiliating defeat could provide the grease that finally would enable the US to push through its demands for Indochinese independence and an American role in planning strategy and training troops. . . . In other words, the secretary of state argued *for* intervention by the United States into the French-Indochina War and for making the *conditional* offer to Laniel at once; he opposed only *immediate, unqualified action* to save Dien Bien Phu.

See Melanie Billings-Yun, *Decision Against War: Eisenhower and Dien Bien Phu, 1954* (New York: Columbia University Press, 1988), pp. 58 and 59, emphasis in original.

18. Memorandum for the Record, January 30, 1954, Meeting of the President's Special Committee on Indochina, in United States Department of Defense, *United States-Vietnam Relations, 1945–1967* (Washington, D.C.: U.S. Government Printing Office, 1971), vol. 9, p. 241; this is the ninth of twelve volumes of a Defense Department study prepared for the House Committee on Armed Services, commonly referred to as the "Pentagon Papers."

19. "Top Secret timetable," John F. Dulles Papers, 1951–59, Subject Series, Box 8, Eisenhower Presidential Library; henceforth referred to as "Dulles Papers." The timetable is undated but was apparently written during General Ely's trip to Washington between March 20, 1954, and March 26, 1954.

20. James Hagerty's diary, April 1, 1954, Hagerty Papers, Diary Entries Series, Box 1.

21. Dwight D. Eisenhower, telegram to Winston Churchill, April 4, 1954, *FRUS 1952–1954*, vol. 13, pt. 1, pp. 1238–1241.

22. Sherman Adams, *Firsthand Report* (New York: Harper, 1961), p. 122. According to Adams, the principle "conditions" were British participation and French commitment to continue to fight.

23. Dulles, "The Threat of a Red Asia," speech on March 29, 1954, quoted in Billings-Yun, *Decision Against War*, p. 62.

24. Richard M. Nixon, *RN: The Memoirs of Richard Nixon* (New York: Grosset and Dunlap, 1978), pp. 152–153, quoted in Ambrose, *Eisenhower*, vol. 2, p. 180.

25. Divine, *Eisenhower and the Cold War*, p. 48.

26. Cyrus Sulzberger, *Seven Continents and Forty Years* (New York: New York Times Books, 1977), quoted in Divine, *Eisenhower and the Cold War*, p. 48.

27. Although General Paul Ély was convinced that the United States would come to the rescue of French forces, Radford later insisted that he had made no promises. Nevertheless, it was clear during their meetings in Washington that Radford favored U.S. intervention. According to Ély, Operation Vulture was Radford's idea ("L'initiative de ce project vint de l'amiral Radford."); see Ély, *Mémoirs: L'Indochine dans la Tourmente* (Paris: Librarie Plon, 1964), p. 77. As Billings-Yun quite reasonably concludes, "one cannot entirely blame this misunderstanding on Ély's rattled nerves or his translator's skills. Radford had given a number of broad hints that Eisenhower would back an intervention plan" (Billings-Yun, *Decision Against War*, p. 50). For another good account of the inception and development of Operation Vulture, see John Prados, *The Sky Would Fall: Operation Vulture: The U.S. Bombing Mission in Indochina, 1954* (New York: Dial Press, 1983).

28. Ambrose, *Eisenhower*, vol. 2, p. 179. See also transcript of telephone conversation between Dulles and Eisenhower, April 5, 1954, Dulles Papers, Telephone Calls Series, Box 10.

29. Eisenhower, telephone conversation, April 5, 1954, Ann Whitman Diary Series, Eisenhower Presidential Library, quoted in Ambrose, *Eisenhower*, vol. 2, p. 197.

30. Dulles's telegram to Ambassador Dillon makes it clear that the administration had not *ruled out* American military intervention, but was simply not ready to undertake it. Dulles suggested in his message that the "military may recommend [an] alternative offer of light planes which can be flown off [of a] French carrier."

See Dulles, telegram to the American Embassy in Paris, April 6, 1954, Dulles Papers, JFD Chronological Series, Box 7.

31. Nathan Twining, Interview, Dulles Oral History Project, Princeton, quoted in Walter LaFeber, *America, Russia, and the Cold War: 1945–1971* (New York: Wiley, 1972), p. 161.

32. A. C. Davis, quoted in Divine, *Eisenhower and the Cold War,* p. 50.

33. Billings-Yun, *Decision Against War,* p. 56.

34. Divine, *Eisenhower and the Cold War,* p. 49; Divine quotes Matthew Ridgway, *Soldier* (New York: Harper, 1956), p. 277. Reflecting later on his recommendation against intervention at Dien Bien Phu, Ridgway wrote, "When the day comes for me to face my Maker and account for my actions, the thing I would be most humbly proud of was the fact that I fought against, and perhaps contributed to preventing, the carrying out of some harebrained tactical schemes which would have cost the lives of some thousands of men. To that list of tragic accidents that fortunately never happened I would add the Indochina intervention" (Ridgway, *Soldier,* p. 278).

35. See Billings-Yun, *Decision Against War,* p. 71.

36. On Humphrey's opposition to Operation Vulture, see Charles Reverdan Scribner, "The Eisenhower and Johnson Administrations' Decisionmaking on Vietnamese Intervention: A Study of Contrasts" (Ph. D. diss., University of California at Santa Barbara, June 1980), pp. 144–145. Also see Humphrey's remarks during the National Security Council meeting on January 8, 1954, in *FRUS 1952–1954,* vol. 13, pt. 1, pp. 947–956, for an indication of his views in the months leading up to the Dien Bien Phu crisis.

37. LaFeber, *America, Russia, and the Cold War,* p. 140.

38. "Memorandum for the Secretary's File," April 5, 1954, Dulles Papers, JFD Chronological Series, Box 7. For a draft of the proposed congressional Joint Resolution, see the Dulles Papers, Subject Series, Box 8. And for another account of this meeting, see LaFeber, *America, Russia, and the Cold War,* pp. 161–162.

39. Geoffrey Warner, "Britain and the Crisis over Dien Bien Phu, April 1954: The Failure of United Action," in Kaplan, Artaud, and Rubin, *Dien Bien Phu and the Crisis of Franco-American Relations,* p. 68, see pp. 55–77 for an extended discussion of the British position on Southeast Asia during this period.

40. Dwight D. Eisenhower, telegram to Dulles, April 23, 1954, Whitman File, Dulles-Herter Series, Box 2. Dulles was in Paris at the time, from whence he reported that the French foreign minis-

ter Georges Bidault "gives the impression of a man close to the breaking point" and that Dien Bien Phu had become "a tremendously emotional thing, and people are no (repeat no) longer capable of reasoning about it"; see John F. Dulles, telegrams to Eisenhower, April 23, 1954, 3:09 P.M. and 6:25 P.M., Whitman File, Dulles-Herter Series, Box 2.

41. Ambrose, *Eisenhower*, vol. 2, p. 181.

42. LaFeber, *America, Russia, and the Cold War*, p. 162.

43. Harold Stassen, from Richard Nixon's notes at the meeting, in Nixon, *RN*, pp. 153–154, quoted in Ambrose, *Eisenhower*, vol. 2, p. 184. Stassen persisted in this view until the fall of Dien Bien Phu. He argued forcefully, in a letter to Dulles, that the administration "should now take the ultimate policy decision that we will not permit the complete fall of Indo-China." He added, "This, of course, means a decision that we will, if necessary, use U.S. combat forces to prevent the complete fall, and the authorization should be obtained from Congress for the Commander-in-Chief to use U.S. combat forces"; see Harold Stassen, letter to John Foster Dulles, May 3, 1954, Dulles Papers, Subject Series, Box 8.

44. "Eyes only" message from McClintock to the President, April 24, 1954, Whitman File, DDE Diary Series, Box 6.

45. "Eyes only" message from Dulles to the president, April 24, 1954, Whitman File, DDE Diary Series, Box 6. Dulles also reports in this message that the fall of Dien Bien Phu would have a "profound effect on EDC"—the European Defense Community that Eisenhower had worked so hard to establish.

46. Sherman Adams summarizes Eisenhower's thought process on the decision not to intervene as follows: "Having avoided one total war with Red China the year before in Korea when he had United Nation support, he was in no mood to provoke another one in Indochina by going it alone in a military action without British and other Western Allies. He was also determined not to become involved militarily in any foreign conflict without the approval of Congress" (Adams, *Firsthand Report*, p. 121, quoted in Scribner, "Eisenhower and Johnson Administrations' Decision-making on Vietnamese Intervention," p. 150).

47. Interview with Dwight D. Eisenhower, quoted in Ambrose, *Eisenhower*, vol. 2, p. 184. This statement indicates the finality of Eisenhower's decision about intervention in Indochina, but he certainly was not reluctant to consider using nuclear weapons elsewhere. Only four days earlier, he "approved recommendations by

the Joint Chiefs that called for 'employing atomic weapons, whenever advantageous . . . against those military targets in China, Hainan and other Communist-held offshore islands' in case of Chinese intervention in Indochina" (Divine, *Eisenhower and the Cold War,* p. 51). At the beginning of April 1954, Eisenhower evidently considered using nuclear weapons in Indochina as well. His diary entry for April 6 consists of notes on only two topics: "H-Bomb" and "Dien Bien Phu"; see diary entry, April 6, 1954, Whitman File, DDE Diary Series, Box 6.

48. Larson, "Eisenhower's World View," p. 43.

49. "Tentative Agenda for the Cabinet Meeting," March 26, 1954, Whitman File, Cabinet Series, Box 3.

50. C. D. Jackson, memorandum to Henry Luce, July 27, 1954, in C. D. Jackson Papers, 1934–1967, Box 56, Eisenhower Presidential Library. Henceforth cited as "Jackson Papers."

51. Janis and Mann (*Decision Making*) identify both "bolstering" and "defensive avoidance" as common responses to the stress of policy crises. See also Lebow's enlightening case studies illustrating these patterns in international crisis decision making in *Between Peace and War*.

52. Shortly before the fall of the French garrison, Eisenhower vented some of his frustration with the French leadership in a long letter to an old friend, General Al Gruenther. France, he complained, "wants still to be considered a world power, but is entirely unready to make the sacrifices necessary to sustain such a position." "The only hope," he bitterly concluded, was for France "to produce a new and inspirational leader—and I do *not* mean one that is 6 feet 5 and who considers himself to be, by some miraculous biological and transmigrative process, the offspring of Clemenceau and Jeanne d'Arc." See Eisenhower, letter to Al Gruenther, April 26, 1954, Whitman File, DDE Diary Series, Box 4. For evidence of the frustration and anger that Ridgway's objections initially provoked, see the declassified transcript of a telephone conversation between Dulles and Eisenhower, March 16, 1954, Dulles Papers, Telephone Calls Series, Box 10. Nevertheless, the president managed to listen to what Ridgway had to say.

53. Eisenhower, quoted by James C. Hagerty, diary entries for January 25, 1954, and March 1, 1954, Hagerty Papers, Diary Entries Series, Box 1, emphasis in original.

54. Millikan and Eisenhower, quoted by James C. Hagerty, diary entry for March 15, 1954, Hagerty Papers, Diary Entries Series, Box 1. See also L. A. Minnich, Memoranda on Legislative

Conferences, March 8, 1954 and May 3, 1954, Whitman File, Legislative Meeting Series, Box 1.

55. Eisenhower, quoted by James C. Hagerty, diary entry for March 29, 1954, Hagerty Papers, Diary Entries Series, Box 1.

56. Eisenhower, quoted in Ewald, *Eisenhower the President,* p. 67.

57. According to E. L. Bartlett, Alaska's delegate to Congress during the battle for statehood, "it was Nate Twining principally who was responsible for delaying statehood on military grounds." See Bartlett, Memorandum, July 5, 1956, E. L. Bartlett Papers, Statehood File, Box 18, Elmer E. Rasmuson Library, University of Alaska, College; quoted in Richard H. Bloedel, "The Alaska Statehood Movement," (Ph. D. Diss., University of Washington, 1974), p. 539.

58. Ernest Gruening, *The Battle for Alaska Statehood* (College: University of Alaska Press, 1967), p. 94.

59. See Bloedel, "Alaska Statehood Movement," p. 539, for elaboration on Seaton's "independent streak."

60. Fred Seaton, Memorandum for Dwight D. Eisenhower, June 24, 1958, Whitman File, Administration Series, Box 32.

61. Ibid.

62. See the covering brief for the "withdrawal" proposal as it was submitted to the president, March 7, 1957, Fred A. Seaton Papers, 1946–72, Subject Series, Box 4, Eisenhower Presidential Library. For the text of Seaton's proposal as it was later delivered to the House Committee on Interior and Insular Affairs (by Hatfield Chilson, since Seaton was at the time confined to the Walter Reed Hospital for treatment of a recurring back injury), see Seaton Papers, 1946–72, Ewald Research Files, Box 2. Provisions for withdrawal were eventually incorporated into section 10 of the Statehood Act.

63. The House of Representatives passed the Alaska Statehood Bill, on May 28, 1968, by a vote of 210–166 (with 51 abstentions).

64. Bloedel, "Alaska Statehood Movement," p. 558.

65. C. W. Snedden, quoted in ibid., p. 559. As some indication of the political capital Seaton was willing to expend, Snedden further remarked that, through the secretary of the interior, "we had trading stock ranging all the way from federal judgeships to new facilities in parks and national monuments to an additional star route on some rural post office" (p. 559).

66. See Dwight D. Eisenhower, diary entry for June 5, 1958,

Whitman File, ACW Diary Series, Box 10. Also see Ewald, *Eisenhower the President*, p. 203.

67. The popular referendum was a condition of the Statehood Bill. Figures on the congressional votes and the referendum are from Gruening, *Battle for Alaska Statehood*, pp. 104 and 106.

68. Eisenhower to William Ewald, quoted in Ewald, *Eisenhower the President*, p. 202.

69. Ewald, *Eisenhower the President*, p. 203.

70. *New York Times*, August 7, 1979, p. A15; also cited in DeMause, *Reagan's America*, p. 22.

71. President Carter's approval rating of 28 percent in July 1979 was, in fact, only four points higher than President Nixon's record low of 24 percent approval during the Watergate scandal—the lowest Gallup Poll approval rating on record. Carter's popularity did rebound somewhat as his re-election campaign against Ronald Reagan progressed, but never much above 40 percent approval. See George C. Edwards, *Presidential Approval: A Sourcebook* (Baltimore: Johns Hopkins University Press, 1990), pp. 153–181.

72. Robert Dallek, *Ronald Reagan: The Politics of Symbolism* (Cambridge: Harvard University Press, 1984), p. 7.

73. Ronald Reagan, "Farewell Address," quoted in Larry Berman, "Looking Back of the Reagan Presidency," in Berman, ed., *Looking Back on the Reagan Presidency* (Baltimore: Johns Hopkins University Press, 1990), p. 5.

74. Barry Posen and Stephen Van Evera, "Reagan Administration Defense Policy: Departure from Containment," in Kenneth Oye, Ronald Lieber, and Donald Rothchild, *Eagle Resurgent?: The Reagan Era in American Foreign Policy* (Boston: Little, Brown, 1983), pp. 75–114. Posen and Van Evera cite Gordon Adams, *The FY 1986 Defense Budget: The Weapons Buildup Continues* (Washington, D.C.: Center on Budget and Policy Priorities, 1985), pp. 45 and 49.

75. Nigel Ashford, "The Conservative Agenda and the Reagan Presidency," in Joseph Hogan, ed., *The Reagan Years: The Record in Presidential Leadership* (Manchester, England: Manchester University Press, 1990), p. 193.

76. For a sampling of these debates, see Norman C. Amaker, *Civil Rights and the Reagan Administration* (Washington, D.C.: Urban Institute Press, 1988); Thomas Muller, *The Impact of Reagan Administration Policies on Regional Income and Employment* (Wash-

ington, D.C.: Urban Institute, 1986); Paul R. Portney, ed., *Natural Resources and the Environment: The Reagan Approach* (Washington, D.C.: Urban Institute Press, 1984); and C. Brant Short, *Ronald Reagan and the Public Lands: America's Conservation Debate, 1979–1984* (College Station: Texas A&M University Press, 1989).

77. Another irony of the Reagan presidency is that the most explosive growth of international debt in the 1980s occurred in the United States itself, and not in Mexico, Brazil, or the other countries discussed in the next section. In a span of four years beginning in 1981, U.S. current accounts went from surplus to the largest deficit in the world (see Benjamin J. Cohen, "An Explosion in the Kitchen? Economic Relations with Other Advanced Industrial States," in Oye, Lieber, and Rothchild, *Eagle Resurgent?* p. 129). This was not a problem Reagan inherited, but one that followed from his commitments to other policies. His failure to reconcile international and domestic (fiscal) priorities constitutes a case of learning failure that will be discussed in chapter 6.

78. Roger S. Leeds and Gale Thompson, "The 1982 Mexican Debt Negotiations: Response to a Financial Crisis," *Foreign Policy Institute Case Studies,* no. 4 (Washington, D.C.: Johns Hopkins Foreign Policy Institute, 1987), p. 10. Leeds and Thompson note, moreover, that "if Mexico failed to pay interest for one year, the net earnings of the money center banks would plummet by one-third" (p. 10). See also Karin Lissakers, "Dateline Wall Street: Faustian Finance," *Foreign Policy* 51 (Summer 1983), pp. 160–175.

79. Donald T. Regan, testimony before U.S. Congress, Committee on Banking, Housing, and Urban Affairs, Subcommittee on International Finance and Monetary Policy, 98th Cong., 1st sess., *International Debt* (Washington, D. C.: U.S. Government Printing Office, 1983), p. 52. Hereafter referred to as U.S. Congress, "*International Debt.*"

As Sue Branford and Bernardo Kucinski have pointed out, the United States' problems were Mexico's problems as well. In particular, President Reagan's aversion to inflation reinforced the Federal Reserve's own preferences, under Paul Volcker, for keeping a tight reign on the money supply. The resulting high interest rates clearly magnified the existing debt problems of many Latin American countries. See Branford and Kucinski, *The Debt Squads: The US, the Banks, and Latin America* (London: Zed Books, 1988), pp. 95–108; and John H. Makin, *The Global Debt Crisis: America's Growing Involvement* (New York: Basic, 1984), pp. 109–153.

80. Joseph Kraft cites an unnamed Treasury Department official, for example, who claimed that Mexican finance minister "Silva Herzog kept describing the troubles to Don Regan, and Regan kept missing the message. Don was like a guy who keeps hearing the same joke over and over again, without getting the punch line"; see Kraft, *The Mexican Rescue* (New York: Group of Thirty, 1984), p. 5. New York Representative Charles Schumer likewise characterized Regan's attitude as "What, me worry" even when "other officials recognized the urgency of the problem." See his statement before the U.S. Congress, House Committee on Banking, Finance, and Urban Affairs, 99th Cong., 1st sess., *U.S. Proposals on International Debt Crisis* (Washington, D.C.: U.S. Government Printing Office, 1986), p. 8; henceforth referred to as U.S. Congress, *"U.S. Proposals on International Debt Crisis."*

Regan's reluctance to act on the debt problem is entirely consistent, however, with the ideological perspective he shared with the president. It would have required remarkable inattentiveness for Regan to have "missed Herzog's message." A more persuasive explanation is that he expected the market to compel changes in Mexican fiscal behavior that would ultimately resolve the crisis without U.S. action.

81. Beryl Sprinkel, quoted in Kraft, *Mexican Rescue*, p. 12. On the similar backgrounds and ideological affinities of the leading economic officials in the Reagan administration, see Cannon, *Reagan*, p. 383; and Darrell Delamaide, *Debt Shock: The Full Story of the World Credit Crisis* (Garden City, New York: Doubleday, 1984), pp. 130–136.

82. Leeds and Thompson, "1982 Mexican Debt Negotiations," pp. 11–13.

83. Ibid., p. 13.

84. Benjamin Cohen, *In Whose Interest?: International Banking and American Foreign Policy* (New Haven: Yale University Press, 1986), p. 213.

85. Ibid., p. 214.

86. Kraft, *Mexican Rescue*, p. 16.

87. Ibid., p. 14. By August 1982, David Stockman had concluded that the combined effect of the administration's tax cut and its continued commitment to a large defense budget would result in a cumulative federal budget deficit over five years of more than $1 trillion. He was consequently inclined to view almost every policy proposal in terms of its effect on this bottom line. See Stock-

man, *The Triumph of Politics: The Inside Story of the Reagan Revolution* (New York: Avon, 1987), pp. 385–386.

88. Kraft, *Mexican Rescue*, p. 16.

89. Rimmer de Vries, quoted in Delamaide, *Debt Shock*, p. 10.

90. Delamaide, *Debt Shock*, p. 17.

91. Indeed, the only two countries in Central or South America that did *not* reschedule their international debts during this period were Colombia and Paraguay; see Branford and Kucinski, *Debt Squads*, pp. 112–115.

92. William Guttman, *Between Bailout and Breakdown: A Modular Approach to Latin America's Debt Crisis* (Washington, D.C.: Center for Strategic and International Studies, 1989), p. 11.

93. Branford and Kucinski (*Debt Squads*, pp. 24–34), for example, attribute a 2.5 percent decline in the supply of major foodstuffs between 1981 to 1984, and increased incidence of disease (particularly diarrhea and parasites in children), to the austerity programs.

94. See *New York Times*, May 21, 1984, p. D1.

95. Branford and Kucinski, *Debt Squads*, p. 119.

96. Cohen, *In Whose Interest?* p. 221.

97. Ibid., p. 231.

98. See U.S. Congress, *U.S. Proposals on International Debt Crisis*, p. 38.

99. James A. Baker, "Statement Before the House Committee on Banking, Finance, and Urban Affairs," in ibid., p. 13.

100. Branford and Kucinski, *Debt Squads*, pp. 119–120.

101. Richard E. Feinberg, "American Power and Third World Economies," in Oye, Lieber, and Rothchild, *Eagle Resurgent?* p. 155.

102. U.S. Congress, *U.S. Proposals on International Debt Crisis*, p. 16.

103. Delamaide, *Debt Shock*, p. 237.

104. Frank Annunzio, statement before the House Committee on Banking, Finance, and Urban Affairs, in U.S. Congress, *U.S. Proposals on International Debt Crisis*, p. 27.

105. See cover story, *Time Magazine*, January 10, 1983.

106. Indeed, profits on loans to Latin America actually grew after 1982. See Branford and Kucinski, *Debt Squads*, pp. 128–129.

107. Kraft, *Mexican Rescue*, p. 17.

108. Delamaide, *Debt Shock*, pp. 100 and 121.

109. Raymond Tanter, *Who's at the Helm? Lessons of Lebanon* (Boulder, Colorado: Westview, 1990).

110. Cannon, *President Reagan,* p. 390. Another detailed discussion of the seesawing political situation in Lebanon, and of the Reagan administration's confused efforts to develop a coherent policy toward it, is Samuel Segev, "The Reagan Plan: A Victim of Conflicting Approaches by the United States and Israel to the Syrian Presence in Lebanon," in Eric J. Schmertz, Natalie Datlof, and Alexej Ugrinsky, eds., *President Reagan and the World* (Westport, Connecticut: Greenwood, 1997), pp. 41–60.

111. Weinberger, quoted in Ralph A. Hallenbeck, *Military Force as an Instrument of U.S. Foreign Policy: Intervention in Lebanon, August 1982 - February 1984* (New York: Praeger, 1991), p. 8; Hallenbeck cites Michael Jansen, *The Battle for Beirut* (Boston: South End Press, 1983), pp. 80–81; and Alexander Haig, *Caveat* (New York: Macmillan, 1984), pp. 338–346.

112. Hallenbeck, *Military Force as an Instrument of U.S. Foreign Policy,* p. 10. See also Haig, *Caveat,* pp. 318–119; and Harold H. Saunders, "An Israeli-Palestinian Peace," *Foreign Affairs* (Fall 1982), pp. 101–121.

113. Cannon, *President Reagan,* p. 394.

114. David C. Martin and John Walcott, *Best Laid Plans: The Inside Story of America's War Against Terrorism* (New York: Touchstone, 1988), p. 93, quoted in Cannon, *President Reagan,* p. 398.

115. Cannon, *President Reagan,* p. 399.

116. Tanter, *Who's at the Helm?* p. 141.

117. Ibid., p. 141.

118. Cannon, *President Reagan,* p. 403.

119. Cannon (ibid., p. 405) suggests that the conflict between Shultz and Weinberger was exacerbated by "Weinberger's fascination with foreign policy and by Shultz's willingness to use military force in behalf of diplomatic objectives. The two men naturally wandered onto each other's turf." See also Hallenbeck, *Military Force as an Instrument of U.S. Foreign Policy,* pp. 138–153; and Agnes G. Korbani, *U.S. Intervention in Lebanon, 1958 and 1982: Presidential Decisionmaking* (New York: Praeger, 1991), pp. 94–96. Segev ("Reagan Plan," in Schmertz, Datlof, and Ugrinsky, *President Reagan and the World,* pp. 50–51) points out the existence of other divisions within the administration as well, such as internal State Department disputes between Shultz and Habib. In David Kimche's acerbic assessment, "the U.S. behaved in Lebanon like an orchestra whose members played different music, and with a conductor who had no idea what was going on," quoted in ibid., p. 51.

120. For an able description of Marine involvement in Lebanon, see Benis M. Frank, *U.S. Marines in Lebanon, 1982–1984* (Washington, D.C.: History and Museums Division, U.S. Marine Corps, 1987).

121. Ronald Reagan, speech on April 23, 1983, quoted in Cannon, *President Reagan*, p. 412.

122. Caspar Weinberger, quoted in Cannon, *President Reagan*, p. 414.

123. Cannon, *President Reagan*, p. 424.

124. See ibid., pp. 426–427; Nancy Reagan, *My Turn*, pp. 242–243.

125. Reagan, quoted in Cannon, *President Reagan*, pp. 443–444.

126. Reagan, *American Life*, p. 462.

127. McFarlane, quoted in Cannon, *President Reagan*, p. 455.

128. According to Colin Powell, Weinberger had never looked "as sad as he did after the Marines were killed" (Cannon, *President Reagan*, p. 444). Weinberger himself emphasized in an interview with Cannon that "it's a source of enormous pain and unhappiness to me that I was not persuasive enough to have the force withdrawn before that tragedy happened" (ibid., note 117, p. 868).

129. Ibid., p. 450. Also see Helen Dewar and Margaret Shapiro, "Hill Leaders Split Over Pulling Out Troops in Beirut," *Washington Post*, January 24, 1984.

130. Shultz, in Martin and Walcott, *Best Laid Plans*, p. 148, quoted in Cannon, *President Reagan*, p. 453.

131. Reagan, *Wall Street Journal*, February 3, 1984, and radio speech, February 4, 1984, quoted in Cannon, *President Reagan*, p. 454.

132. Cannon, *President Reagan*, p. 455. See also Hallenbeck, *Military Force as an Instrument of U.S. Foreign Policy*, p. 131.

133. Stuyvesant Wainwright, interview with Richard Fenno, 1961, quoted in Greenstein, *Hidden-Hand Presidency*, p. 16.

CHAPTER 5. GROUPTHINK

1. Janis himself cites Pearl Harbor and Watergate as instances of groupthink; see his *Groupthink* and, on Watergate, also see Bertrand H. Raven, "The Nixon Group," *Journal of Social Issues* 30 (1974), pp. 297–320. On the *Challenger* disaster, see James K.

Esser and J. S. Lindoerfer, "Groupthink and the Space Shuttle Challenger Accident: Toward a Quantitative Case Analysis," *Journal of Behavioral Decision Making* 2 (1989), pp. 167–177.

2. Randall S. Peterson, et al., "Group Dynamics in Top Management Teams: Groupthink, Vigilance, and Alternative Models of Organizational Failure and Success," *Organizational Behavior and Human Decision Processes* 73 (1998), pp. 272–305.

3. See, for example, Raymond J. Aldag and S. R. Fuller, "Beyond Fiasco: A Reappraisal of the Groupthink Phenomenon and a New Model of Group Decision Processes," *Psychological Bulletin* 113 (1993), pp. 533–552; Longley and Pruitt, "Groupthink"; 't Hart, *Groupthink in Government;* and 't Hart, Stern, and Sundelius, *Beyond Groupthink.* On efforts to test the theory, see also W. Park, "A Review of the Research on Groupthink," *Journal of Behavioral Decision Making* 3 (1990), pp. 229–245.

4. Among the more "journalistic" discussions of groupthink are J. Heller, "The Dangers of Groupthink," *Guardian,* January 31, 1983; and Steve Smith, "Groupthink and the Hostage Rescue Mission," *British Journal of Political Science* 14 (1984), pp. 117–123.

5. See J. A. Courtright, "A Laboratory Investigation of Groupthink," *Communication Monographs* 45 (1978), pp. 229–246; and Mattie L. Flowers, "A Laboratory Test of Some Implications of Janis' Groupthink Hypothesis," *Journal of Personality and Social Psychology* 35 (1977), pp. 888–896. An innovative approach that combines some of the virtues of historical research on natural groups and quantitative measurement is described in Philip E. Tetlock, et al., "Assessing Political Group Dynamics: A Test of the Groupthink Model," *Journal of Personality and Social Psychology* 63 (1992), pp. 403–425.

6. Janis, *Victims of Groupthink* (1972 edition), p. 9.

7. Sloan Wilson's novel, *The Man in the Gray Flannel Suit* (New York: Simon & Schuster, 1955) evokes many of these generalizations. See also Diggins, *Proud Decades,* pp. 177–188.

8. The figures for weekly earnings are calculated in constant 1960 dollars for an average wage earner with three dependents; see Diggins, *Proud Decades,* pp. 178–180.

9. Harold G. Vatter, *The U.S. Economy in the 1950s: An Economic History* (Chicago: University of Chicago Press, 1963), pp. 7–8.

10. U.S. gold holdings were $22.87 billion in 1951, roughly the same ($22.86 billion) in 1957, but had decreased to $19.58 billion

by 1959; see "Foreign Economic Policy Issues" briefing paper, November 10, 1959, U.S. Council on Foreign Economic Policy, Office of the Chairman, Records 1954–61, CFEP Papers Series, Eisenhower Presidential Library (henceforth cited as "CFEP Records 1954–61"). Data on short-term, foreign liabilities are also given in C. Edward Galbreath's memorandum for Clarence Randall, June 26, 1959, CFEP Records 1954–61, Chronological File, Box 1.

11. See table 9-1, "United States Balance of Payments, 1951–1960," in Vatter, *U.S. Economy in the 1950s,* pp. 260–261.

12. See C. Edward Galbreath, background paper on the U.S. balance of payments, March 23, 1960, CFEP Records 1954–61, CFEP Papers Series, Box 1; and Galbreath, memorandum for Clarence Randall, June 26, 1959, CFEP Records 1954–61, Chronological File, Box 1.

13. George Humphrey, letter to President Eisenhower, April 15, 1955, Whitman File, Administration Series, Box 21.

14. Ibid.

15. Dwight Eisenhower, letter to George Humphrey, April 26, 1955, Whitman File, Administration Series, Box 21.

16. Minutes of Cabinet meeting, April 20, 1956, Whitman File, Cabinet Series, Box 7. See also Cabinet Secretary Maxwell Rabb's memo to Governor Adams, April 18, 1956, Whitman File, Cabinet Series, Box 7.

17. Minutes of Cabinet meeting, April 20, 1956, Whitman File, Cabinet Series, Box 7. Eisenhower also suggested during this meeting that the principal danger associated with the gold outflow was simply that other countries might use this gold to purchase goods from the Soviet Union, thus turning an issue of economic policy into one of international, anticommunist strategy with which he was personally more concerned.

18. Letter from Russell Leffingwell, February 18, 1957, Whitman File, Administration Series, Box 23; and George Humphrey, letter to President Eisenhower, May 14, 1957, Whitman File Administration Series, Box 23. Both are quoted in Kaufman, *Trade and Aid,* p. 178.

19. Kaufman, *Trade and Aid,* p. 178.

20. Ibid., p. 18.

21. Ibid., p. 24.

22. This report was prepared by Walt Rostow and Max Millikan who were both, at the time, professors at MIT's Center for International Studies. According to Kaufman (*Trade and Aid,* p. 50), it was widely read and "highly influential."

23. C. D. Jackson, letter to Nelson Rockefeller, November 10, 1955, Jackson Papers, 1934–67, Box 75; also quoted in Kaufman, *Trade and Aid*, p. 66. Kaufman (*Trade and Aid*, p. 226, note 37) points out that "Rockefeller said he would forward Jackson's letter to the president."

24. Kaufman, *Trade and Aid*, pp. 95 and 96.

25. Ibid., p. 106. Congress ultimately approved a DLF budget authorization for only two years and for only $625 million in 1959.

26. See Randall's "summary of Fairless Committee recommendations," and Eisenhower's letter to Randall, March 3, 1957, both in CFEP Records 1954–61, CFEP Papers Series, Box 2. In many cases, Randall's recommendations were simply that further studies be conducted. He did specifically reject, however, the Fairless Committee proposal that in "foreign assistance programs a higher priority should be given to those countries which have joined in the collective security system." Doing so would have made it more difficult to provide aid to the very countries that were at particular risk of "succumbing" to communism.

27. C. D. Jackson, February 6, 1957, Jackson Papers, 1934–67, Box 56, quoted in Walt W. Rostow, *Eisenhower, Kennedy, and Foreign Aid* (Austin: University of Texas Press, 1985), p. 124.

28. Like Humphrey, Dodge favored limiting (if not eliminating outright) foreign aid programs, a preference that might have stemmed from Dodge's background as a budget director. See Rostow, *Eisenhower, Kennedy, and Foreign Aid*, p. 94.

29. Both Arthur Burns and Raymond Saulnier, who succeeded Burns in 1956, make this orientation of the CEA clear in interviews with Erwin C. Hargrove; see Hargrove and Samuel Morley, *The President and the Council of Economic Advisors: Interviews with CEA Chairmen* (Boulder, Colorado: Westview, 1984), pp. 111–115 and 144–147. See also Iwan Morgan's discussion of Burns's role as an economic advisor in *Eisenhower versus "the Spenders": The Eisenhower Administration, the Democrats and the Budget, 1953–60* (London: Pinter, 1990), pp. 6–8.

30. Milton Eisenhower spent considerable time in Latin America, where he became convinced that American "aid can be decisive in helping Latin Americans build better institutions, increase income, and purge injustice from their society. We must be swift and generous." See Milton Eisenhower, *The Wine Is Bitter* (Garden City, New York: Doubleday, 1963), pp. xii-xiii.

31. In addition to Kaufman (*Trade and Aid*, pp. 101–112) and Rostow (*Eisenhower, Kennedy, and Foreign Aid*, pp. 125–138), see

also Russell Edgerton, *Sub-Cabinet Politics and Policy Commitment: The Birth of the Development Loan Fund* (Syracuse: Inter-University Case Program, 1970). On the diversity of Eisenhower's economic advisors' views, see also Morgan, *Eisenhower versus "the Spenders."*

32. Somewhat earlier, in 1954, Dodge was replaced as budget director by Rowland Hughes. Hughes and his successors, Perceval Brundage and Maurice Stans, were also conservative but not as influential with the president as Dodge.

33. Rostow, *Eisenhower, Kennedy, and Foreign Aid,* p. 118. Dulles himself expressed his frustration with Humphrey and Dodge in a conversation with C. D. Jackson on April 14, 1956: "The really effective axis in Washington today is the Humphrey-Dodge axis, and Dodge's committee—another one of those coordinating things—is a disaster as far as getting any of the things I want done. There are days when a great many of these problems cannot be approached from the viewpoint of a Middle Western banker-businessman, and that is the experience and the attitude of Humphrey and of Dodge, and in a sense of Herbert Hoover, and their many allies all over the place." See Jackson, letter to Henry Luce, April 16, 1956, Jackson Papers, 1934 67, Box 56; quoted in Rostow, *Eisenhower, Kennedy, and Foreign Aid,* pp. 257–268.

34. Hargrove and Morley, *President and the Council of Economic Advisors,* p. 124.

35. Adams, *Firsthand Report,* p. 381. Eisenhower himself called 1958 "the worst year of his life" (Ambrose, *Eisenhower,* vol. 2, p. 511).

36. Kaufman, *Trade and Aid,* p. 176. For a detailed statistical description of these trends, see Robert Anderson, Memorandum for the President, August 24, 1959, Whitman File, Administration Series, Box 2.

37. In fact, were it not for several countries' debt prepayments to the United States in 1959, the payments deficit would have exceeded $4 billion; see C. Edward Galbreath, Memorandum to Council on Foreign Economic Policy, March 23, 1960, CFEP Records 1954–61, CFEP Papers Series, Box 1.

38. See C. Edward Galbreath, Memorandum for Clarence Randall, March 4, 1960, CFEP Records 1954–61, Chronological File, Box 1.

39. See C. Edward Galbreath, Memorandum for Clarence Randall, August 4, 1959; and Clarence Randall, letter to Thomas Mann (assistant secretary of state), August 3, 1959, both in CFEP Records 1954–61, Chronological File, Box 1.

40. C. Edward Galbreath, Memorandum to Council on Foreign Economic Policy, June 2, 1960, CFEP Records 1954–61, Policy Papers Series, Box 16.

41. See Clarence Randall, letter to Herbert Hoover, May 4, 1960, CFEP Records 1954–61, Chronological File, Box 1.

42. C. Edward Galbreath, Memorandum to Council on Foreign Economic Policy, June 2, 1960, CFEP Records 1954–61, Policy Papers Series, Box 16.

43. Kaufman, *Trade and Aid,* pp. 180 and 181.

44. The president issued a directive on November 16, 1960, calling on all government agencies to reduce the number of dependents abroad. For reports on compliance with this directive, see the three "Agency Reports—Gold Directive" folders in White House Office, Office of the Staff Secretary, Subject Series, Alphabetical Subseries, Box 1, Eisenhower Presidential Library. A memorandum for the record from A. J. Goodpaster, located in the third of these folders and dated December 12, 1960, describes the president's displeasure over the failure of some departments to reduce adequately their personnel abroad.

45. See Kaufman, *Trade and Aid,* p. 183.

46. Treasury Department briefing paper on "Foreign Financial Issues Facing the United States," undated (probably late 1960), Whitman File, Administration Series, Box 3. At about the same time, on November 9, 1960, Treasury Secretary Anderson reported that "by now we have almost a gold panic situation," quoted in Raymond J. Saulnier, *Constructive Years: The U.S. Economy under Eisenhower* (Lanham, Maryland: University Press of America, 1991), p. 122.

47. Joanne Gowa, *Closing the Gold Window: Domestic Politics and the End of Bretton Woods* (Ithaca: Cornell University Press, 1983), p. 42. See also Robert Triffin, *Gold and the Dollar Crisis* (New Haven: Yale University Press, 1961).

48. Figure 5–1 is calculated using data from the *International Economic Report of the President* (Washington, D.C.: U.S. Government Printing Office, 1973), table 20, p. 86. U.S. gold reserves fell from $22.86 billion in 1957 to $16.95 billion in 1961 and to $12.07 billion by 1967. For data on American gold reserves, see International Monetary Fund, *International Financial Statistics Yearbook* (Washington, DC: International Monetary Fund, 1979), vol. 32, pp. 426–427.

49. Ambrose, *Eisenhower,* vol. 2, p. 607.

50. Saulnier, *Constructive Years,* p. 121.

51. Stephen Rabe has argued, for example, that this internal cohesion led to rigid foreign policies toward Latin America incapable of responding to rapid changes in the region (e.g., the rise of Fidel Castro). See Rabe, *Eisenhower and Latin America: The Foreign Policy of Anticommunism* (Chapel Hill: University of North Carolina Press, 1988), esp. p. 113; also see Thomas Zoumaras, "Eisenhower's Foreign Economic Policy: The Case of Latin America," in Melanson and Mayers, *Reevaluating Eisenhower,* pp. 155–191.

52. Clarence Randall, letter to Robert Anderson, July 31, 1959, CFEP Records 1954 61, Chronological File, Box 1.

53. On the Cabinet's approval of Anderson's request, see Robert Gray, Record of Action, Cabinet Paper, March 19, 1959, Whitman File, Cabinet Series, Box 13. Morgan describes Anderson's somewhat blasé attitude about the gold outflows in *Eisenhower versus "the Spenders,"* p. 129.

54. Kaufman, *Trade and Aid,* p. 193. Morgan also holds that "with hindsight it is evident that devaluation would have been the appropriate response to the changing realities of the international economy" (Morgan, *Eisenhower versus "the Spenders,"* pp. 174–175).

55. Saulnier, "Oral History Interview," in Hargrove and Morley, *President and the Council of Economic Advisors,* pp. 127–130.

56. The Randall Commission was created to support the administration's initial stance in favor of trade over aid; the Fairless Committee was established in response to the Senate's decision to create its own committee to investigate American foreign economic policy.

57. See Dwight D. Eisenhower, diary entry for July 23, 1959, Whitman File, ACW Diary Series, Box 10.

58. Joseph McCarthy, *Congressional Record,* 82nd Cong., 1st sess., June 14, 1951, pp. 6556–6603, quoted in Robert Griffith, *The Politics of Fear* (Lexington: University Press of Kentucky, 1970), p. 145. This attack on Marshall is not particularly consistent with McCarthy's earlier descriptions of the general as "a pathetic thing" who was nothing more than a pawn of Acheson (Griffith, *Politics of Fear,* p. 144).

59. Emmet Hughes recalls that the president was enthusiastic about inserting a paragraph in the Milwaukee speech in praise of Marshall. Hughes was happy to oblige, and he, Robert Cutler, and Gabriel Hauge were all dismayed that Eisenhower chose to

remove the reference to Marshall in the speech. Hauge even considered resigning from the campaign. See Hughes, *Ordeal of Power,* pp. 41–44; and Ambrose, *Eisenhower,* vol. 1, pp. 563–567.

60. Ambrose, *Eisenhower,* vol. 1, p. 567.

61. Hughes, *Ordeal of Power,* pp. 43–44.

62. Eisenhower, *New York Times,* June 6, 1952, quoted in Greenstein, *Hidden-Hand Presidency,* p. 161.

63. Eisenhower, letter to Paul Helms, March 9, 1954, Whitman File, DDE Diary Series, Box 6, emphasis in original.

64. Bryce Harlow describes as follows an illustrative occasion on which he wrote a press release for Eisenhower:

> It had to be issued quickly, and I wrote up a legal-size, double-spaced statement and we came running to give it to him as it was a rush item of some kind. I rushed in and sat down beside him, and he then picked up his pen and struck out a word, put it back, handed the paper to me and said, "Bryce, I want to explain what I did there. I struck out the word 'deliberately.' Let me tell you something: don't ever attack a man's motives. Don't ever attack a man's motives because he will never forgive you for that. You can attack his judgment forever, you can argue with him forever, and he will respect you for that. Remember that in the future writing for me" (Harlow, "'Compleat' President," in Thompson, *Eisenhower Presidency,* p. 162).

65. Eisenhower, diary entry, April 1, 1953, Whitman File, DDE Diary Series, Box 9; also Ferrell, *Eisenhower Diaries,* pp. 233–234.

66. Greenstein, *Hidden-Hand Presidency,* p. 165.

67. Ibid., pp. 167–168. Harold Stassen's account, which reveals surprisingly little pique at Eisenhower's handling of the episode, is contained in his memoirs; see Stassen and Marshall Houts, *Eisenhower: Turning the World toward Peace* (St. Paul, Minnesota: Merrill/Magnus, 1990), pp. 243–252.

68. Ambrose, *Eisenhower,* vol. 2, p. 81.

69. The majority of Americans stated, at the time, that they approved of McCarthy's activities. See Anthony James Joes, "Eisenhower Revisionism and American Politics," in Joann P. Krieg, ed., *Dwight D. Eisenhower: Soldier, President, Statesman* (New York: Greenwood, 1987), p. 288.

70. C. D. Jackson, personal diary entry, November 3, 1953, Jackson Papers, 1934 67, Box 56.

71. See Sherman Adams, *Firsthand Report*, p. 151.

72. Eisenhower, letter to Paul Reed (chairman of General Electric), June 17, 1953, Whitman File, DDE Diary Series, Box 3; Eisenhower, quoted in C. D. Jackson's log entry for December 2, 1953, Jackson Papers, 1934–67, Box 56.

73. Thorough descriptions of McCarthy's accusations and the army-McCarthy hearings that followed are contained in Griffith, *Politics of Fear*, pp. 243–269; and Richard M. Fried, *Men Against McCarthy* (New York: Columbia University Press, 1976), pp. 279–289. McCarthy's private criticism of the army actually began somewhat earlier after his former aide, Schine, was inducted into the army.

74. Griffith, *Politics of Fear*, p. 246.

75. Ambrose, *Eisenhower*, vol. 2, p. 161; and Fried, *Men Against McCarthy*, p. 279.

76. Fried, *Men Against McCarthy*, p. 279.

77. Ambrose, *Eisenhower*, vol. 2, p. 160.

78. *New York Times*, February 24, 1954.

79. James C. Hagerty, diary entry, February 24, 1954, Hagerty Papers, 1953–61, Diary Entries Series, Box 1; also reproduced in Robert H. Ferrell, ed., *The Diary of James C. Hagerty: Eisenhower in Mid-Course, 1954–55* (Bloomington: Indiana University Press, 1983), p. 19.

80. Hagerty, diary entry, February 25, 1954, Hagerty Papers, 1953–61, Diary Entries Series, Box 1.

81. Since the congressional investigation into the Peress case had, by March, devolved into a personal battle between Stevens and McCarthy, Eisenhower objected not only to McCarthy's tendency to bully witnesses but also to his "judging his own case" as the chair of the Investigations Subcommittee. In a news conference, Eisenhower proclaimed that "in America, if a man is a party to a dispute, directly or indirectly, he does not sit in judgment on his own case." The next day, the *New York Times* headlined: "President Opposes McCarthy as Judge in His Own Dispute." See Greenstein, *Hidden-Hand Presidency*, pp. 200–201.

82. Telephone conversation between Dwight Eisenhower and Deputy Attorney General Rogers (Attorney General Brownell was not in the office when Eisenhower called), March 2, 1954, Whitman File, DDE Diary Series, Box 5. By this point, the attorney general had been at work for some time preparing a legal foundation to block McCarthy's demands on the executive branch. See Her-

bert Brownell, with John P. Burke, *Advising Ike: The Memoirs of Attorney General Herbert Brownell* (Lawrence: University Press of Kansas, 1993), pp. 257–259.

83. Greenstein, *Hidden-Hand Presidency*, p. 187.

84. See Hagerty, diary entry, May 28, 1954, Hagerty Papers, 1953–61, Diary Entries Series, Box 1; and Greenstein, *Hidden-Hand Presidency*, pp. 209–210. In this diary entry, Hagerty describes a White House staff meeting during which the president was "really mad" and said about McCarthy's request, "This amounts to nothing but a wholesale subversion of public service. McCarthy is making exactly the same plea of loyalty to him that Hitler made to the German people."

85. Dwight D. Eisenhower, letter to Bill Robinson, March 12, 1954, Whitman File, DDE Diary Series, Box 6.

86. See Hagerty's diary entries for March and April 1954, in Ferrell, *Diary of James C. Hagerty*, pp. 23–50.

87. George Bender, a member of Congress running at the time for an Ohio Senate seat, quoted in Richard M. Fried, *Nightmare in Red: The McCarthy Era in Perspective* (New York: Oxford University Press, 1990), p. 140.

88. Griffith, *Politics of Fear*, p. 263, footnote 57.

89. See James Hagerty, diary entry for March 16, 1955, published in Ferrell, *Diary of James C. Hagerty*, pp. 210–212. Also see the memorandum on "Events leading up to so-called 'break' made by Senator McCarthy with the President, December 7, 1954," Whitman File, Administration Series, Box 25.

90. Fried, *Nightmare in Red*, p. 141.

91. Ibid., p. 16.

92. See Kenneth O'Reilly, *Hoover and the Un-Americans: The FBI, HUAC, and the Red Menace* (Philadelphia: Temple University Press, 1983). Also see Larry Ceplair and Steven Englund, *The Inquisition in Hollywood: Politics in the Film Community, 1930–1960* (Garden City, New York: Anchor, 1980); Sigmund Diamond, *Compromised Campus* (New York: Oxford University Press, 1992); Ellen Schrecker, *No Ivory Tower: McCarthyism and the Universities* (New York: Oxford University Press, 1986); Ellen Schrecker, *Many Are the Crimes: McCarthyism in America* (Boston: Little, Brown, 1998); and the now-dated but nevertheless valuable David Caute, *The Great Fear: The Anti-Communist Purge under Truman and Eisenhower* (New York: Simon & Schuster, 1978).

93. See Frank Donner, *The Age of Surveillance* (New York:

Knopf, 1981); Fried, *Nightmare in Red*, pp. 189–192; and O'Reilly, *Hoover and the Un-Americans*.

94. In 1969, the HUAC renamed itself the House Internal Security Committee. In 1975, its responsibilities were assumed by the House Judiciary Committee.

95. Ambrose, *Eisenhower*, vol. 2, p. 64, also see p. 81.

96. Fried, *Nightmare in Red*, p. 133.

97. Brownell, *Advising Ike*, p. 248. Brownell's ambivalence about the McCarthy era internal security programs is clear in his memoirs. He concludes they were necessary, but also that they "lacked reasonable standards, fair procedures, and constitutional protections"; the result was that they "had effects on individuals who posed no threat to national security" (p. 248).

98. Unanswerable or not, many have ventured opinions on the matter. Among those who contend that Eisenhower did all he could, and managed the threat of McCarthyism rather skillfully, are William Ewald, in *Who Killed Joe McCarthy?* (New York: Simon & Schuster, 1984), and Fred Greenstein, in *Hidden-Hand Presidency*. Others pointed to Eisenhower's great popularity and argued that he could have done much more to support the opponents of McCarthy's abuses. In fact, Army Secretary Stevens own assistant, John Kane, resigned in protest over the lack of support for his office from the White House. See Thomas C. Reeves, *The Life and Times of Joe McCarthy: A Biography* (New York: Stein and Day, 1982), p. 561.

99. Eisenhower, *Mandate for Change*, p. 330.

100. See also Ambrose's discussion of Eisenhower's abandonment of General Zwicker, in *Eisenhower*, vol. 2, pp. 164–165.

101. See Ambrose, *Eisenhower*, vol. 2, pp. 131–35, 141–42, and 166–68; and Fried, *Nightmare in Red*, pp. 179–180.

102. Greenstein, *Hidden-Hand Presidency*, p. 193.

103. On Eisenhower's deliberations between April 9, 1954, and 11, 1954, about the Oppenheimer case, see Ambrose, *Eisenhower*, vol. 2, pp. 166–167.

104. Janis, *Groupthink*.

105. Harlow, "The 'Compleat' President," in Thompson, *Eisenhower Presidency*, pp. 147–148.

106. Ibid., p. 148. See also Greenstein, *Hidden-Hand Presidency*, pp. 43–46; and, on Eisenhower's emotional commitment to resolving economic problems in the latter years of his presidency, Morgan, *Eisenhower versus "the Spenders."*

CHAPTER 6. DEADLOCK

1. Nathan, *Administrative Presidency,* pp. 69–93; and Hargrove, "Reagan Understands How to Be President."

2. Blumenthal, *Our Long National Daydream,* p. 3. Blumenthal's comments are taken from an essay, "Reagan the Unassailable," that he originally wrote while a correspondent for the *New Republic.*

3. I. M. Destler, "Reagan and the World: An 'Awesome Stubborness,'" in Jones, *Reagan Legacy,* p. 247.

4. Paul E. Peterson and Mark Rom, "Lower Taxes, More Spending, and Budget Deficits," in Jones, *Reagan Legacy,* p. 215.

5. Destler, "Reagan and the World," p. 247.

6. Stockman, *Triumph of Politics,* p. 118, emphasis in original. See pp. 116–119 for an account of the January 30 meeting with Weinberger, Schneider, and Carlucci.

7. For a more detailed discussion of the tax cut, see Cannon, *President Reagan,* pp. 232–279; Stockman, *Triumph of Politics,* pp. 248–290; and, on the administration's later efforts at tax reform, Jeffrey H. Birnbaum and Alan S. Murray, *Showdown at Gucci Gulch: Lawmakers, Lobbyists, and the Unlikely Triumph of Tax Reform* (New York: Vintage, 1987).

8. Stockman, *Triumph of Politics,* p. 285.

9. Ibid., p. 295.

10. Ibid.

11. See Schieffer and Gates, *Acting President,* pp. 144–145.

12. Anderson, *Revolution,* p. 246. See also Campbell, *Managing the Presidency,* pp. 69–70 for another account of the close relationship between the OMB and the White House during the first half of 1981.

13. Anderson, *Revolution,* p. 230, see also pp. 267–268. Anderson goes on to note, "I often reminded the cabinet councils of the president's campaign promises and his personal views on specific policy issues, and soon became known as the conscience of the administration to some, and as an irritating nag to others" (p. 230). Anderson thus seems almost to have gone out of his way to court "groupthink."

14. Stockman, *Triumph of Politics,* p. 119.

15. Ibid., pp. 119–122; and Anderson, *Revolution,* p. 249. As Anderson notes, the "Budget Working Group was effective. Billions of dollars of federal budget cuts which were appealed to the board

and denied were not appealed to the president. The board played an important role in choking off the normal, instinctive moves of the federal bureaucracy" (p. 249).

16. Regan's account, in his memoirs, of the debate over the money supply evokes a game of "chicken." "Volcker," he claims, was "possessed of an almost messianic desire to drive inflation out of the economy" and thus "pursued restrictive policies that created large, unpredictable swings in the money supply. Thus Congress was stomping on the accelerator of the economy while Volcker was simultaneously slamming on the brakes. The Administration, given the scary job of holding the steering wheel of the skidding jalopy, was sorely tempted to throw up its hands and cover its eyes" (Regan, *For the Record*, pp. 191–192).

17. The Senate rejected the administration's proposed cut in early retirement benefits by a 96–0 vote. Even in this case, however, the president's advisors carefully kept him out of the fray. See Stockman, *Triumph of Politics*, pp. 194–209, for an account of administration decision making on the proposed social security cut.

18. Ibid., p. 293.

19. Regan, quoted in ibid., p. 297, emphasis in original; see also Regan, *For the Record*, pp. 193–195. By June 1981, the rivalry between Stockman and Regan had become difficult to paper over. After discovering that Stockman was partly responsible for a press leak on the administration's tax policy, Regan exploded. "*God damn it!* This is the final straw," he told Stockman. "You're not going to get away with this. I'm going straight to the President. . . . This is the last time you're going to undercut me. . . . I've had it up to my ears. We're going to settle right now who's in charge of economic policy" (Stockman, *Triumph of Politics*, p. 262).

20. Stockman, *Triumph of Politics*, p. 296.

21. Ibid., p. 319; for Stockman's account of his dispute with Weinberger over the defense budget, see pp. 299–324.

22. Ibid., pp. 323–324.

23. Ibid., p. 339. See also Regan, *For the Record*, pp. 193–206.

24. Stockman, *Triumph of Politics*, p. 341.

25. Regan, *For the Record*, p. 197.

26. Reagan, *American Life*, p. 315.

27. Regan, *For the Record*, p. 210.

28. Stockman, *Triumph of Politics*, p. 97.

29. Ibid., p. 345–346, emphasis in original.

30. William Greider, "The Education of David Stockman," *Atlantic Monthly* 248 (December 1981), pp. 27–54.

31. Reagan, *American Life*, p. 317.

32. Regan, *For the Record*, p. 203.

33. Ibid., pp. 209 and 210.

34. Stockman, *Triumph of Politics*, p. 391.

35. Edwards, *Presidential Approval*, pp. 107–108. Eisenhower averaged a similar 65 percent approval rating during his presidency (pp. 153–156).

36. On the ethics scandals during the Reagan administration, see Dugger, *On Reagan*, pp. 25–42.

37. James Schlesinger, "Reykjavik and Revelations: A Turn of the Tide?" in William G. Hyland, ed., *America and the World: 1986* (New York: Council on Foreign Relations, 1987), p. 441; cited in Destler, "Reagan and the World," p. 256.

38. Charles-Philippe David, *Foreign Policy Failure in the White House: Reappraising the Fall of the Shah and the Iran-Contra Affair* (Lanham, Maryland: University Press of America, 1993); and 't Hart, *Groupthink in Government*. Also consistent with the idea of groupthink, Theodore Draper describes the group that formulated the arms-for hostages plans as a "junta"; see Draper, "The Rise of an American Junta," *New York Review of Books*, October 8, 1987, pp. 47–58; Draper, "The Fall of an American Junta," *New York Review of Books*, October 22, 1987, pp. 45–57; and Draper, *A Very Thin Line: The Iran-Contra Affairs* (New York: Hill and Wang, 1991). My own account of the way decision making during the first phase of the Iran-Contra affair (before it became public) resembled groupthink is given in Paul A. Kowert, "Leadership and Learning in Political Groups: The Management of Advice in the Iran-Contra Affair," *Governance: An International Journal of Policy and Administration* 14, 2 (April 2001), pp. 201–232.

39. Cannon, *President Reagan*, p. 557.

40. Deaver planned to leave the White House himself, and he may have felt that Baker's move to Treasury would make his own departure easier. Nancy Reagan depended heavily on both Baker and Deaver, however, and the plan clearly required her approval. Deaver convinced her that Baker would soon leave his post anyway and that, since Regan got along well with the president, he would be a good replacement. See ibid. (pp. 553–588), for a more detailed discussion of the structural changes in the White House staff in 1985. For a clear statement of Mrs. Reagan's own impor-

tance to the president, see Neustadt, *Presidential Power and the Modern Presidents,* pp. 312–313.

41. As Regan put it, the president "seemed to be absorbing a fait accompli rather than making a decision. One might have thought that the matter had already been settled by some absent party" (Regan, *For the Record,* p. 255).

42. See ibid., p. 261. Of course, several of the president's other Cabinet officials, including Shultz and Weinberger, could meet with him easily enough. Yet Regan's proximity to the president allowed him to be present at these meetings as well.

43. Ibid., pp. 262–264.

44. Schieffer and Gates, *Acting President,* p. 199.

45. John Tower, Edmund Muskie, and Brent Scowcroft, *Report of the President's Special Review Board, February 26, 1987* (Washington, D.C.: U.S. Government Printing Office, 1987); published by the *New York Times* as *The Tower Commission Report* (New York: Times Books, 1987), p. 79; henceforth cited as "*Tower Commission Report.*"

46. See *Tower Commission Report,* p. 67. Before Robert McFarlane was replaced by Admiral Poindexter as national security advisor, McFarlane also met regularly with the president to discuss initiatives to free the hostages. It was McFarlane who first brought the possibility of an arms trade to the president's attention, while Reagan was convalescing shortly after his prostate cancer operation. See *Tower Commission Report,* pp. 129–145; Schieffer and Gates, *Acting President,* pp. 231–232; and Congressional Quarterly, *The Iran-Contra Puzzle* (Washington, D.C.: Congressional Quarterly, 1987), pp. A9–A10.

47. *Tower Commission Report,* p. 81.

48. Ibid., pp. 138–148; Congressional Quarterly, *Iran-Contra Puzzle,* p. A10. TOW missiles are tube-launched, optically tracked, wire-guided missiles intended to be used primarily against tanks. Shultz later testified before the Tower Commission that he had opposed the missile sale: "I said in the meeting that it's a mistake. I said it had to be stopped" (*Tower Commission Report,* p. 145). Shultz and Weinberger also reiterated this position in another meeting two days later (August 8).

49. Congressional Quarterly, *Iran-Contra Puzzle,* p. A10. The plan presented to the president on August 6 had its origins in a revised Special National Intelligence Estimate on Iran prepared by the CIA in May 1985. On this basis, two NSC staffers (Donald Fortier and Howard Teicher) prepared a National Security Decision

Directive—the object of Weinberger's comment—suggesting that arms sales to Iran might curry favor with Iranian "moderates." Also see Draper, *Very Thin Line,* p. 150.

50. McFarlane testified before the Tower Commission that the president's approval of the initial arms sale came in a phone call shortly after the August 8 meeting (*Tower Commission Report,* pp. 145–148). For another discussion of McFarlane's first presentation of the arms-for-hostages initiative to the president and of the president's reaction, see Cannon, *President Reagan,* pp. 613–619.

51. Congressional Quarterly, *Iran-Contra Puzzle,* p. A15. Also see Draper, *Very Thin Line,* pp. 225–229; and *Tower Commission Report,* pp. 177–188.

52. Cannon, *President Reagan,* pp. 635–636. For an account of this meeting, see also Draper, *Very Thin Line*, pp. 247–249; and *Tower Commission Report,* pp. 219–228.

53. Cannon, *President Reagan,* pp. 637–638.

54. *Tower Commission Report,* pp. 81–82.

55. Stanley Sporkin, quoted in Cannon, *President Reagan,* p. 637.

56. It remains unclear whether Reagan himself knew anything about North's plans to divert profits from the arms sales to the Contras. In his videotaped deposition for Admiral Poindexter's trial, Reagan specifically denied any knowledge of such a diversion. See Ronald Reagan, deposition in the case of *United States of America v. John M. Poindexter* (U.S. District Court, District of Columbia), taken at the U.S. District Court, Central District of California, February 16–17, 1990.

57. Cannon, *President Reagan,* p. 639. According to William Casey's testimony before Congress, the draft of this finding "was not circulated among the national security planning group as required; and several key administration officials were not informed that Reagan had signed it." See National Security Archive, *The Chronology* (New York: Warner Books, 1987), p. 576.

58. McFarlane's unsuccessful trip to Teheran had actually been in May. In response to the early news reports, based on the *Al-Shiraa* story, McFarlane simply denied that he had traveled to Iran in October.

59. National Security Archive, *Chronology*, pp. 544 and 545; the National Security Archive cites Reuters, November 6, 1986.

60. *Tower Commission Report,* p. 480.

61. Ronald Reagan, televised address, November 13, 1986, quoted in *Tower Commission Report,* pp. 502 and 503.

62. Cannon, *President Reagan,* p. 681.

63. Regan, quoted in Bernard Weintraub, "Criticism on Iran and Other Issues Put Reagan's Aides on Defensive," *New York Times,* November 16, 1986.

64. Cannon, *President Reagan,* p. 586; and Draper, *Very Thin Line,* p. 477. Shultz was also unhappy with Regan, who he believed had protected the president from the truth for too long.

65. By her own admission, Mrs. Reagan "was furious" after she read Weintraub's interview with Regan in the *New York Times.* See Nancy Reagan, *My Turn,* p. 314.

66. Regan, *For the Record,* pp. 3–24; Nancy Reagan, *My Turn,* pp. 312–313. During the president's convalescence, Regan decided to use a helicopter to commute from the White House to the Bethesda Naval Hospital, provoking another dispute. Nancy Reagan felt that "it was inappropriate for anyone other than the president to use the helicopter except in an emergency" (Nancy Reagan, *My Turn,* p. 313). Regan objected that traveling by car would take 40 minutes each way, but in the end he gave in to Mrs. Reagan's wishes (Regan, *For the Record,* pp. 14–15).

67. Mrs. Reagan's consultations with her astrologer, Joan Quigley, were another point of contention between the first lady and the chief of staff. Quigley advised Mrs. Reagan about whether specific dates were "safe" or "dangerous" for the president. Donald Regan was thus obliged, as he recalls sarcastically in his memoirs, to keep "a color-coded calendar on my desk (numerals highlighted in green ink for 'good' days, red for 'bad' days, yellow for 'iffy' days) as an aid to remembering when it was propitious to move the President of the United States from one place to another, or schedule him to speak in public, or commence negotiations with a foreign power" (Regan, *For the Record,* p. 4).

68. Ibid., p. 30.

69. Ibid., p. 30, emphasis in original.

70. Draper, *Very Thin Line,* pp. 470 and 472.

71. Cannon, *President Reagan,* p. 691; and Lawrence E. Walsh, *Firewall: The Iran Contra Conspiracy and Cover-up* (New York: Norton, 1997), pp. 374–375.

72. Regan, *For the Record,* p. 36.

73. Draper, *Very Thin Line,* p. 478.

74. See U.S. Congress, House Select Committee to Investigate Covert Arms Transactions with Iran and Senate Select Committee On Secret Military Assistance to Iran and the Nicaraguan Opposition, 100th Cong., 1st sess., *Report of the Congressional Commit-*

tees Investigating the Iran-Contra Affair (Washington, D.C.: U.S. Government Printing Office, 1987); reprinted under the same title by the *New York Times*, Joel Brinkley and Stephen Engelberg, eds. (New York: Times Books, 1988), see pp. 260–261.

75. Reagan, *American Life*, p. 529.

76. Draper, *Very Thin Line*, p. 485.

77. Mayer and McManus (*Landslide*, p. 359) report the results of a *Wall Street Journal-NBC News* poll to this effect.

78. Even conservative members of Congress, such as Utah Senator Orrin Hatch, had begun to call for Regan to resign. As Hatch put it, "He did not protect the president. He did not inform the president. What is worse, he did not assure that he was informed himself" (Mayer and McManus, *Landslide*, p. 362). On the evening of December 4, Mrs. Reagan and Michael Deaver convened a meeting in the White House, also attended by William Rogers and Robert Strauss, to discuss Regan. The four talked with the president for two hours, and Strauss, Deaver, and Mrs. Reagan in particular felt Regan should leave. Strauss summed up his position in this way: "I have no quarrel with Don Regan. . . . But you've got two serious problems right now, and he's not helping you with either one. First, you've got a political problem on the Hill, and Don Regan has no constituency and no allies there. Second, you've got a serious media problem, and Regan has no friends there, either. . . . You're in a hell of a mess, Mr. President, and you need a chief of staff who can help you" (Nancy Reagan, *My Turn*, p. 321). See also Cannon, *President Reagan*, pp. 722–725.

79. Edwin Feulner, quoted in Mayer and McManus, *Landslide*, pp. 370–371.

80. Mayer and McManus, *Landslide*, p. 371.

81. Regan, *For the Record*, p. 71.

82. Nancy Reagan, *My Turn*, p. 319.

83. Cannon, *President Reagan*, p. 725.

84. Kenneth Khachigian, quoted in Mayer and McManus, *Landslide*, p. 371.

85. Mayer and McManus, *Landslide*, p. 374.

86. Ibid., p. 379. On February 8, during yet another clash over whether the president should hold a press conference, their argument became so acrimonious that Regan actually hung up on Mrs. Reagan. For the accounts of both parties, which agree substantially, see Regan, *For the Record*, pp. 100–101; and Nancy Reagan, *My Turn*, p. 326.

87. Regan, *For the Record*, p. 108.

88. Ibid., p. 109.
89. *Tower Commission Report*, p. 81.
90. Regan, *For the Record*, p. 416.
91. Meese, quoted in Mayer and McManus, *Landslide*, p. 385. For a discussion of improvements in policy coordination within the Reagan administration after Baker's arrival, see Kowert, "Leadership and Learning in Political Groups."
92. Cannon, *President Reagan*, p. 710.
93. Mayer and McManus, *Landslide*, p. 378.
94. Edwin Meese claimed while testifying at Oliver North's trial, in fact, that impeachment "was a concern." Meese, quoted in Cannon, *President Reagan*, p. 704; Cannon cites George Lardner Jr., "Meese Details White House Crisis," *Washington Post*, March 29, 1989.
95. One aspect of the closed learning style, as noted in chapter 2, is the tendency to emphasize the role of fate or powerful others over one's own role in events (external locus of control). Reagan's emphasis on external causes of the crisis, such as the press, is thus consistent with a closed learning style.
96. Reagan, *American Life*, p. 541.
97. Regan, *For the Record*, p. 109.
98. Janis and Mann, *Decision Making*, pp. 52–58 and 107–133. Janis and Mann argue that defensive avoidance occurs when a decision maker is faced with a problem that poses serious risks and for which no solution is realistically apparent. In these circumstances, decision makers typically deny the existence of the problem or blame it on others. For closed leaders in particular, too much diversity of opinion or dissent may suggest that no solution is possible, thus producing the conditions for defensive avoidance.
99. See Cannon, *President Reagan*, pp. 678 and 719; and Stockman, *Triumph of Politics*, pp. 388–389.
100. Cannon, *President Reagan*, p. 738. Nevertheless, by the end of 1988, Reagan's public approval rating once again exceeded 60 percent (Edwards, *Presidential Approval*, p. 113).

CHAPTER 7. CONCLUSION

1. Niccolò Machiavelli, *The Prince*, trans. William K. Marriott (New York: Dutton, 1958), ch. 23.
2. Ibid. Maximilian I (1459–1519), Holy Roman Emperor and German king, succeeded his father Emperor Frederick III in 1493.

Military campaigns and "marriage diplomacy" led to his involvement in French and Italian politics.

3. Janis also acknowledges, though only as a brief caveat, that this advice may not be suitable in all circumstances; see Janis, *Groupthink*, p. 262. His later work, *Crucial Decisions*, pays greater attention to possible interactions between personality and structural constraints on the policy-making process; see esp. pp. 203–229.

4. Excerpt from *Milinda-pa-ha*, quoted in Aaron Wildavsky, *Speaking Truth to Power: The Art and Craft of Policy Analysis* (Boston: Little, Brown, 1979), p. 402. Milinda (Menendes) was a Bactrian king and heir to territory in Afghanistan, Pakistan, and northwest India earlier conquered by Alexander the Great.

5. This complaint is voiced strongly, for example, by Alexander George (*Presidential Decisionmaking in Foreign Policy*, p. 166); and by Burke and Greenstein (*How Presidents Test Reality*, p. 21).

6. This is also a simplification, of course, since leaders are not really conveniently divided into the two distinct categories of *open* and *closed*. Most of them probably fall somewhere in a middle range. The most closed individuals, those totally incapable of hearing advice, are not likely to rise to high positions of leadership. Likewise, those so committed to openness that they shy away from making even simple decisions on their own are not likely to become leaders, although they might conceivably make good technical advisors. It makes more sense to conceive of learning style as a continuum, ranging from closed to open. This is the assumption of the preceding chapters, although differences between Eisenhower and Reagan were often treated in categorical terms to simplify presentation of the main argument. In practice, as a result of both "self-selection" and competition for leadership positions, leaders are typically open enough to take advice and closed enough to make up their own minds about it.

7. Kowert, "Leadership and Learning in Political Groups," articulates political hypotheses about learning similar to those advanced here. In addition, see Paul D. Hoyt and Jean A. Garrison, "Political Manipulation within the Small Group: Foreign Policy Advisers in the Carter Administration," in 't Hart, Stern, and Sundelius, *Beyond Groupthink*, pp. 249–274; and D. Thompson, "Moral Responsibility of Public Officials: The Problem of Many Hands," *American Political Science Review* 74 (1980), pp. 905–916. Research on majority and minority influence in decision groups also emphasizes the distribution of power within groups. Two of

the more important studies of majority and minority influence are Serge Moscovici, "Social Influence and Conformity," in Gardner Lindzey and Elliot Aronson, eds., *The Handbook of Social Psychology* (New York: Random House, 1985), vol. 2, pp. 347–412; and Charlan Jeanne Nemeth, "Differential Contributions of Majority and Minority Influence," *Psychological Review* 93 (1986), pp. 23–32. Again, however, political scientists themselves have had relatively little to say about the effects of the distribution of power within organizations on decision making. Most studies of minority influence follow the usual pattern of drawing on basic research and theories formulated by psychologists and applying them to political groups.

At a somewhat different level than that of the advisory group, Graham Allison's classic study of governmental politics, *Essence of Decision: Explaining the Cuban Missile Crisis* (Boston: Little, Brown, 1971), makes a similar point about the importance of political considerations to governmental decision making and problem solving. No one should be surprised to discover that political organizations routinely face internal as well as external political battles. Yet, as two later assessments make clear, efforts to derive theoretical propositions from Allison's insights have not progressed rapidly. See Jonathan Bendor and Terry Hammond, "Rethinking Allison's Models," *American Political Science Review* 86 (1992), pp. 301–321; and David Welch, "The Organizational Process and Bureaucratic Politics Paradigms," *International Security* 17 (1992), pp. 112–146.

8. Johnson, *Managing the White House.*

9. In principle, formality does not require political distance or hierarchy. Egalitarian norms within a group might also be formalized, but leaders who prefer collegial groups are probably less likely to insist on formality. This distinction between *formality* and *hierarchy* is discussed further in the next section.

10. Nixon did approve of the change in alert status when he was informed of it the following morning. See Stephen Ambrose, *Nixon: Ruin and Recovery* (New York: Simon & Schuster, 1991), vol. 3, pp. 234–257; Patrick Haney, "The Nixon Administration and Middle East Crises: Theory and Evidence of Presidential Management of Foreign Policy Decision-Making," *Political Research Quarterly* 48 (1994), pp. 939–959; and Haney, *Organizing for Foreign Policy Crises,* pp. 75–79. Henry Kissinger's own version of events is vague on when exactly Nixon was informed; see Kissinger, *The White House Years* (Boston: Little, Brown, 1979).

11. Hess, *Organizing the Presidency*, pp. 27–43.

12. See ibid., pp. 140–168. As Hess puts it, "power centers existed in the White House—in the Office of Management and Budget, the Domestic Policy staff, the National Security Council, and the Council of Economic Advisors—but no hierarchy. No one supervised how all the pieces fitted together philosophically or operationally until halfway through the president's term" (p. 142). Also see Kessel, "Structures of the Carter White House"; and Moens, *Foreign Policy Under Carter*.

13. James Fallows, "The Passionless Presidency," *Atlantic* (May 1979), p. 39.

14. On the classification of Nixon as a relatively closed leader, see Kowert, "Where *Does* the Buck Stop?"

15. See Hess, *Organizing the Presidency*, p. 102; also Herbert Y. Schandler, *The Unmaking of a President* (Princeton: Princeton University Press, 1977). For another example of "ritualized" dissent, see 't Hart's brief discussion of the city of Amsterdam's costly decision to proceed with plans to build an opera house annex to City Hall (t' Hart, *Groupthink in Government*, pp. 184–185).

16. See Alexander George, *Presidential Decisionmaking in Foreign Policy*, pp. 191–208.

17. Roger Hilsman, *To Move a Nation* (Garden City, New York: Doubleday, 1967), p. 6, quoted in 't Hart, *Groupthink in Government*, p. 152. On the lessons Kennedy learned about the importance of a trusted inner circle of advisors after the Bay of Pigs fiasco, also see Hess, *Organizing the Presidency*, p. 81.

18. Robert Albanese and David D. Van Fleet, "Rational Behavior in Groups: The Free-Riding Tendency," *Academy of Management Review* 10 (1985), pp. 244–255; Stephen G. Harkins and Kate Szymanski, "Social Loafing and Social Facilitation: New Wine in Old Bottles," in Clyde Hendrick, ed., *Group Processes and Intergroup Relations*, *Review of Personality and Social Psychology* (Newbury Park, California: Sage, 1987), vol. 9, pp. 167–188; and Steven Prentice-Dunn and Ronald W. Rogers, "Deindividuation and the Self-Regulation of Behavior," in Paul B. Paulus, ed., *Psychology of Group Influence*, 2d ed. (Hillsdale, New Jersey: Lawrence Erlbaum, 1989), pp. 87–109.

19. Some psychological studies suggest that the natural size of groups is relatively small, typically less than ten people, and often only two or three. See John M. Levine and Richard L. Moreland, "Progress in Small Group Research," *Annual Review of Psychology* 41 (1990), p. 596. It would be interesting to know whether this

pattern also holds true in more "communitarian" societies, such as China or Japan, where one might expect the typical group to be larger.

20. Hess, *Organizing the Presidency*, p. 189.

21. Ibid., p. 178.

22. For assessments of the openness of modern presidents, see Kowert, "Where *Does* the Buck Stop?" Again, this is not to say that politically unpopular outcomes are inevitable for closed leaders or that closed leaders are never able to tolerate dissent. For an example to the contrary, see Betty Glad and Jean A. Garrison, "Ronald Reagan and the Intermediate Nuclear Forces Treaty: Whatever Happened to the 'Evil Empire'?" in Schmertz, Datlof, and Ugrinsky, eds., *President Reagan and the World*, pp. 91–107.

23. Hess, *Organizing the Presidency*, p. 142.

24. Alexander George, *Presidential Decisionmaking in Foreign Policy*, p. 2.

25. Hess makes a similar argument in *Organizing the Presidency*, p. 14. He suggests that overconfidence may follow re-election as well and offers the additional examples of Roosevelt's court-packing plan in 1937 and Johnson's escalation of the Vietnam War in 1965.

26. Thomas Gilovich, *How We Know What Isn't So: The Fallibility of Human Reason in Everyday Life* (New York: Free Press, 1991), p. 186. Also see Robert Nisbett and Lee Ross, *Human Inference: Strategies and Shortcomings of Social Judgment* (Englewood Cliffs, New Jersey: Prentice-Hall, 1980).

27. Stephen Jay Gould, *An Urchin in the Storm: Essays About Books and Ideas* (New York: Norton, 1987), p. 245; quoted in Gilovich, *How We Know What Isn't So*, p. 6.

Bibliography

Abelson, Robert P., "Whatever Became of Consistency Theory?" *Personality and Social Psychology Bulletin* 9 (1983), pp. 37–54.

Adams, Gordon, *The FY 1986 Defense Budget: The Weapons Buildup Continues* (Washington, D.C.: Center on Budget and Policy Priorities, 1985).

Adams, Sherman, *Firsthand Report* (New York: Harper, 1961).

Adorno, T. W., et al., *The Authoritarian Personality* (New York: Harper, 1950).

Albanese, Robert and David D. Van Fleet, "Rational Behavior in Groups: The Free-Riding Tendency," *Academy of Management Review* 10 (1985), pp. 244–255.

Aldag, Raymond J. and S. R. Fuller, "Beyond Fiasco: A Reappraisal of the Groupthink Phenomenon and a New Model of Group Decision Processes," *Psychological Bulletin* 113 (1993), pp. 533–552.

Allison, Graham, *Essence of Decision: Explaining the Cuban Missile Crisis* (Boston: Little, Brown, 1971).

Allport, Gordon W., *Personality: A Psychological Interpretation* (New York: Holt, 1937).

——, *The Nature of Prejudice* (Boston: Addison-Wesley, 1954).

Amaker, Norman C., *Civil Rights and the Reagan Administration* (Washington, D.C.: Urban Institute Press, 1988).

Ambrose, Stephen E., *The Supreme Commander: The War Years of General Dwight D. Eisenhower* (New York: Doubleday, 1970).

——, *Eisenhower: Soldier, General of the Army, President-Elect, 1890–1952* (New York: Simon & Schuster, 1983), vol. 1.

231

————, *Eisenhower: the President* (New York: Simon & Schuster, 1984), vol. 2.

————, *Nixon: Ruin and Recovery* (New York: Simon & Schuster, 1991), vol. 3.

Anderson, John R., *Cognitive Psychology and Its Implications* (San Francisco: W. H. Freeman & Co., 1980).

Anderson, Lynn R., "Groups Would Do Better Without Humans," *Personality and Social Psychology Bulletin* 4 (1978), pp. 557–558.

Anderson, Martin, *Revolution: The Reagan Legacy* (Stanford: Hoover Institution Press, 1990).

Anderson, Patrick, *The President's Men* (Garden City, New York: Doubleday, 1968).

Anthony, R. N., *The Management Control Function* (Boston: Harvard Business School Press, 1988).

Artaud, Denise, "France Between the Indochina War and the European Defense Community," in Lawrence S. Kaplan, Denise Artaud, and Mark R. Rubin, *Dien Bien Phu and the Crisis of Franco-American Relations, 1954–1955* (Wilmington, Delaware: Scholarly Resources Books, 1990), pp. 251–268.

Ashford, Nigel, "The Conservative Agenda and the Reagan Presidency," in Joseph Hogan, ed., *The Reagan Years: The Record in Presidential Leadership* (Manchester: Manchester University Press, 1990).

Baars, Bernard J., *The Cognitive Revolution in Psychology* (New York: Guilford, 1986).

Backteman, Gunnar and David Magnusson, "Longitudinal Stability of Personality Characteristics," *Journal of Personality* 49, 2 (June 1981), pp. 148–160.

Barber, James David, *The Lawmakers* (New Haven: Yale University Press, 1965).

————, *The Presidential Character: Predicting Performance in the White House* (Englewood Cliffs, New Jersey: Prentice-Hall, 1972).

Basgall, Jo Ann and C. R. Snyder, "Excuses in Waiting: External Locus of Control and Reactions to Success-Failure Feedback," *Journal of Personality and Social Psychology* 54 (1988), pp. 656–662.

Bem, Daryl J. and A. Allen, "On Predicting Some of the People Some of the Time," *Psychological Review* 81 (1974), pp. 88–104.

Bendor, Jonathan and Terry Hammond, "Rethinking Allison's Models," *American Political Science Review* 86 (1992), pp. 301–321.

Berman, Larry, ed., *Looking Back on the Reagan Presidency* (Baltimore: Johns Hopkins University Press, 1990).

Billings-Yun, Melanie, *Decision Against War: Eisenhower and Dien Bien Phu, 1954* (New York: Columbia University Press, 1988).

Birnbaum, Jeffrey H. and Alan S. Murray, *Showdown at Gucci Gulch: Lawmakers, Lobbyists, and the Unlikely Triumph of Tax Reform* (New York: Vintage, 1987).

Block, Jack, *Lives Through Time* (Berkeley: Bancroft, 1971).

Bloedel, Richard H., "The Alaska Statehood Movement" (Ph. D. diss., University of Washington, 1974).

Blumenthal, Sidney, *Our Long National Daydream: A Political Pageant of the Reagan Era* (New York: Harper & Row, 1988).

Boorstin, Daniel, *The Genius of American Politics* (Chicago: University of Chicago Press, 1953).

Bower, Gordon H. and Ernest R. Hilgard, *Theories of Learning* (Englewood Cliffs, New Jersey: Prentice-Hall, 1981).

Boyarsky, Bill, *The Rise of Ronald Reagan* (New York: Random House, 1968).

Branford, Sue and Bernardo Kucinski, *The Debt Squads: The US, the Banks, and Latin America* (London: Zed Books, 1988).

Breslauer, George W. and Philip E. Tetlock, eds. *Learning in U.S. and Soviet Foreign Policy* (Boulder, Colorado: Westview, 1991).

Brodie, Bernard, "A Psychoanalytic Interpretation of Woodrow Wilson," *World Politics* 9 (1957), pp. 413–422.

Bronner, Rolf, *Decision Making Under Time Pressure* (Lexington, Massachussets: Heath, 1982).

Brownell, Herbert, with John P. Burke, *Advising Ike: The Memoirs of Attorney General Herbert Brownell* (Lawrence: University Press of Kansas, 1993).

Burger, Jerry, "Desire for Control and Achievement-Related Behaviors," *Journal of Personality and Social Psychology* 48 (1985), pp. 1520–1533.

———, "Desire for Control and Conformity to a Perceived Norm," *Journal of Personality and Social Psychology* 53 (1987), pp. 355–360.

Burke, John P., *The Institutional Presidency: Organizing and Managing the White House from FDR to Clinton* (Baltimore: Johns Hopkins University Press, 2000).

Burke, John P. and Fred I. Greenstein, *How Presidents Test Reality: Decisions on Vietnam, 1954 and 1965* (New York: Russell Sage Foundation, 1989).

Buys, Christian J., "Humans Would Do Better Without Groups," *Personality and Social Psychology Bulletin* 4 (1978), pp. 123–125.

Campbell, Bruce A., "On the Utility of Trait Theory in Political Science," *Micropolitics* 1, 2 (1981), pp. 177–190.

Campbell, Colin, *Managing the Presidency: Carter, Reagan, and the Search for Executive Harmony* (Pittsburgh: University of Pittsburgh Press, 1986).

Cannon, Lou, *Reagan* (New York: Perigee, 1982).

———, *President Reagan: The Role of a Lifetime* (New York: Simon & Schuster, 1991).

Caro, Robert, *The Years of Lyndon Johnson: Means of Ascent* (New York: Knopf, 1990).

Cattell, Raymond B., *Personality and Learning Theory: The Structure of Personality in Its Environment* (New York: Springer, 1979), vol. 1.

Caute, David, *The Great Fear: The Anti-Communist Purge under Truman and Eisenhower* (New York: Simon & Schuster, 1978).

Ceplair, Larry and Steven Englund, *The Inquisition in Hollywood: Politics in the Film Community, 1930–1960* (Garden City, New York: Anchor, 1980).

Church, George J., "The President's Men," *Time*, December 14, 1981, pp. 16–22.

Clark, Margaret S. and Alice M. Isen, "Toward Understanding the Relationship Between Feeling States, Judgments, and Behavior," in Albert Hastorf and Alice Isen, eds., *Cognitive Social Psychology* (New York: Elsevier North-Holland, 1982), pp. 73–108.

Cohen, Benjamin J., "An Explosion in the Kitchen? Economic Relations with Other Advanced Industrial States," in Kenneth Oye, Ronald Lieber, and Donald Rothchild, *Eagle Resurgent?: The Reagan Era in American Foreign Policy* (Boston: Little, Brown, 1983), pp. 115–143.

———, *In Whose Interest?: International Banking and American Foreign Policy* (New Haven: Yale University Press, 1986).

Colquhoun, W. P. and D. W. J. Corcoran, "The Effects of Time of Day and Social Isolation on the Relationship Between Temperament and Performance," *British Journal of Social and Clinical Psychology* 3 (1964), pp. 226–231.

Congressional Quarterly, *Trade: U.S. Policy Since 1945* (Washington, D.C.: Congressional Quarterly, 1984).

———, *The Iran-Contra Puzzle* (Washington, D.C.: Congressional Quarterly, 1987).

Conkin, Paul Keith, *Big Daddy from the Pedernales: Lyndon Baines Johnson* (Boston: Twayne Publishers, 1986).

Conley, James J. "Longitudinal Stability of Personality Traits: A Multitrait-Multimethod-Multioccasion Analysis," *Journal of Personality and Social Psychology* 49, 5 (1985), pp. 1266–1282.

Costa, Paul T. and Robert R. McCrae, "Still Stable After All these Years," in P. B. Baltes and O. G. Brim, eds., *Life Span Development and Behavior* (New York: Academic Press, 1980), vol. 3, pp. 65–102.

Courtright, J. A., "A Laboratory Investigation of Groupthink," *Communication Monographs* 45 (1978), pp. 229–246.

Crabb, Cecil and Kevin Mulcahy, *Presidents and Foreign Policy Making: From FDR to Reagan* (Baton Rouge: Louisiana State University Press, 1986).

Dallek, Robert, *Ronald Reagan: The Politics of Symbolism* (Cambridge: Harvard University Press, 1984).

David, Charles-Philippe, *Foreign Policy Failure in the White House: Reappraising the Fall of the Shah and the Iran-Contra Affair* (Lanham, Maryland: University Press of America, 1993).

Davis, Kenneth S., *Soldier of Democracy: A Biography of Dwight Eisenhower* (Garden City, New York: Doubleday, Doran, 1945).

Davis, William L. and E. Jerry Phares, "Internal-External Control as a Determinant of Information-Seeking in a Social Influence Situation," *Journal of Personality* 35, 4 (1967), pp. 547–561.

Deaver, Michael K., with Mickey Herskowitz, *Behind the Scenes* (New York: Morrow, 1987).

Delamaide, Darrell, *Debt Shock: The Full Story of the World Credit Crisis* (Garden City, New York: Doubleday, 1984).

DeMause, Lloyd, *Reagan's America* (New York: Creative Roots, 1984).

DeMause, Lloyd and Henry Ebel, eds., *Jimmy Carter and American Fantasy: Psychohistorical Explorations* (New York: Two Continents, 1977).

Dessler, David, "What's at Stake in the Agent-Structure Debate?" *International Organization* 43, 3 (1989), pp. 441–473.

Destler, I. M., "Reagan and the World: An 'Awesome Stubborness,'" in Charles O. Jones, ed., *The Reagan Legacy: Promise and Performance* (Chatham, New Jersey: Chatham House, 1988), pp. 241–261.

Dewar, Helen and Margaret Shapiro, "Hill Leaders Split Over Pulling Out Troops in Beirut," *Washington Post*, January 24, 1984.

Diamond, Sigmund, *Compromised Campus* (New York: Oxford University Press, 1992).

Diggins, John Patrick, *The Proud Decades: America in War and in Peace, 1941–1960* (New York: Norton, 1988).

Digman, John M., "Personality Structure: Emergence of the Five-Factor Model," *Annual Review of Psychology* 41 (1990), pp. 417–440.

Divine, Robert A., *Eisenhower and the Cold War* (New York: Oxford University Press, 1981).

Dollinger, Stephen J., Leilani Greening, and Barbara Tylenda, "Psychological-Mindedness as 'Reading Between the Lines': Vigilance, Locus of Control, and Sagacious Judgment," *Journal of Personality* 53 (1985), pp. 603–625.

Donner, Frank, *The Age of Surveillance* (New York: Knopf, 1981).

Draper, Theodore, "The Rise of an American Junta," *New York Review of Books*, October 8, 1987, pp. 47–58.

———, "The Fall of an American Junta," *New York Review of Books*, October 22, 1987, pp. 45–57.

———, *A Very Thin Line: The Iran-Contra Affairs* (New York: Hill and Wang, 1991).

Dugger, Ronnie, *On Reagan: The Man & His Presidency* (New York: McGraw-Hill, 1983).

Duram, James, *A Moderate Among Extremists: Dwight D. Eisenhower and the School Desegregation Crisis* (Chicago: Nelson-Hall, 1981).

Eckstein, Harry, "Case Study and Theory in Political Science," in Fred Greenstein and Nelson Polsby, eds., *Handbook of Political Science* (Reading, Massachusetts: Addison-Wesley, 1975), vol. 7, pp. 79–138.

Eden, Colin and Jim Radford, *Tackling Strategic Problems: The Role of Group Decision Support* (London: Sage, 1990).

Edgerton, Russell, *Sub-Cabinet Politics and Policy Commitment:*

The Birth of the Development Loan Fund (Syracuse: Inter-University Case Program, 1970).

Edwards, George C., *Presidential Approval: A Sourcebook* (Baltimore: Johns Hopkins University Press, 1990).

Eisenhower, Dwight D., *Crusade in Europe* (Garden City, New York: Doubleday, 1948).

——, *Mandate for Change: The White House Years, 1953–1956* (Garden City, New York: Doubleday, 1963).

——, *Waging Peace: The White House Years, 1956–1961* (Garden City, New York: Doubleday, 1965).

——, *At Ease: Stories I Tell to Friends* (Garden City, New York: Doubleday, 1967).

Eisenhower, Milton, *The Wine Is Bitter* (Garden City, New York: Doubleday, 1963).

Ellis, Henry C. and James B. Franklin, "Memory and Personality: External Versus Internal Locus of Control and Superficial Organization in Free Recall," *Journal of Verbal Learning and Verbal Behavior* 22 (1983), pp. 61–74.

Ély, Paul, *Mémoirs: L'Indochine dans la Tourmente* (Paris: Librarie Plon, 1964).

Erikson, Erik, *Young Man Luther: A Study in Psychoanalysis and History* (New York: Norton, 1958).

Esser, James K. and J. S. Lindoerfer, "Groupthink and the Space Shuttle Challenger Accident: Toward a Quantitative Case Analysis," *Journal of Behavioral Decision Making* 2 (1989), pp. 167–177.

Estes, William K., *Models of Learning, Memory, and Choice* (New York: Praeger, 1982).

Etheredge, Lloyd S., *Can Governments Learn?* (New York: Pergamon, 1985).

Evans, Charles R. and Kenneth L. Dion, "Group Cohesion and Performance: A Meta-Analysis," *Small Group Research* 22 (1991), pp. 175–186.

Ewald, William B., *Eisenhower the President: Crucial Days, 1951–1960* (Englewood Cliffs, New Jersey: Prentice-Hall, 1981).

——, "A Biographer's Perspective," in Kenneth Thompson, ed., *The Eisenhower Presidency: Eleven Intimate Perspectives of Dwight D. Eisenhower* (Lanham, Maryland: University Press of America, 1984), pp. 15–37.

——, *Who Killed Joe McCarthy?* (New York: Simon & Schuster, 1984).

Eysenck, Hans J., *Dimensions of Personality* (London: Routledge and Kegan Paul, 1947).

——, *The Biological Basis of Personality* (Springfield, Illinois: Charles C. Thomas, 1967).

Eysenck, Hans J. and S. B. G. Eysenck, "On the Unitary Nature of Extraversion," in Hans J. Eysenck, *Eysenck on Extraversion* (New York: Wiley, 1973).

Fallows, James, "The Passionless Presidency," *Atlantic Monthly* May 1979, pp. 33–48.

Ferrell, Robert H., *The Eisenhower Diaries* (New York: Norton, 1981).

——, ed., *The Diary of James C. Hagerty: Eisenhower in Mid-Course, 1954–55* (Bloomington: Indiana University Press, 1983).

Feinberg, Richard E., "American Power and Third World Economies," in Kenneth Oye, Ronald Lieber, and Donald Rothchild, *Eagle Resurgent?: The Reagan Era in American Foreign Policy* (Boston: Little, Brown, 1983), pp. 145–165.

Festinger, Leon, *A Theory of Cognitive Dissonance* (Stanford: Stanford University Press, 1966).

Fiske, Susan and Shelley Taylor, *Social Cognition* (New York: Random House, 1984).

FitzGerald, Frances, "A Critic at Large: Memoirs of the Reagan Era," *New Yorker*, January 16, 1989, p. 91.

Flowers, Matie L., "A Laboratory Test of Some Implications of Janis's Groupthink Hypothesis," *Journal of Personality and Social Psychology* 35 (1977), pp. 888–896.

Fox, William, *Effective Group Problem Solving* (San Francisco: Jossey-Bass, 1988).

Frank, Benis M., *U.S. Marines in Lebanon, 1982–1984* (Washington, D.C.: History and Museums Division, U.S. Marine Corps, 1987).

Freud, Sigmund and William C. Bullitt, *Thomas Woodrow Wilson, Twenty-Eighth President of the United States: A Psychological Study* (Boston: Houghton Mifflin, 1967).

Fried, Richard M., *Men Against McCarthy* (New York: Columbia University Press, 1976).

——, *Nightmare in Red: The McCarthy Era in Perspective* (New York: Oxford University Press, 1990).

Geen, Russell G., "Preferred Stimulation Levels in Introverts and Extraverts: Effects on Arousal and Performance," *Journal of Personality and Social Psychology* 46 (1984), pp. 1303–1312.

Geen, Russell G., Eugene McCown, and James Broyles, "Effects of Noise on Sensitivity of Introverts and Extraverts to Signals in a Vigilance Task," *Personality and Individual Differences* 6, 2 (1985), pp. 237–241.

George, Alexander, "The Case for Multiple Advocacy in Making Foreign Policy," *American Political Science Review* 66 (1972), pp. 751–785.

————, "Case Studies and Theory Development: The Method of Structured, Focused Comparison," in Paul G. Lauren, *Diplomacy: New Approaches in History, Theory and Policy* (New York: Free Press, 1979), pp. 43–68.

————, *Presidential Decisionmaking in Foreign Policy: the Effective Use of Information and Advice* (Boulder, Colorado: Westview, 1980).

George, Alexander and Juliette George, *Woodrow Wilson and Colonel House: A Personality Study* (New York: John Day, 1956; reprint, New York: Dover, 1964).

Gilovich, Thomas, *How We Know What Isn't So: The Fallibility of Human Reason in Everyday Life* (New York: Free Press, 1991).

Glad, Betty, *Jimmy Carter: In Search of the Great White House* (New York: Norton, 1980).

Glad, Betty and Jean A. Garrison, "Ronald Reagan and the Intermediate Nuclear Forces Treaty: Whatever Happened to the 'Evil Empire'?" in Eric J. Schmertz, Natalie Datlof, and Alexej Ugrinsky, eds., *President Reagan and the World* (Westport, Connecticut: Greenwood, 1997), pp. 91–107.

Goldberg, Lewis R., "The Structure of Phenotypic Personality Traits," *American Psychologist* 48 (1993), pp. 26–34.

Golding, S. L., "Flies in the Ointment: Methodological Problems in the Analysis of Percentage of Variance Due to Persons and Situations," *Psychological Bulletin* 82 (1975), pp. 278–288.

Goldstein, Judith, *Ideas, Interests, and American Trade Policy* (Ithaca: Cornell University Press, 1993).

Goodpaster, Andrew, "Organizing the White House," in Kenneth Thompson, ed., *The Eisenhower Presidency: Eleven Intimate Perspectives of Dwight D. Eisenhower* (Lanham, Maryland: University Press of America, 1984), pp. 63–87.

Gould, Stephen Jay, *An Urchin in the Storm: Essays About Books and Ideas* (New York: Norton, 1987).

Gowa, Joanne, *Closing the Gold Window: Domestic Politics and the End of Bretton Woods* (Ithaca: Cornell University Press, 1983).

Gray, Jeffrey A., "The Psychophysiological Basis of Introversion-Extraversion," *Behavior Research and Therapy* 8 (1970), pp. 249–266.

Green, Richard and Jonathan Mack, "Would Groups Do Better Without Social Psychologists? A Response to Buys," *Personality and Social Psychology Bulletin* 4 (1978), pp. 561–563.

Greenstein, Fred I., *Personality and Politics: Problems of Evidence, Inference, and Conceptualization* (Chicago: Markham, 1969; reprint, Princeton: Princeton University Press, 1987).

———, "Eisenhower as an Activist President: A Look at New Evidence," *Political Science Quarterly* 94 (1979–1980), pp. 575–599.

———, *The Hidden Hand Presidency: Eisenhower as Leader* (New York: Basic, 1982).

———, "Ronald Reagan—Another Hidden-Hand Ike?" *PS: Political Science and Politics* 23, 1 (1990), pp. 7–13.

———, "Political Style and Political Leadership: The Case of Bill Clinton," in Stanley A. Renshon, ed., *The Clinton Presidency: Campaigning, Governing, and the Psychology of Leadership* (Boulder, Colorado: Westview, 1995), pp. 137–147.

Greenstein, Fred I. and John P. Burke, *How Presidents Test Reality: Decisions on Vietnam, 1954 and 1965* (New York: Russell Sage Foundation, 1989).

Greider, William, "The Education of David Stockman," *Atlantic Monthly* 248 (December 1981), pp. 27–54.

Griffith, Robert, *The Politics of Fear* (Lexington: University Press of Kentucky, 1970).

Gruening, Ernest, *The Battle for Alaska Statehood* (College: University of Alaska Press, 1967).

Guttman, William, *Between Bailout and Breakdown: A Modular Approach to Latin America's Debt Crisis* (Washington, D.C.: Center for Strategic and International Studies, 1989).

Haas, Ernst B., "Collective Learning: Some Theoretical Speculations," in George W. Breslauer and Philip E. Tetlock, eds., *Learning in U.S. and Soviet Foreign Policy* (Boulder, Colorado: Westview, 1991), pp. 62–99.

Haig, Alexander, *Caveat* (New York: Macmillan, 1984).

Haney, Patrick, "The Nixon Administration and Middle East Crises: Theory and Evidence of Presidential Management of Foreign Policy Decision-Making," *Political Research Quarterly* 48 (1994), pp. 939–959.

————, *Organizing for Foreign Policy Crises* (Ann Arbor: University of Michigan Press, 1997).

Hall, Peter, *The Political Power of Economic Ideas: Keynesianism across Nations* (Princeton: Princeton University Press, 1989).

Hallenbeck, Ralph A., *Military Force as an Instrument of U.S. Foreign Policy: Intervention in Lebanon, August 1982 - February 1984* (New York: Praeger, 1991).

Hargrove, Erwin C., "Reagan Understands How to Be President," *U.S. News & World Report*, April 27, 1981, pp. 23–24.

Hargrove, Erwin C. and Samuel Morley, *The President and the Council of Economic Advisors: Interviews with CEA Chairmen* (Boulder, Colorado: Westview, 1984).

Harkins, Stephen G. and Kate Szymanski, "Social Loafing and Social Facilitation: New Wine in Old Bottles," in Clyde Hendrick, ed., *Group Processes and Intergroup Relations, Review of Personality and Social Psychology* (Newbury Park, California: Sage, 1987), vol. 9, pp. 167–188.

Harlow, Bryce, "The 'Compleat' President," in Kenneth Thompson, ed., *The Eisenhower Presidency: Eleven Intimate Perspectives of Dwight D. Eisenhower* (Lanham, Maryland: University Press of America, 1984), pp. 145–162.

Harr, Karl G., "Eisenhower's Approach to National Security Decisionmaking," in Kenneth Thompson, ed., *The Eisenhower Presidency: Eleven Intimate Perspectives of Dwight D. Eisenhower* (Lanham, Maryland: University Press of America, 1984), pp. 89–111.

Heider, Fritz, *The Psychology of Interpersonal Relations* (New York: Wiley, 1958).

Heller, J., "The Dangers of Groupthink," *Guardian*, January 31, 1983.

Herek, Gregory M., Irving Janis, and Paul Huth, "Decision Making During International Crises: Is the Quality of Process Related to Outcome?" *Journal of Conflict Resolution* 31, 2 (June 1987), pp. 203–225.

Hermann, Margaret, ed., *A Psychological Examination of Political Leaders* (New York: Free Press, 1977).

Hermann, Margaret G. and Thomas Preston, "Presidents, Advisers, and Foreign Policy: The Effects of Leadership Style on Executive Arrangements," *Political Psychology* 15 (1994), pp. 75–96.

————, "Presidents and Their Advisers: Leadership Style, Advisory Systems, and Foreign Policy Making," in Eugene Wittkopf, ed., *Domestic Sources of American Foreign Policy* (New York: St. Martin's, 1988).

Hess, Stephen, *Organizing the Presidency* (Washington, D.C.: Brookings, 1976, 2d ed., 1988).

Hilsman, Roger, *To Move a Nation* (Garden City, NY: Doubleday, 1967).

Hogan, Joseph, ed., *The Reagan Years: The Record in Presidential Leadership* (Manchester: Manchester University Press, 1990).

Holbo, Paul S. and Robert W. Sellen, eds., *The Eisenhower Era: The Age of Consensus* (Hinsdale, Illinois: Dryden Press, 1974).

Holsti, Ole R., *Crisis Escalation War* (Montreal: McGill-Queen's University Press, 1972).

Hook, Sidney, *The Hero in History* (New York: John Day, 1943).

Hormuth, S. E., "The Sampling of Experiences *in situ*," *Journal of Personality* 54 (1986), pp. 262–293.

Horvath, F. E., "Psychological Stress: A Review of Definitions and Experimental Research," in L. von Bertalanffy and Anatol Rapoport, *General Systems Yearbook* 4 (Ann Arbor, Michigan: Society for General Systems Research, 1959).

Houts, Arthur C., Thomas D. Cook, and William R. Shadish, "The Person-Situation Debate: A Critical Multiplist Perspective," *Journal of Personality* 54, 1 (March 1986), pp. 52–105.

Hoyt, Paul D. and Jean A. Garrison, "Political Manipulation within the Small Group: Foreign Policy Advisers in the Carter Administration," in Paul 't Hart, Eric Stern, and Bengt Sundelius, *Beyond Groupthink: Political Group Dynamics and Foreign Policymaking* (Ann Arbor: University of Michigan Press, 1997), pp. 249–274.

Hughes, Emmet John, *The Ordeal of Power: A Political Memoir of the Eisenhower Years* (New York: Atheneum, 1963).

Humphreys, Michael S. and William Revelle, "Personality, Motivation, and Performance: A Theory of the Relationship Between Individual Differences and Information Processing," *Psychological Review* 91 (1984), pp. 153–184.

Hyland, William B., ed., *America and the World, 1986* (New York: Council on Foreign Relations, 1987).

Immerman, Richard H., "Eisenhower and Dulles: Who Made the Decisions?" *Political Psychology* 1, 2 (1979), pp. 21–38.

———, *The CIA in Guatemala: The Foreign Policy of Intervention* (Austin: University of Texas Press, 1982).

————, ed., *John Foster Dulles and the Diplomacy of the Cold War* (Princeton: Princeton University Press, 1990).

————, "Prologue: Perceptions by the United States of its Interests in Indochina," in Lawrence S. Kaplan, Denise Artaud, and Mark R. Rubin, *Dien Bien Phu and the Crisis of Franco-American Relations, 1954–1955* (Wilmington, Delaware: Scholarly Resources Books, 1990), pp. 1–26.

Ingold, Charles H., "Locus of Control and Use of Public Information," *Psychological Reports* 64 (1989), pp. 603–607.

International Monetary Fund, *International Financial Statistics Yearbook* (Washington, D.C.: International Monetary Fund, 1979), vol. 32.

Irish, Marian D., "The Organization Man in the Presidency," *Journal of Politics* 20 (1958), pp. 259–277.

Janis, Irving, *Groupthink: Psychological Studies of Policy Decisions and Fiascoes*, 2d ed., (Boston: Houghton Mifflin, 1982).

————, *Crucial Decisions: Leadership in Policymaking and Crisis Management* (New York: Free Press, 1989).

Janis, Irving and Leon Mann, *Decision Making: A Psychological Analysis of Conflict, Choice, and Commitment* (New York: Free Press, 1977).

Jansen, Michael, *The Battle for Beirut* (Boston: South End Press, 1983).

Jervis, Robert, *Perception and Misperception in International Politics* (Princeton: Princeton University Press, 1976).

Joes, Anthony James, "Eisenhower Revisionism and American Politics," in Joann P. Krieg, ed., *Dwight D. Eisenhower: Soldier, President, Statesman* (New York: Greenwood, 1987).

Johnson, Richard Tanner, *Managing the White House: An Intimate Study of the Presidency* (New York: Harper & Row, 1974).

Johnson, Rossall J., "Conflict Avoidance Through Acceptable Decisions," *Human Relations* 27 (1974), pp. 71–82.

Jones, Charles O., ed., *The Reagan Legacy: Promise and Performance* (Chatham, New Jersey: Chatham House, 1988).

Jung, Carl G., *Psychological Types* (London: Routledge and Kegan Paul, 1923).

Kahin, George McT., *Intervention: How America Became Involved in Vietnam* (New York: Knopf, 1986).

Kaplan, Lawrence S., Denise Artaud, and Mark R. Rubin, *Dien Bien Phu and the Crisis of Franco-American Relations, 1954–1955* (Wilmington, Delaware: Scholarly Resources Books, 1990).

Kaufman, Burton, *Trade and Aid: Eisenhower's Foreign Economic Policy 1953–1961* (Baltimore: Johns Hopkins University Press, 1982).

Kellerman, Henry, *Group Cohesion: Theoretical and Clinical Perspectives* (New York: Grune & Stratton, 1981).

Kessel, John H., "The Structures of the Carter White House," *American Journal of Political Science* 27 (1983), pp. 431–463.

———, "The Structures of the Reagan White House," *American Journal of Political Science* 28 (1984), pp. 231–258.

Kinnard, Douglas, *President Eisenhower and Strategy Management* (Washington, D.C.: Pergamon-Brassey, 1977).

Kissinger, Henry, *The White House Years* (Boston: Little, Brown, 1979).

Kittle, Robert A., "After 3 Months: Report Card on Reagan," *U.S. News & World Report*, April 27, 1981, pp. 20–22.

Kitts, Kenneth and Betty Glad, "Presidential Personality and Improvisational Decision Making: Eisenhower and the 1956 Hungarian Crisis," in Shirley Anne Warshaw, ed., *Reexamining the Eisenhower Presidency* (Westport, Connecticut: Greenwood, 1993), pp. 183–208.

Korbani, Agnes G., *U.S. Intervention in Lebanon, 1958 and 1982: Presidential Decisionmaking* (New York: Praeger, 1991).

Kowert, Paul A., "Between Reason and Passion: A Systems Theory of Foreign Policy Learning" (Ph. D. diss., Cornell University, 1992).

———, "Where *Does* the Buck Stop?: Assessing the Impact of Presidential Personality," *Political Psychology* 17 (1996), pp. 421–452.

———, "Leadership and Learning in Political Groups: The Management of Advice in the Iran-Contra Affair," *Governance: An International Journal of Policy and Administration* 14, 2 (April 2001), pp. 201–232.

Kowert, Paul A. and Daryl J. Bem, "Assessing the Personality of Public Figures: Profiles of Six Postwar American Presidents," forthcoming.

Kraft, Joseph, *The Mexican Rescue* (New York: Group of Thirty, 1984).

Krasner, Stephen, "Are Bureaucracies Important? (Or Allison Wonderland)" *Foreign Policy* 7 (1971), pp. 159–179.

Kravitz, David, et al., "Humans Would Do Better Without Other Humans," *Personality and Social Psychology Bulletin* 4 (1978), pp. 559–560.

Kuwahara, Yasuo, *Decision-Making Structures and Processes in Multinationals in Japan* (Geneva: International Labour Office, 1985).

Kymlicka, B. B. and Jean V. Matthews, *The Reagan Revolution?* (Chicago: Dorsey Press, 1988).

LaFeber, Walter, *America, Russia, and the Cold War: 1945–1971* (New York: Wiley, 1972).

Lardner, George Jr., "Meese Details White House Crisis," *Washington Post*, March 29, 1989, p. A5.

Larson, Arthur, *Eisenhower: The President Nobody Knew* (New York: Scribner, 1968).

——, "Eisenhower's World View," in Kenneth Thompson, ed., *The Eisenhower Presidency: Eleven Intimate Perspectives of Dwight D. Eisenhower* (Lanham, Maryland: University Press of America, 1984), pp. 39–59.

Larson, Carl E. and Frank M.J. LaFasto, *Teamwork: What Must Go Right, What Can Go Wrong* (Newbury Park, California: Sage, 1989).

Larson, Deborah, *Origins of Containment* (Princeton: Princeton University Press, 1985).

Lasswell, Harold D., *Power and Personality* (New York: Norton, 1948).

——, *Politics: Who Gets What, When, How* (New York: Meridian, 1958).

Lazarus, Richard S., James Deese, and Sonia F. Osler, "The Effects of Psychological Stress Upon Performance," *Psychological Bulletin* 49 (1952), pp. 293–317.

Leahey, Thomas H. and Richard J. Harris, *Human Learning* (Englewood Cliffs, New Jersey: Prentice-Hall, 1985).

Le Bon, Gustave, *The Crowd* (London: T. Fisher Unwin, 1896).

Lebow, Richard Ned, *Between Peace and War: The Nature of International Crisis* (Baltimore: Johns Hopkins University Press, 1981).

Leeds, Roger S. and Gale Thompson, "The 1982 Mexican Debt Negotiations: Response to a Financial Crisis," *Foreign Policy Institute Case Studies* (Washington, D.C.: Johns Hopkins Foreign Policy Institute, 1987), no. 4.

Lefcourt, Herbert M., *Locus of Control: Current Trends in Theory and Research* (Hillsdale, New Jersey: Lawrence Erlbaum, 1982).

Lerner, Max, "The Big Mangling Machine," *Chicago Sun-Times*, June 26, 1971.

Levine, John M. and Richard L. Moreland, "Progress in Small Group Research," *Annual Review of Psychology* 41 (1990), pp. 585–634.

Lissakers, Karin, "Dateline Wall Street: Faustian Finance," *Foreign Policy* 51 (Summer 1983), pp. 160–175.

Longley, J. and Dean G. Pruitt, "Groupthink: A Critique of Janis' Theory," *Review of Personality and Social Psychology* 1 (1980), pp. 74–93.

Lowi, Theodore J., *The Personal President: Power Invested, Promise Unfulfilled* (Ithaca: Cornell University Press, 1985).

Lyon, Peter, *Eisenhower: Portrait of the Hero* (Boston: Little, Brown, 1974).

Makin, John H., *The Global Debt Crisis: America's Growing Involvement* (New York: Basic, 1984).

Maraniss, David, *First in His Class: A Biography of Bill Clinton* (New York: Simon & Schuster, 1995).

Martin, David C. and John Walcott, *Best Laid Plans: The Inside Story of America's War Against Terrorism* (New York: Touchstone, 1938).

Mayer, Jane and Doyle McManus, *Landslide: The Unmaking of the President, 1984–1988* (New York: Houghton Mifflin, 1988).

Mazlish, Bruce and E. Diamond, *Jimmy Carter: A Character Portrait* (New York: Simon & Schuster, 1979).

McClelland, Peter D., *Causal Explanation and Model Building in History, Economics, and the New Economic History* (Ithaca: Cornell University Press, 1975).

McCrae, Robert R. and Paul T. Costa, *Emerging Lives, Enduring Dispositions: Personality in Adulthood* (Boston: Little, Brown, 1984).

———, *Personality in Adulthood* (New York: Guilford, 1990).

McCrae, Robert and Oliver P. John, "An Introduction to the Five Factor Model and Its Applications," *Journal of Personality* 60 (1992), pp. 175–215.

Medin, Douglas, "Theories of Discrimination Learning and Learning Set," in William K. Estes, ed., *Handbook of Learning and Cognitive Processes: Approaches to Human Learning and Motivation* (Hillsdale, New Jersey: Lawrence Erlbaum, 1976), vol. 3, pp. 131–169.

Melanson, Richard and David Mayers, *Reevaluating Eisenhower: American Foreign Policy in the 1950s* (Urbana: University of Illinois Press, 1987).

Miller, Judith and Laurie Mylroie, *Saddam Hussein and the Crisis in the Gulf* (New York: Times Books, 1990).

Minix, Dean A., *Small Groups and Foreign Policy Decision-Making* (Washington, D.C.: University Press of America, 1982).

Mischel, Walter, *Personality and Assessment* (New York: Wiley, 1968).

Mischel, Walter and P. K. Peake, "Beyond Déjà Vu in the Search for Cross-Situational Consistency," *Psychological Review* 98 (1982), pp. 730–755.

Moens, Alexander, *Foreign Policy Under Carter: Testing Multiple Advocacy Decision Making* (Boulder, Colorado: Westview, 1990).

Morgan, Iwan, *Eisenhower versus "the Spenders": the Eisenhower Administration, the Democrats and the Budget, 1953–60* (London: Pinter, 1990).

Moscovici, Serge, "Social Influence and Conformity," in Gardner Lindzey and Elliot Aronson, eds., *The Handbook of Social Psychology* (New York: Random, 1985), vol. 2, pp. 347–412.

Moskowitz, D. S., "Comparison of Self-Reports, Reports by Knowledgeable Informants, and Behavioral Observation Data," *Journal of Personality* 54 (1986), pp. 294–317.

Muller, Thomas, *The Impact of Reagan Administration Policies on Regional Income and Employment* (Washington, D.C.: Urban Institute Press, 1986).

Myers, Isabel Briggs, *Gifts Differing: Understanding Personality Type* (Palo Alto, California: Consulting Psychologists Press, 1980, 1993).

Nathan, Richard P., "A Disengaged Presidency," *Newsweek*, September 7, 1981, pp. 21–23.

———, *The Administrative Presidency* (New York: Macmillan, 1986).

National Security Archive, *The Chronology* (New York: Warner Books, 1987).

Nau, Henry R., *The Myth of America's Decline: Leading the World Economy into the 1990s* (New York: Oxford University Press, 1990).

Nelson, Michael, ed., *The Presidency and the Political System* (Washington, D.C.: Congressional Quarterly, 1990).

Nemeth, Charlan Jeanne, "Differential Contributions of Majority and Minority Influence," *Psychological Review* 93 (1986), pp. 23–32.

Neustadt, Richard, *Presidential Power: The Politics of Leadership* (New York: Wiley, 1960).

———, *Presidential Power and the Modern Presidents* (New York: Free Press, 1990).

New York Times, *The Tower Commission Report* (New York: Times Books, 1987).

Nisbett, Richard and Lee Ross, *Human Inference: Strategies and Shortcomings of Social Judgment* (Englewood Cliffs, New Jersey: Prentice-Hall, 1980).

Nixon, Richard M., *RN: The Memoirs of Richard Nixon* (New York: Grosset & Dunlap, 1978).

Nuttin, Joseph and Anthony G. Greenwald, *Reward and Punishment in Human Learning* (New York: Academic Press, 1968).

Odell, John, *U.S. International Monetary Policy: Markets, Power, and Ideas as Sources of Change* (Princeton: Princeton University Press, 1982).

Onuf, Nicholas, *World of Our Making: Rules and Rule in Social Theory and International Relations* (Columbia: University of South Carolina Press, 1989).

O'Reilly, Kenneth, *Hoover and the Un-Americans: The FBI, HUAC, and the Red Menace* (Philadelphia: Temple University Press, 1983).

Orman, John, *Comparing Presidential Behavior: Carter, Reagan, and the Macho Presidential Style* (New York: Greenwood, 1987).

Oye, Kenneth, Ronald Lieber, and Donald Rothchild, *Eagle Resurgent?: The Reagan Era in American Foreign Policy* (Boston: Little, Brown, 1983).

Park, W., "A Review of the Research on Groupthink," *Journal of Behavioral Decision Making* 3 (1990), pp. 229–245.

Parkes, Katharine R., "Locus of Control, Cognitive Appraisal, and Coping in Stressful Episodes," *Journal of Personality and Social Psychology* 46 (1984), pp. 655–668.

Patterson, Bradley H., "An Overview of the White House," in Kenneth Thompson, ed., *The Eisenhower Presidency: Eleven Intimate Perspectives of Dwight D. Eisenhower* (Lanham, Maryland: University Press of America, 1984), pp. 113–141.

———, "Eisenhower's Innovations in White House Staff Structure and Operations," in Shirley Anne Warshaw, ed., *Reexamining the Eisenhower Presidency* (Westport, Connecticut: Greenwood, 1993), pp. 33–56.

Paulus, Paul B., ed., *Psychology of Group Influence*, 1st ed. (Hillsdale, New Jersey: Lawrence Erlbaum, 1980).

————, *Psychology of Group Influence*, 2d ed., (Hillsdale, New Jersey: Lawrence Erlbaum, 1989).

Peterson, Paul E. and Mark Rom, "Lower Taxes, More Spending, and Budget Deficits," in Charles O. Jones, ed., *The Reagan Legacy: Promise and Performance* (Chatham, New Jersey: Chatham House, 1988), pp. 213–240.

Peterson, Randall S. et al., "Group Dynamics in Top Management Teams: Groupthink, Vigilance, and Alternative Models of Organizational Failure and Success," *Organizational Behavior and Human Decision Processes* 73 (1998), pp. 272–305.

Pfiffner, James P., *The Managerial Presidency* (Pacific Grove, California: Brooks/Cole, 1991).

Phares, E. Jerry, "Differential Utilization of Information as a Function of Internal-External Control," *Journal of Personality* 36 (1968), pp. 649–662.

————, *Locus of Control in Personality* (Morristown, New Jersey: General Learning Press, 1976).

Pittman, Thane S. and Paul R. D'Agostino, "Motivation and Cognition: Control Deprivation and the Nature of Subsequent Information Processing," *Journal of Experimental Social Psychology* 25 (1989), pp. 465–480.

Portney, Paul R., ed., *Natural Resources and the Environment: The Reagan Approach* (Washington, D.C.: Urban Institute Press, 1984).

Posen, Barry and Stephen Van Evera, "Reagan Administration Defense Policy: Departure from Containment," in Kenneth Oye, Ronald Lieber, and Donald Rothchild, *Eagle Resurgent?: The Reagan Era in American Foreign Policy* (Boston: Little, Brown, 1983), pp. 75–114.

Postman, Leo, "Methodology of Human Learning," in William K. Estes, ed., *Handbook of Learning and Cognitive Processes: Approaches to Human Learning and Motivation* (Hillsdale, New Jersey: Lawrence Erlbaum, 1976), vol. 3, pp. 11–69.

Prados, John, *The Sky Would Fall: Operation Vulture: The U.S. Bombing Mission in Indochina, 1954* (New York: Dial Press, 1983).

Prentice-Dunn, Steven and Ronald W. Rogers, "Deindividuation and the Self-Regulation of Behavior," in Paul B. Paulus, ed., *Psychology of Group Influence*, 2d ed. (Hillsdale, New Jersey: Lawrence Erlbaum, 1989), pp. 87–109.

Pruessen, Ronald, *John Foster Dulles: The Road to Power* (New York: Free Press, 1982).

Pruitt, Dean G., "Choice Shifts in Group Discussion: An Introductory Review," *Journal of Personality and Social Psychology* 20 (1971), pp. 339–360.

Rabe, Stephen, *Eisenhower and Latin America: The Foreign Policy of Anticommunism* (Chapel Hill: University of North Carolina, 1988).

Raven, Bertram H., "The Nixon Group," *Journal of Social Issues* 30 (1974), pp. 297–320.

Reagan, Nancy, with William Novak, *My Turn: The Memoirs of Nancy Reagan* (New York: Random House, 1989).

Reagan, Ronald W., *Where's the Rest of Me?* (New York: Karz Publishers, 1981).

———, *An American Life* (New York: Simon & Schuster, 1990).

Reeves, Thomas C., *The Life and Times of Joe McCarthy: A Biography* (New York: Stein and Day, 1982).

Regan, Donald T., *For the Record: From Wall Street to Washington* (New York: St. Martin's, 1988).

Renshon, Stanley A., ed., *The Political Psychology of the Gulf War: Leaders, Publics, and the Process of Conflict* (Pittsburgh: University of Pittsburgh Press, 1993).

———, ed., *The Clinton Presidency: Campaigning, Governing, and the Psychology of Leadership* (Boulder, Colorado: Westview, 1995).

Riecken, H. W., "The Effect of Talkativeness on Ability to Influence Group Solutions of Problems," *Sociometry* 2 (1958), pp. 309–321.

Ridgway, Matthew, *Soldier* (New York: Harper, 1956).

Rockman, Bert A., "The Style and Organization of the Reagan Presidency," in Charles O. Jones, ed., *The Reagan Legacy: Promise and Performance* (Chatham, New Jersey: Chatham House, 1988), pp. 3–29.

Rokeach, Milton, *The Open and Closed Mind* (New York: Basic, 1960).

Rostow, Walt W., *Eisenhower, Kennedy, and Foreign Aid* (Austin: University of Texas Press, 1985).

Rotter, Julian B., *Social Learning and Clinical Psychology* (Englewood Cliffs, NJ: Prentice-Hall, 1954).

———, "Generalized Expectancies for Internal Versus External Control of Reinforcement," *Psychological Monographs* 80, 1 (1966), whole no. 609.

Ryan, T. A., "Intention and Kinds of Learning," in Gery d'Ydewalle and Willy Lens, eds., *Cognition in Human Motivation and Learning* (Hillsdale, New Jersey: Lawrence Erlbaum, 1981), pp. 59–85.

Saulnier, Raymond J., *Constructive Years: The U.S. Economy under Eisenhower* (Lanham, Maryland: University Press of America, 1991).

Saunders, Harold H., "An Israeli-Palestinian Peace," *Foreign Affairs* (Fall 1982), pp. 101–121.

Schandler, Herbert Y., *The Unmaking of a President* (Princeton: Princeton University Press, 1977).

Schieffer, Bob and Gary Paul Gates, *The Acting President* (New York: Dutton, 1989).

Schlesinger, James, "Reykjavik and Revelations: A Turn of the Tide?" in William G. Hyland, ed., *America and the World: 1986* (New York: Council on Foreign Relations, 1987).

Schmertz, Eric J., Natalie Datlof, and Alexej Ugrinsky, eds., *President Reagan and the World* (Westport, Connecticut: Greenwood, 1997).

Schrecker, Ellen, *No Ivory Tower: McCarthyism and the Universities* (New York: Oxford University Press, 1986).

———, *Many Are the Crimes: McCarthyism in America* (Boston: Little, Brown, 1998).

Scribner, Charles Reverdan, "The Eisenhower and Johnson Administrations' Decisionmaking on Vietnamese Intervention: A Study of Contrasts" (Ph. D. diss., University of California at Santa Barbara, June 1980).

Segev, Samuel, "The Reagan Plan: A Victim of Conflicting Approaches by the United States and Israel to the Syrian Presence in Lebanon," in Eric J. Schmertz, Natalie Datlof, and Alexej Ugrinsky, eds., *President Reagan and the World* (Westport, Connecticut: Greenwood, 1997), pp. 41–60.

Shaffer, Leigh, "On the Current Confusion of Group-Related Behavior and Collective Behavior: A Reaction to Buys," *Personality and Social Psychology Bulletin* 4 (1978), pp. 564–567.

Shapiro, Michael, *Language and Poltical Understanding: The Politics of Discursive Practices* (New Haven: Yale University Press, 1981).

Sheehy, Gail, *Character: America's Search for Leadership* (New York: Bantam, 1990).

Short, C. Brant, *Ronald Reagan and the Public Lands: America's Conservation Debate, 1979–1984* (College Station: Texas A&M University Press, 1989).

Simon, Herbert A., "Rationality as Process and as Product of Thought," *American Economic Review (Papers and Proceedings)* 68 (1978), pp. 1–16.

————, "Motivational and Emotional Controls of Cognition," *Annual Review of Psychology* 30 (1979), pp. 29–39.

Simonton, Dean Keith, "Presidential Personality: Biographical Use of the Gough Adjective Check List," *Journal of Personality and Social Psychology* 51 (1986), pp. 149–160.

Skowronek, Stephen, "Notes on the Presidency in the Political Order," *Studies in American Political Development* (New Haven: Yale University Press, 1986), vol. 1, pp. 286–302.

————, "Presidential Leadership in Political Time," in Michael Nelson, ed., *The Presidency and the Political System* (Washington, D.C.: Congressional Quarterly, 1990), pp. 117–161.

Smith, Steve, "Groupthink and the Hostage Rescue Mission," *British Journal of Political Science* 14 (1984), pp. 117–123.

Snyder, Jack, *The Ideology of the Offensive: Military Decision Making and the Disasters of 1914* (Ithaca: Cornell University Press, 1984).

Stassen, Harold and Marshall Houts, *Eisenhower: Turning the World toward Peace* (St. Paul, Minnesota: Merrill/Magnus, 1990).

Stein, Janice Gross and Raymond Tanter, *Rational Decision Making: Israel's Security Choices, 1967* (Columbus: Ohio State University Press, 1980).

Stockman, David, *The Triumph of Politics: The Inside Story of the Reagan Revolution* (New York: Avon, 1987).

Suedfeld, Peter, "Are Simple Decisions Always Worse?" *Society* 25, 5 (1988), pp. 25–27.

Suedfeld, Peter and Philip Tetlock, "Integrative Complexity of Communications in International Crises," *Journal of Conflict Resolution* 21 (1977), pp. 169–184.

Sulzberger, Cyrus, *Seven Continents and Forty Years* (New York: New York Times Books, 1977).

't Hart, Paul, *Groupthink in Government: A Study of Small Groups and Policy Failures* (Amsterdam: Swets and Zeitlinger, 1990; reprint, Baltimore: Johns Hopkins University Press, 1994).

't Hart, Paul, Eric Stern, and Bengt Sundelius, *Beyond Groupthink: Political Group Dynamics and Foreign Policymaking* (Ann Arbor: University of Michigan Press, 1997).

Tanter, Raymond, *Who's at the Helm?: Lessons of Lebanon* (Boulder, Colorado: Westview, 1990).

Tarrow, Sidney, *Democracy and Disorder: Protest and Politics in Italy 1965–1975* (Oxford: Clarendon Press, 1989).

———, *Struggle, Politics, and Reform: Collective Action, Social Movements, and Cycles of Protest*, Occasional Paper no. 21, Western Societies Program (Ithaca: Center for International Studies, Cornell University, 1989).

Taylor, A. J. P., *From Napoleon to Lenin* (New York: Harper & Row, 1966).

Taylor, R. N., "Psychological Determinants of Bounded Rationality: Implications for Decision-Making Strategies," *Decision Sciences* 6 (1975), pp. 409–429.

Tetlock, Philip E., "Integrative Complexity of American and Soviet Foreign Policy Rhetoric: A Time-Series Analysis," *Journal of Personality and Social Psychology* 49, 6 (1985), pp. 1565–1585.

———, "Monitoring the Integrative Complexity of American and Soviet Policy Rhetoric: What Can Be Learned?" *Journal of Social Issues* 44, 2 (1988), pp. 101–131.

———, "Learning in U.S. and Soviet Foreign Policy: In Search of an Elusive Concept," in George W. Breslauer and Philip E. Tetlock, eds., *Learning in U.S. and Soviet Foreign Policy* (Boulder, Colorado: Westview, 1991), pp. 20–61.

Tetlock, Philip E. et al., "Assessing Political Group Dynamics: A Test of the Groupthink Model," *Journal of Personality and Social Psychology* 63 (1992), pp. 403–425.

Thompson, D., "Moral Responsibility of Public Officials: The Problem of Many Hands," *American Political Science Review* 74 (1980), pp. 905–916.

Thompson, Kenneth, *The Eisenhower Presidency: Eleven Intimate Perspectives of Dwight D. Eisenhower* (Lanham, Maryland: University Press of America, 1984).

———, "The Strengths and Weaknesses of Eisenhower's Leadership," in Richard Melanson and David Mayers, *Reevaluating Eisenhower: American Foreign Policy in the 1950s* (Urbana: University of Illinois Press, 1987), pp. 13–30.

Tower, John, Edmund Muskie, and Brent Scowcroft, *Report of the President's Special Review Board, February 26, 1987* (Washington, D.C.: U.S. Government Printing Office, 1987).

Trice, Ashton D. and Judith Price-Greathouse, "Locus of Control and AIDS Information-Seeking in College Women," *Psychological Reports* 60 (1987), pp. 665–666.

Triffin, Robert, *Gold and the Dollar Crisis* (New Haven: Yale University Press, 1961).

Tuchman, Barbara, *The Guns of August* (New York: Dell, 1962).

Turner, Marlene E. and Anthony R. Pratkanis, "Twenty-Five Years of Groupthink Theory and Research: Lessons from the Evaluation of a Theory," *Organizational Behavior and Human Decision Processes* 73, 2/3 (February/March 1998), pp. 105–115.

United States Congress, *International Debt*, 98th Cong., 1st sess. (Washington, D.C.: U.S. Government Printing Office, 1983).

————, *U.S. Proposals on International Debt Crisis*, 99th Cong., 1st sess. (Washington, D.C.: U.S. Government Printing Office, 1986).

————, *Report of the Congressional Committees Investigating the Iran-Contra Affair*, 100th Cong., 1st sess. (Washington, D.C.: U.S. Government Printing Office, 1987).

United States Department of Defense, *United States-Vietnam Relations, 1945–1967* (Washington, D.C.: U.S. Government Printing Office, 1971), vol. 9.

Vacc, Nicholas A. and Nancy Nesbitt Vacc, "Cognitive Complexity-Simplicity as a Determinant of Internal-External Locus of Control," *Psychological Reports* 52 (1983), pp. 913–914.

Van der Linden, Frank, *The Real Reagan* (New York: Morrow, 1981).

Vatter, Harold G., *The U.S. Economy in the 1950s: An Economic History* (Chicago: University of Chicago Press, 1963).

Vertzberger, Yaacov Y. I., "Foreign Policy Decisionmakers as Practical-intuitive Historians: Applied History and Its Shortcomings," *International Studies Quarterly* 30 (1986), pp. 223–247.

Vogel, Ezra F., ed., *Modern Japanese Organization and Decisionmaking* (Berkeley: University of California Press, 1975).

Walcott, Charles E. and Karen M. Hult, *Governing the White House: From Hoover through LBJ* (Lawrence: University Press of Kansas, 1995).

Walsh, Lawrence E., *Firewall: The Iran-Contra Conspiracy and Cover-up* (New York: Norton, 1997).

Warner, Geoffrey, "Britain and the Crisis over Dien Bien Phu, April 1954: The Failure of United Action," in Lawrence S. Kaplan, Denise Artaud, and Mark R. Rubin, *Dien Bien Phu and the Crisis of Franco-American Relations, 1954–1955* (Wilmington, Delaware: Scholarly Resources Books, 1990), pp. 55–77.

Warshaw, Shirley Anne, ed., *Reexamining the Eisenhower Presidency* (Westport, Connecticut: Greenwood, 1993).

Weber, Max, *Economy and Society*, eds. Guenther Roth and Claus Wittich (Berkeley: University of California Press, 1978).

Weintraub, Bernard, "Criticism on Iran and Other Issues Put Reagan's Aides on Defensive," *New York Times*, November 16, 1986.

Welch, David, "The Organizational Process and Bureaucratic Politics Paradigms," *International Security* 17 (1992), pp. 112–146.

Wendt, Alexander E., "The Agent-Structure Problem in International Relations Theory," *International Organization* 41, 3 (1987), pp. 335–370.

Werner, Emmy E., "Resilient Offspring of Alcoholics: A Longitudinal Study from Birth to Age 18," *Journal of Studies on Alcohol* 44 (1986), pp. 34–40.

Werner, Paul D. and Lawrence A. Pervin, "The Content of Personality Inventory Items," *Journal of Personality and Social Psychology* 51, 3 (1986), pp. 622–628.

Wilke, Henk A. M. and Roel W. Meertens, *Group Performance* (London: Routledge, 1994).

Williams, Lloyd, *The Congruence of People and Organizations* (Westport, Connecticut: Quorum Books, 1993).

Wilson, Sloan, *The Man in the Gray Flannel Suit* (New York: Simon & Schuster, 1955).

Worchel, S., W. Wood, and J. Simpson, eds., *Group Process and Productivity* (Newbury Park, California: Sage, 1992).

Yerkes, Robert M. and J. D. Dodson, "The Relation of Strength of Stimulus to Rapidity of Habit Formation," *Journal of Comparative Neurology and Psychology* 18 (1908), pp. 459–482.

Zaccaro, Stephen J. and Charles A. Lowe, "Cohesiveness and Performance on an Additive Task: Evidence for Multidimensionality," *Journal of Social Psychology* 128 (1988), pp. 547–558.

Zander, Alvin, *Making Groups Effective* (San Francisco: Jossey-Bass, 1994).

Zoumaras, Thomas, "Eisenhower's Foreign Economic Policy: The Case of Latin America," in Richard Melanson and David Mayers, *Reevaluating Eisenhower: American Foreign Policy in the 1950s* (Urbana: University of Illinois Press, 1987), pp. 155–191.

Zuckerman, Marvin, ed., *Biological Bases of Sensation Seeking, Impulsivity, and Anxiety* (Hillsdale, New Jersey: Lawrence Erlbaum, 1983).

Index

For references to notes, the note number is given in parentheses.